PROVOCATIONS OF VIRTUE

PROVOCATIONS OF VIRTUE

Rhetoric, Ethics, and the Teaching of Writing

JOHN DUFFY

UTAH STATE UNIVERSITY PRESS
Logan

© 2019 by University Press of Colorado

Published by Utah State University Press
An imprint of University Press of Colorado
245 Century Circle, Suite 202
Louisville, Colorado 80027

 ASSOCIATION of UNIVERSITY PRESSES   The University Press of Colorado is a proud member of
the Association of University Presses.

The University Press of Colorado is a cooperative publishing enterprise supported,
in part, by Adams State University, Colorado State University, Fort Lewis College,
Metropolitan State University of Denver, University of Colorado, University of Northern
Colorado, Utah State University, and Western State Colorado University.

∞ This paper meets the requirements of the ANSI/NISO Z39.48-1992 (Permanence of
Paper).

ISBN: 978-1-60732-826-1 (paperback)
ISBN: 978-1-60732-827-8 (ebook)
DOI: https://doi.org/10.7330/9781607328278

Library of Congress Cataloging-in-Publication Data

Names: Duffy, John, 1955– author.
Title: Provocations of virtue : rhetoric, ethics, and the teaching of writing / John Duffy.
Description: Logan : Utah State University Press, [2019] | Includes bibliographical refer-
    ences and index.
Identifiers: LCCN 2018046157 | ISBN 9781607328261 (pbk.) | ISBN 9781607328278
    (ebook)
Subjects: LCSH: English language—Rhetoric—Study and teaching (Higher) | Rhetoric—
    Moral and ethical aspects. | Virtue.
Classification: LCC PE1404 .D84 2019 | DDC 808/.042071—dc23
LC record available at https://lccn.loc.gov/2018046157

The University Press of Colorado gratefully acknowledges the generous support of the
Institute for Scholarship in the Liberal Arts at Notre Dame University toward the publication of this book.

Cover image © Clash_Gene/Shutterstock.com

To Sean and Devin.

Defenceless under the night
Our world in stupor lies;
Yet, dotted everywhere,
Ironic points of light flash out
Wherever the Just
Exchange their messages
—WH Auden

CONTENTS

ACKNOWLEDGMENTS

A great many people contributed to the completion of this book. I am indebted to everyone who listened, who read early and later drafts, who offered necessary criticism, and who questioned, tested, pushed, and heartened me when I most needed it.

I am grateful first of all to Michael Spooner of Utah State University Press, who encouraged me to begin this book and who generously granted me the time to finish it. Thanks also to Rachael Levay of Utah State University Press and Laura Furney of University Press of Colorado, both of whom helped see this work through to publication. A special thank you to is owed to Anya Hawke for her scrupulous reading of the manuscript.

I am indebted as well to my colleagues in the field, especially Lois Agnew and Paula Mathieu, who allowed me to join them on several panels at the CCCC conference, and whose excellent work provided a spur and model for my own. I owe a great debt to Mary P. Sheridan, who invited me to join a Watson Conference colloquium at the University of Louisville, where I first presented some of these ideas, and where I received invaluable critiques from Bruce Horner, Gesa Kirsch, Jonathan Alexander, Wendy S. Herford, Paula Mathieu, Jeff Grabill, Juan Guerra, and from the graduate students in the Rhetoric and Composition program, especially Drew Holladay and Rachel Gramer. At various points along the way, I benefited from conversations with more colleagues than I can recount, but especially Catherine Prendergast, Shannon Carter, Patrick Berry, Russel Durst, Bronwyn Williams, Joe Harris, John Gallagher, David Jolliffe, Eli Goldblatt, Rebecca Nowacek, Julie Nelson Cristoph, Doug Hesse, Bob Yagelski, Bonnie Smith Whitehouse, Asao Inoue, Jill Swiencicki, David Martins, Barbara Lowe, Frank Farmer, Jared Colton, Linda Adler-Kassner, Eileen Schell, Paul Kei Matsuda, John Schilb, Scott Barnett, and Hugh Burns. Not all of these colleagues endorsed my understandings of virtue, rhetoric, and the teaching of writing; several pushed back emphatically and persuasively. I learned from each of them.

I was privileged to have the opportunity to rehearse some of my inchoate ideas at several colleges and universities, including the University of Illinois, Texas A&M-Commerce, Indiana University South Bend, Stanford University, Syracuse University, University of Cincinnati, Indiana University, University of Connecticut, University of Denver, Rochester Institute of Technology, St. John Fisher College, The United States Air Force Academy, Purdue University, and St. Mary's College. I am grateful to the faculty and students who attended those talks and asked me tough, insightful questions that made me think harder and more clearly. I am grateful as well to the College of Arts and Letters at the University of Notre Dame, which gave me an academic year to read and reflect on questions of ethics and rhetoric.

At Notre Dame, I have been fortunate to work with colleagues committed to ethical discourse and teaching. I owe thanks to Cyril O'Regan, who first explained to me what I was trying to do, and who took the time to read and comment on an early and acutely inadequate draft. I am grateful to William Mattison, who read the chapter on the virtues, and who graciously pointed out my misunderstandings and wrong turns, and to Jean Porter, who shared some of her vast knowledge of the virtues with me. Thanks also to Mark Roche, whose enthusiasm for this project in its early stages helped persuade me to continue with it.

A special sort of gratitude is owed to my colleagues in the University Writing Program at Notre Dame, from whom I have learned more than I can say. Patrick Clauss read the entire manuscript in draft, offering meticulous, insightful commentary. Matthew Capdevielle read early drafts and helped me just as he has helped thousands of writers in his role as director of the University Writing Center. My colleagues Nicole MacLaughlin, Erin McLaughlin, Beth Capdevielle, Damian Zurro, and Ed Kelly exemplify daily what it means to be a committed and ethical teacher. Much of my thinking about the ethics of writing is the result of conversations with my students at Notre Dame. I am indebted to all of them, but especially April Feng and Rebecca Feng.

A special, unpayable debt is owed to Norbert Elliot, who was reader, counselor, and friend. Bryan Trabold read everything I sent his way and asked all the right questions, even before I understood what those questions might be. Michael K. Lecky remains, as he has been throughout my adult life, the reader over my shoulder: my teacher, my first editor, my word-conscience.

One afternoon when the leaves were turning yellow, before I had spoken to anyone else about this project, I took a walk with Kathleen Opel and described the book I wanted to write. She urged me to write it. I am fortunate to be walking beside her still.

PROVOCATIONS OF VIRTUE

INTRODUCTION

Let us begin with a few episodes in the everyday life of public discourse in the United States:

ONE: When the city of New Orleans began removing monuments commemorating the Confederacy, a decision that precipitated heated debate, legal challenges, death threats, and violent protests, the action so upset Republican State Representative Karl Oliver in neighboring Mississippi that he took to Facebook in May 2017 to express his displeasure. Oliver wrote:

> The destruction of these monuments, erected in the loving memory of our family and fellow Southern Americans, is both heinous and horrific. If the, and I use this term extremely loosely, "leadership" of Louisiana wishes to, in a Nazi-ish fashion, burn books or destroy historical monuments of OUR HISTORY, they should be LYNCHED! Let it be known, I will do all in my power to prevent this from happening in our State. (Wang 2017)

Oliver included with his post a picture of the Confederate General Robert E. Lee, whose statue was the last of the monuments to be removed. Before he deleted his post two days later, many people had weighed in to support or excoriate Oliver's comments, including two fellow Mississippi lawmakers, Representatives John Read and Doug McLeod, both of whom "liked" the post. Oliver later issued an apology, acknowledging his use of the word "lynched" was wrong. "I humbly ask for your forgiveness," Oliver wrote (ibid.). He did not address comparing New Orleans city officials to Nazis.

TWO: As a controversial bill expanding a school voucher program in the state of Arizona was being sent in April 2017 to Governor Doug Ducey for his signature, Democratic Representative Jesus Rubalcava was outraged. Rubalcava, an elementary school teacher, was among a number of Democratic and moderate Republican critics of the bill, which they viewed as an effort to "dismantle" public education because it would redirect money from public to private and religious schools (Sanchez, O'Dell, and Rau 2017). Writing to a Facebook friend about the bill's sponsor, Republican Senator Debbie Lesko, Rubalcava stated, "I wanted to punch her in the throat." (Sanchez and Pitzl, 2017). Lesko,

DOI: 10.7330/9781607328278.c000

a self-identified survivor of domestic violence, said she found Rubalcava's comment, "very disturbing and totally inappropriate." After initially defending his Facebook post, Rubalcava subsequently removed it and made a public apology to Lesko and his colleagues in the legislature.

THREE: When media critic Anita Sarkeesian, the founder of *Feminist Frequency*, a website on which she analyzes patriarchy and misogyny in gaming culture, launched a fundraising campaign in 2012 for her *Tropes vs. Women in Video Games* video series, she became the subject of a vicious online harassment campaign, much of it gender-based. Sarkeesian's webpage was hacked, her Wikipedia page vandalized with sexual and violent imagery, and she received multiple rape and death threats, including a message from someone who had tracked down her home address and threatened to kill her and her parents (McDonald 2014). To illustrate the vitriol regularly directed at her, Sarkeesian published on her blog a collection of the tweets she received in a single week. Sarkeesian's "content warning for misogyny" noted the tweets included "gender insults, victim blaming, incitement to suicide, sexual violence, rape and death threats" (Sarkeesian 2015).

FOUR: On March 31, 2009, the influential conservative pundit Erick Erickson published a short piece on his blog, *Red State*, expressing his exasperation with a Washington State law prohibiting the sale of dishwasher detergent containing phosphates, a measure designed to prevent water pollution. Arguing that phosphate-free detergents did not effectively clean dishes placed in the dishwasher, and that some Washington residents were driving across state lines to buy detergents containing phosphates, Erickson decried the law as "lunacy." "At what point," Erickson asked, "do the people tell the politicians to go to hell? At what point do they get off the couch, march down to their state legislator's house, pull him outside, and beat him to a bloody pulp for being an idiot?" Warning that "rage" was building in response to "government control" of people's lives, Erickson concluded, "Were I in Washington State, I'd be cleaning my gun right about now waiting to protect my property from the coming riots or the government apparatchiks coming to enforce nonsensical legislation" (Erickson 2009).

FIVE: On November 2, 2018, the fact-checkers for the *Washington Post* marked an ironic milestone. President Donald J. Trump, elected to roughly two years earlier, had surpassed 6,000 in his catalog of what the fact-checkers described as "false or misleading claims" (Kessler, Rizzo, and Kelly 2018). Noting that in the first nine months of his presidency, the president had made 1,318 false or misleading claims, an average of five a day, the fact checkers stated that "the flood of presidential misinformation" increased dramatically in the seven weeks leading up the 2018 midterm elections. In that period, according to the fact checkers, the president made a total of 1,419 false or misleading claims, or an average of 30 a day. The fact checkers confessed to being overwhelmed by the pace of the president's false and misleading statements. After one Trump rally, the fact checkers wrote that "the burden of keeping up with this verbiage" was "too daunting for our deadline."

• • •

Welcome to public discourse in the contemporary United States: intolerant and irrational, venomous and violent, divisive and dishonest. What is perhaps most startling about the episodes above, or any of the other mendacious, rage-driven examples I might have referenced, is how utterly routine they have become in the context of contemporary public argument in the United States. With each passing news cycle, it seems, there are fresh reports of the demonization, incendiary metaphors, and virulent historical analogies that now characterize public discourse. Cable television, talk radio, and countless portals on the Internet have made toxic rhetoric a fact of everyday life, an emotional release, a form of entertainment, and a corporate product.

More, such rhetoric has managed to undermine discourses grounded in rational argument and logical proofs, formerly considered authoritative. Our toxic public arguments have contributed to a rhetorical climate in which we no longer share common understandings of the nature of a fact, or what counts as evidence, or how to interpret what evidence may be presented.[1] Even scientific matters, such as climate change and the safety of vaccines, are subject to rancorous, ideologically driven debate.

Indeed, many people in the United States seem to have lost confidence in the very existence of factual information that stands apart from partisan interests, while the institutions formerly entrusted with supplying such information—those of government, science, public schools, higher education, traditional media, and others—are regarded with suspicion and even contempt by large numbers of people. A study by the Pew Research Center (2015) found "the American public is deeply cynical about government, politics and the nation's leaders," while a Gallup survey reported, "Americans' confidence in major institutions continues to lag below historical averages," with confidence in newspapers and organized religion dropping to record lows (Norman 2016). Perhaps this loss of faith explains the conspiracy theories that routinely achieve wide purchase among sections of the public: George W. Bush was responsible for 9/11; Barack Obama was born in Kenya; Hillary Clinton operated a pedophilia ring from the basement of a Washington, DC, pizzeria.

Nor is the deepening distrust of empirical reality confined to the darker fringes of US life. The 2016 presidential campaign and subsequent election of Donald J. Trump ushered into US political and cultural life a new vocabulary of "post-truth," "alternative facts," and "fake news." Mr. Trump himself, regardless of whether or not one agreed with his politics, routinely trafficked in falsehoods throughout his unconventional campaign and into his presidency, such as when he claimed without evidence that millions of illegal votes prevented him from the winning the popular vote in the election (Jacobson 2016), or when he falsely asserted that Barack Obama had wiretapped his phones (Heigl 2017), or when he implied that Texas Senator Ted Cruz's father may have been implicated in the assassination of John F. Kennedy, a claim the fact-checking organization Politifact called "incorrect and ridiculous" (Jacobson and Qiu 2016).

Perhaps the rhetorical moment was most succinctly captured by Trump surrogate Scottie Nell Hughes, who was interviewed on NPR's *Diane Rehm* show just days after Trump's victory. Responding to critics who accused Trump of repeatedly lying throughout his campaign, Hughes said:

> And so one thing that has been interesting this entire campaign season to watch is that people that say facts are facts, they're not really facts. Everybody has a way, it's kind of like looking at ratings or looking at a glass of half-full water. Everybody has a way of interpreting them to be the truth or not true. There's no such thing, unfortunately, anymore of facts. And so Mr. Trump's tweet amongst a certain crowd, a large—a large part of the population, are truth. (*Rehm* 2017)

Hughes was widely reviled for her statement, "There's no such thing, unfortunately, anymore of facts," but she accurately described a juncture in contemporary US public argument.

Surveys of public attitudes indicate widespread pessimism regarding the state of public discourse. A 2017 study by NPR/PBS News Hour/Marist, for example, found that 70 percent of Americans believe the tone of political discourse has declined since the election of President Trump, a finding that held true across both major political parties (Santhanam 2017). A study by the public relations firm Weber Shandwick (2016) offered even more discouraging numbers, reporting that 95 percent of respondents say the lack of civility is a problem in the United States, with 70 percent saying incivility has reached "crisis" proportions. While the term "civility" can obscure more than it reveals, as I shall discuss presently, studies of "incivility" suggest that it lowers political trust (Mutz and Reeves 2005), promotes negative attitudes toward political leaders

(Cappella and Jamieson 1997), and leads to increasing suspicion among Americans of one another (Rodin and Steinberg 2003). Perhaps it is not surprising, then, that a report by the Pew Research Center (2017) on political polarization in the United States asserts that the partisan divide on political values reached "record levels" during Barack Obama's presidency, and that "the gaps have grown even larger" during Donald Trump's first year as president.

Vituperative rhetoric, of course, is nothing new in US political life. In his book, *Scandal and Civility: Journalism and the Birth of American Democracy*, historian Marcus Daniel reminds us that, "there was no golden age of American politics when public spirited men debated issues of great moment with a rationality as sharply honed as their classical rhetoric, when public debate was conducted within well understood and widely accepted limits of civility . . . On the contrary, scandal and incivility have always been part of American politics" (Daniel 2009, 5). Historian Thomas Bender supplies a similar narrative, writing, "Nineteenth-century politics was rife with insult; reasoned argument was often eclipsed by spectacle, liquor and corruption" (Bender 2003, 27). And communication scholars Judith Rodin and Stephen P. Steinberg recall that abusive discourse has deep roots in US history, observing that Presidents Jefferson, Lincoln, Cleveland, and the Theodore Roosevelt were subject to "vicious" and "uncivil" attacks (Rodin and Steinberg 2003, 3).

Nor was such discourse necessarily destructive. Daniel argues that the "tempestuous, fiercely partisan, and highly personal" politics of the eighteenth century post-revolutionary United States contributed to the creation of a "vibrant and iconoclastic culture of political dissent" and "the emergence of a more democratic social and political order" (6). In similar spirit, Bruce Thornton, a research fellow at the Hoover Institute, writes in "Three Cheers for Incivility," that the "dislike of political rancor is at the heart of a dislike of democracy" and that efforts to "moderate or police, based on some subjective notions of 'civility' or decorum, the clashing expressions of passionate beliefs often is an attempt to limit the freedom to express those beliefs, and a way to benefit one faction at the expense of others" (Thornton 2015).

Yet if we properly reject nostalgia for a golden age that never was, neither should we dismiss the badly degraded condition of our present public argument. In the last twenty-five years, social scientists Jefferey M. Berry and Sarah Sobieraj contend in their meticulously researched book, *The Outrage Industry: Political Opinion Media and the New Incivility*, the discourse of what the authors call "outrage," characterized by "hallmark venom, vilification of opponents, and hyperbolic reinterpretations of events," has moved from its marginal position in the broader media landscape to become "a new genre of political opinion media" (Berry and Sobieraj 2014, 5). Nor can the corrosive state of contemporary public argument, insists communications scholar Clarke Rountree, be understood as simply the latest expression of the invective, constructive or otherwise, that has long characterized political rhetoric in the United States (Rountree 2013a). Rather, Rountree argues, it represents something "completely new," a product of developments in media, political party affiliations, campaign finance laws, and what Rountree calls "our post-9/11 culture of fear" (431).

Whatever the causes, we appear to have arrived at a historical and cultural moment in which there is little place in our civic arguments for deliberative language that might explore ambiguities, express doubt, admit error, or accommodate ideas that contradict our own. We seem increasingly incapable, as scholar Danielle S. Allen puts it, of "talking to strangers," or constructively engaging with those who disagree with us questions of war and peace, wealth and poverty, sickness and health (Allen 2004). The result is arguments reduced to assertions and counter-assertions, claims and counter-claims, often expressed in language that is shrill, irrational, duplicitous, and violent. The discourse of "crisis" is cheaply purchased in US public affairs—we are told of the literacy crisis, the economic crisis, the environmental crisis, and others—but if we are not experiencing a crisis of public argument, one that divides along political, cultural, economic, and demographic lines, we are near the edge of something like it.

What does all this mean for teachers of writing, and for the discipline of Writing Studies?[2]

WRITING STUDIES AND PUBLIC ARGUMENT

The state of contemporary public argument presents an unsettling paradox to those of us who identify, whether as teachers, scholars, administrators, or others, with the discipline of Writing Studies. By many measures, our discipline has never been more robust. Once a derided outlier in departments of English, today Writing Studies is characterized by major scholarship, vigorous graduate programs, and well-organized national advocacy associations. The first-year writing course, the central project of the discipline for much of its existence, continues to be the subject of serious scholarly work, serving as a site for pedagogical innovations that link the teaching of writing to political activism (Kahn and Lee 2010), community engagement (Mathieu 2005), multilingualism

(Matsuda 2012), digital rhetoric (Berry, Hawisher, and Selfe 2012), and so much more.

Yet despite the sustained scholarship devoted to the study and teaching of writing, despite the highly-trained Writing Studies faculty leading writing programs across the nation, and despite the impressive numbers of students enrolled in our courses each year, we seem to have little influence on the conduct of US public argument. The principles we teach are largely absent from the public square, and our conceptions of rhetoric as methods of inquiry and community building seem as so much folklore, appealing mythologies that have little purchase in the worlds beyond our classrooms. Moreover, as historians, journalists, and others are called upon to analyze the problems of public discourse, we in Writing Studies are largely incidental to the discussion, our disciplinary expertise unacknowledged or obscured by perceptions of our work as a form of remedial service. In conversations concerning the character of public discourse, I mean to say, we are mostly irrelevant.

This disconnection of our work from the conduct of public discourse is symptomatic of a greater disciplinary problem: our failure to explain to the general public, to colleagues in other disciplines, to our students, and perhaps even to ourselves what we do, why our work matters, and what is at stake in the teaching of writing. We have not successfully communicated what David W. Smit termed our "teleological reason for being" (Smit 2011, 1). We appear to have no prevailing disciplinary narrative, and our diverse and contending theories, methods, and pedagogies, Smit argued in *The End of Composition Studies*, "have no common theoretical basis, no shared assumptions about the nature and value of writing, and no communal sense of what kinds of writing should be taught and learned" (Smit 2004, 223). Moreover, the pluralism that so invigorates the discipline paradoxically threatens to isolate us within increasingly specialized discourses that have little to say to one another. As one respondent put it in an April 2014 WPA-listserv discussion on engaging the public, "Unless I miss my mark, the sea of folks out there teaching composition do not even form a cohesive group themselves. I'm just saying I'm confused about who we are . . ." Perhaps it is no surprise we continue to debate among ourselves the identity of the discipline and its future (Hansen 2011).

There are advantages to such contentions, certainly. Debates over disciplinary identities can be a sign of intellectual vitality, and the refusal of "grand narratives" has encouraged the development of approaches to writing research and teaching that are grounded in the political, cultural, and material realities of learners. Rejecting what Deborah H.

Holdstein has described as "a prudent, if sometimes misguided, desire to promote a narrow scope or focus" (Holdstein 2005, 406), we have become an intellectually capacious discipline, one that has made space for such diverging standpoints as classical rhetoric and cultural studies, expressivist pedagogy and critical theory, feminist pedagogy and queer studies. In what Lance Massey calls "The (Dis)Order of Composition" (Massey 2011) we continue to grow.

Nor are we lacking in white papers, outcome statements, and other such documents that attempt to articulate our disciplinary priorities. The *WPA Outcomes Statement for First-Year Composition (3.0)* (2014), for example, provides a cogent representation of "the writing knowledge, practices, and attitudes that undergraduate students develop in first-year composition." Similarly, *The Framework for Success in Postsecondary Writing* (2011), endorsed by the Council of Writing Program Administrators, the National Council of Teachers of English (NCTE), and the National Writing Project (2011), provides a description of "the rhetorical and twenty-first-century skills as well as habits of mind and experiences that are critical for college success" (1). Our writing textbooks, too, may be said to offer a collective representation of aims, language, and practices common to the writing classroom.

However, such efforts have not resulted the formation of a prevailing disciplinary narrative, or a common set of assumptions concerning the nature and value of writing. As Writing Studies is undermined by the same forces destabilizing higher education generally—budget cuts and rising tuitions, a growing reliance on adjunct labor, and increasing public skepticism about the value of a postsecondary education—we have yet to offer a common vision, a shared rationale for our work. We are constrained in telling our story because we are not agreed on just what the story is. What are teaching when we teach writing? Why are we teaching it? What is the ultimate purpose, the *telos* of our work? We appear to lack a shared language for answering such questions.

However, such a language, or so I will argue in this book, has historically been available to us and is available to us still, if we would reclaim it. It is a language derived from the particulars of our classroom practices, but one that provides a common rationale for the intellectual project of our discipline. I refer to the language of *ethics*, that branch of philosophy given over to questions of how to live a good life. What does it mean to be a good person? What kind of person do I want to be? How should I live my life?

Such questions are relevent in the context of the writing class because to teach writing is to teach the communicative practices, such as making claims, offering evidence, and considering counter-arguments, among others, through which writers propose and navigate human relationships. And it is in the context of navigating these human relationships that we are necessarily engaged, students and teachers, with the values, attitudes, and actions that fall within the domain of the ethical. "At the point when you begin to write," James E. Porter has written, "you begin to define yourself ethically. You make a choice about what is the right thing to do—even if that choice is a tentative and contingent one" (Porter 1998, 150).

I do not mean by this that we *should* teach rhetorical ethics in our classrooms, or that we are *obliged* to do so. Rather, I am suggesting that as teachers of writing we are *always* and *already* engaged in the teaching of rhetorical ethics; that the teaching of writing *necessarily* and *inevitably* involves us in ethical deliberation and decision-making. I am proposing that the very act of sitting down to write places before the writer and teacher of writing those questions that speak to the kinds of people we choose to be, the sorts of relationships we seek to establish with others, and the kinds of communities in which we wish to live. Have I been truthful in making these claims? Have I been fair-minded in considering views that oppose my own? Shall I use this inflammatory metaphor in my essay? Why or why not? When we discuss such questions with students, when we engage them in conversations about why they make some choices over others and what principles might guide their choices, we are in effect teaching ethics; more specifically, we are teaching practices of ethical discourse. We are teaching students what it means to be, in the ethical sense, a "good writer" in the twenty-first century.

To say that writing and the teaching of writing involve ethical reflection and decision-making is not to suggest that individual writers should be judged as ethical or unethical, in the sense of being moral, upright, honest, and so forth. Nor it is to say that writers necessarily reflect on ethical concerns as they write. They may or may not. Neither is it to assert, finally, that every text can be regarded as ethical or unethical based on its content. Many texts, perhaps most, are devoid of the subject matter typically associated with ethics. Rather, to say writing involves ethical choices is to say that when creating a text the writer addresses others. And that, in turn, initiates a relationship between writer and readers, one that entangles writers, and those who would teach writing, in the questions, problems, and choices associated with ethical reflection and reasoning.

And it is in the discourse of ethics that we teachers of writing find a language that, should we choose to reclaim and share it with our students, will expand and complicate students' understandings of what it means to write, showing students that what they write ultimately says as much about the kinds of people they are as it does about the content and effects of their texts. More, the discourse of ethics offers us, teachers of writing, a common narrative, a story we might tell to students, to colleagues in other disciplines, to deans, to legislators, and to the general public, about what it is we teach, why our work matters, and what is at stake in the teaching of writing in the twenty-first century. Finally, the teaching of ethical rhetoric, should we acknowledge and embrace it in our classrooms, provides a vocabulary with which our students might learn to "talk to strangers" and perhaps begin to repair the broken state of our public arguments.

These, at any rate, are the claims I will argue in this book. Before going further, however, we need to say what we mean by the word, "ethics."

WHAT DO WE MEAN BY ETHICS?

Until recently, ethics was defined in Western philosophy by one of the two preeminent moral theories, the so-called "Big Two": deontology, the ethics of rules and obligations, and consequentialism, the ethics of outcomes and results. In recent decades, these theories have been challenged by the emergence of postmodern ethics, which has become the dominant ethical paradigm throughout much of the humanities (Berlin 1990; Porter 1998). Each of these theories provides a moral framework, or a set of principles, for guiding ethical decision-making in the course of everyday life: What is the right thing to do in this situation? What are the consequences of taking that action, or not taking it? How do I decide between irreconcilable truths?

Applied to the writing classroom, each moral theory offers students and teachers a set of principles for guiding ethical decision-making when reading or composing texts. Each provides, to say it another way, an understanding of "the good" that informs a conception of "the good writer." And yet none of these frameworks, the deontological, the consequential, or the postmodern, provides a fully adequate account of how writers might define themselves ethically as they make choices, recalling James Porter's apt phrase, about "the right thing to do."

I recommend in this book a different conception of ethics for the writing course, one derived from a moral theory that is both old and new, discarded and recovered, and one that inevitably engages us in discussions of truthfulness, accountability, open-mindedness, courage, practical wisdom, justifiable anger, and more. There is a word for such qualities. They are examples of what Aristotle in the *Nicomachean Ethics* called "virtues," from the Greek *arête,* or, broadly, "excellence," and they are today the subject of that branch of moral philosophy known as "virtue ethics." A virtue, according to Rosalind Hursthouse, one of the most prominent contemporary philosophers of virtue, is "the concept of something that makes it possessor good; a virtuous person is a morally good, excellent, or admirable person who acts and reacts well, rightly, as she should—she gets things right" (Hursthouse 1999, 13). For Richard White, in *Radical Virtues: Moral Wisdom and the Ethics of Contemporary Life,* "the virtues, including justice, courage, and compassion, are the ways in which we typically grasp the nature of goodness" (White 2008, 1).

Plato and Aristotle analyzed the virtues in their writings, and philosophers from Confucius to Alasdair MacIntyre have explored virtue-based approaches to ethics. Virtue ethics, which Philip Cafaro notes is sometimes described as "the ethical system that takes 'virtue' or 'the virtues' as its primary ethical category" (Cafaro 2015, 442, n.1), offers an alternative to ethical traditions grounded in the rules of deontology or the anticipated outcomes of consequentialism. More, virtue ethics offers a moral theory that takes us beyond the resolute skepticism of postmodernism. And it is in the language of the virtues, in what I will call "rhetorical virtues,"[3] by which I mean the discursive enactments of truthfulness, accountability, open-mindedness, and the like, that students and teachers of writing can find "principles for action,"[4] or rationales for making ethical decisions in the writing class.

Talk of "virtue" may sound strange, or worse, to our modern ears, having faded, Brian Treanor writes, "from common use and public language, to the more narrow and private sphere of sexual or religious morality" (Treanor 2014, 15). Certainly, the term has little purchase in Writing Studies. While we have embraced Aristotle's *Rhetoric,* we have mostly ignored his *Ethics.* Perhaps this is because "we postmodern skeptical academics," as Patricia Bizzell wrote more than two decades ago, "are habitually fearful that any talk of teaching virtue will tend to introduce exclusions, as socially privileged groups in our diverse nation arrogate to themselves the right to define what virtue is taught" (Bizzell 1992b, 6). If we are to teach an ethics of virtue, I understand Bizzell to be asking, whose virtues are we teaching?

Perhaps, too, we are wary of the historical and ideological inflections of the word, which has been associated with the subjugation of women, with neo-conservative ideology, and with an exclusively—and therefore exclusionary—Christian worldview. Feminist philosophers, for example, have made a compelling case that virtue-based ethical theories have historically accommodated concepts of "feminine virtues" central to the subordination and control of women (Jaggar 1991; Grimshaw 1993). Others have argued that the concept of virtue has been appropriated by neo-conservatives who have used it as a racialized discourse through which to shift conversations about poverty and inequality away from social causes and toward the supposed "individual character deficiencies" of the poor, particularly African Americans (Tessman 2001, 89). And then there are the theological undercurrents of the word, perhaps most clearly illustrated by the Catholic Saint Thomas Aquinas's ([1911] 1981) conception of the "theological virtues" of faith, hope, and charity, which are said to be imparted by God and therefore available only to believers—meaning non-believers are effectively excluded from the virtuous life. In short, there are reasons why the term "virtue" is not exactly trending in Writing Studies.

Yet while these historical, ideological, and theological attachments can inform our considerations of virtue, they need not restrict our understanding of the term, nor foreclose to us its possibilities. Recent work in feminist virtue ethics, critical virtue ethics, and non-Western virtue theories, as I discuss in chapter 3, offer evocative and expansive interpretations of the term that complicate the ways we might read and use the notion of virtue. Indeed, I will argue that while the history of virtue has complicated the term, we may yet find, those of us who teach writing, that the provocations of virtue are ultimately affirming, generative, and rich with possibility.

In discussing virtue in this book, I will make a distinction between two kinds of virtues. What I will call *virtues of rhetorical practice* refers to the virtues enacted in the practices we teach, our claims, evidence, counterarguments, and the rest. What I shall term *virtues of rhetorical interpretation* refers to the virtues we judge to be enacted in the readings we undertake or in the rhetorical situations to which we respond. So, for examples of the latter, we might speak of the virtues of justice and righteous indignation expressed in Martin Luther King, Jr.'s "Beyond Vietnam" speech, which called for an end to the war (King 1967), or the virtues of courage and compassion enacted in Mary Fisher's "A Whisper of AIDS" speech at the 1992 Republican National Convention (Fisher 1992). While both the virtues of practice and interpretation express the qualities, traits, or dispositions through which we might, in White's phrase, "grasp the nature of goodness," I am primarily concerned in this book with virtues of rhetorical practice.

THIS, NOT THESE

Let me say what I am not proposing in this book. First, I am not proposing that we teach in our classes established codes or standards of behavior associated with a particular culture, religious faith, or ideology. Virtue ethics, which Rebecca L. Walker and Philip J. Ivanhoe describe as "an umbrella term covering a plurality of theoretical and even anti-theoretical" approaches to ethics (Walker and Ivanhoe 2007a, 3), resists the application of such codes and standards, locating the rightness of wrongness of actions in the character of moral agents whose judgments are informed by the particulars of situation. I am not recommending to writers or teachers of writing, then, a set of rules or standard practices to follow.

Neither am I advocating that we renounce previous practices, approaches, or pedagogies for teaching writing. I am not calling for writing programs and teachers to discard previous knowledge, abandon what has worked, and reinvent themselves and their classrooms. Rather, I am suggesting that whatever theoretical and pedagogical approaches may prevail in a given writing program or classroom—whether expressivism, critical pedagogy, writing about writing, or others—ethical questions and considerations will inevitably be present, percolating under the surface or boiling over it. I am proposing that programs and teachers of writing address these questions and considerations directly and intentionally, integrating them into ongoing discussions and making explicit what is often left implicit in the writing class. I suggest ways such conversations might be structured in chapter 5.

Finally, I am not offering in this book yet another jeremiad on the decline of civility and the need to restore it to public life. Certainly, there is much to admire about civility, which Stephen L. Carter defines as "the sum of the many sacrifices we are called to make for the sake of living together" (Carter 1998, 11), and which John A. Hall (Hall 2013) describes as a "precondition" of truth and moral development. In Writing Studies, the scholar Craig Rood has argued thoughtfully and persuasively for what he calls "rhetorical civility," which he defines in part as "the rhetorical practices committed to understanding and being understood, respecting and being respected" (Rood 2013, 344). Conceived in such terms, civility is more than the historical association with manners, etiquette, and politeness; it is beyond these a precondition of democratic practice and a set of shared norms that offer an alternative to violence (Hall). Indeed, Cheshire Calhoun contends that civility should be understood as a virtue, one that communicates, Calhoun writes, "basic moral attitudes of respect, tolerance, and considerateness" (Calhoun 2000, 255).

Yet civility can also be an equivocal if not a masking word, obscuring more than it reveals. In contexts of asymmetrical power, civility can function as a politically regressive term used to preserve an unjust social and economic order. Nancy Welch, for example, has observed that civility can function "to hold in check agitation against a social order that is undemocratic . . . and unequal in distribution of wealth" (Welch 2012, 36). Welch takes as her example the 1912 Bread and Roses Strike, in which striking immigrant millworkers in Lawrence, Massachusetts were condemned as unruly and "uncivil" by Lawrence's social elites and textile barons. Nina M. Lozano-Reich and Dana L. Cloud have similarly argued that when privileged interests exclude as "uncivil" those voices deemed controversial or subversive, the call to civility may function as a strategy "to effectively silence and punish marginalized groups" (Lozano-Reich and Cloud 2009, 223). In this view, civility can serve to check legitimate expressions of protest, while accusations of incivility can be used to manage public discourse in ways that serve the interests of dominant classes. The meaning of civility, it would seem, is conditioned by those who call for it, and those who are called upon to observe it.

The virtues, in contrast, offer a vocabulary that is explicit, exacting, and wide in scope. While the language of virtue expresses, for example, attitudes of respect, tolerance, and considerateness—those attitudes prized in civility—the vocabulary of virtue also encompasses demands for justice, judgment, and righteous anger. There are times and places, the language of virtue allows, when the attitudes of respect, tolerance, and considerateness that characterize civility may not be possible or appropriate. A virtue-based conception of discourse recognizes that rude, confrontational, even incendiary speech can be a necessary and, indeed, an ethical response to inequality, oppression, environmental destruction, and other abuses. What is called for in a virtue-based ethics of writing is the quality of what Aristotle termed *phronesis*, or practical wisdom, the ability of know when such speech or writing is called for, at whom it should be directed, and how it may best be expressed. An ethics of rhetorical virtue, then, demands more than mere civility.

REASONS TO DOUBT

There are good reasons to doubt this project. I will discuss just three. We can doubt the value of argument. In making the case for the explicit teaching of rhetorical ethics, I focus primarily on the teaching of argument, which I define, quoting Douglas Walton, as "the giving of reasons to support or criticize a claim that is questionable, or open to doubt"

(Walton 2006, 1). I concentrate on teaching argument rather than, say, narrative or poetics,[5] because argument is the common currency of many college writing programs, the subject of our classes, curricula, and textbooks; because it is the dominant discourse throughout academia, the genre in which our students will most often be asked to write after leaving our classrooms; and because I hold the view that argument remains, despite everything, an essential means through which to participate in civic conversation and promote a more just and inclusive society.

But perhaps this view is wrong. The rationale for making arguments rests on the assumption that the giving of good reasons grounded in relevant evidence can result in changes of attitudes or behaviors, that is, persuasion. Recent research, however, suggests the opposite outcome is just as likely, if not more so.

A study by political scientists Brendan Nyhan and Jason Reifler found that when people were presented with factual information that contradicted their deeply held beliefs, not only were they unlikely to be persuaded, they effectively doubled down on their beliefs (Nyhan and Reifler 2010). Nyhan and Reifler call this "the backfire effect," in which corrections to a belief actually increase the original misperceptions. Rather than effecting persuasion through the reasoned presentation of claims and evidence, the ideal of many writing courses, arguments may cause listeners or readers to become even more entrenched in their views, even when it can be conclusively demonstrated these views are grounded in misinformation.

Perhaps, too, the teaching of argument is politically regressive. Writing Studies scholar Todd DeStigter (DeStigter 2015) has questioned the widely held assumption that argumentative writing promotes critical thinking, provides training in the rational deliberation essential for a functioning democracy, and offers students a form of cultural capital enabling upward social and academic mobility. Instead, DeStigter writes, the "cognitive ideal" (15) of argumentation taught in secondary and higher education rests on epistemological assumptions, rooted in the writings of Kant and Descartes, which hold that there exist "real truths" accessible through abstract reasoning processes. However, modern philosophy, asserts DeStigter, has exposed rationality as just another discourse masquerading as truth, and argument as just another culturally privileged mode of communication. Rather than enabling practices of deliberative democracy and promoting upward mobility, according to DeStigter, argument can have an adverse effect, limiting what counts as legitimate political discourse by excluding, for example, the discourse practices of minority groups, thereby inhibiting actions that might address economic inequality. DeStigter recommends that teachers of writing recognize "more agonistic and even revolutionary models of public activism," in which people might do "impolite, illegal, or even violent things in their struggle for justice" (24).

Next, we can doubt reason. Recent research in human cognition suggests that the purpose of reasoning is not to assess the validity of claims or discover impartial truths but has instead developed for the more competitive purpose of enabling one group of people to prevail over another (Mercier 2011b; Mercier and Sperber 2011; Mercier and Landemore 2012). In what has become known as "the argumentative theory of reasoning" (Mercier and Landemore 2012, 243), people who argue are not seeking consensus or promoting understanding but are instead intent on persuading others of the validity of their views, that is, winning. More, the cognitivists suggest that what are generally perceived as fallacies of reasoning, such as confirmation bias, the tendency to interpret information in a way that supports one's preconceptions, are not design flaws in the system but are instead products of human evolution. Patricia Cohen explains that "bias, lack of logic and other supposed flaws that pollute the stream of reason are instead social adaptations that enable one group to persuade (and defeat) another" (Cohen 2011). Truth and accuracy, in this conception of argument, are mostly incidental.

This suggests that teaching students, as many of us do, to view the research process as an opportunity for inquiry and exploration, and not as a pretext to confirm pre-existing biases, effectively places us at odds with human evolutionary development. And attempting to reform students' reasoning processes by persuading them to abandon their biases is akin to proclaiming, cognitive scientist Hugo Mercier has written, "hands were made for walking and that everybody should be taught that" (Mercier n.d.).

Finally, we can doubt the possibility of virtuous discourse. As if cognitive and ideological objections to argument were not enough, there is, for lack of a better term, the realist objection. Let us concede there is something quixotic, if not naïve, in the notion of a virtuous public discourse, particularly one rooted in the everyday practices of the first-year writing class. For one thing, history is not abounding with examples of enlightened public argument, and even the ancient Greeks, from whom we inherit much of our thinking on rhetoric, virtue, and democracy, created a society that oppressed women, discriminated against immigrants, and sold their enemies into slavery. Moreover, to argue that teaching the rhetorical virtues of honesty, accountability, practical wisdom, and the like will somehow liberate our society from its addiction to toxic public discourse, to say nothing of promoting a more just and inclusive democracy, seems to call for extended periods of magical thinking. More, it runs the risk of reviving, zombie-like, the literacy myth, or the fiction that certain privileged forms of literacy practice can overcome the structural barriers that maintain social and economic inequalities (Graff and Duffy 2016).

Yet if there are reasons to doubt, there are equally reasons to counterbalance such doubts. A study by the political scientists Thomas Wood and Ethan Porter (Wood and Porter 2016), for example, tested 8,100 subjects on 36 issues for evidence of Nyhan and Reifler's backfire effect. On only one issue—the presence of weapons of mass destruction in Iraq in 2003—did the researchers find evidence of a cognitive backfire, or a refusal of participants to acknowledge their own misconceptions. "By and large," the authors write, "citizens heed factual information, even when such information challenges their partisan and ideological commitments." Wood and Porter's study suggests that we may not yet fully understand the interactions of persuasion, ideology, and cognition, and that discounting the role of argument in promoting the common good may be, at the very least, premature.

DeStigter's critique of argument, moreover, may be interpreted not so much as a rejection of the genre but a call for its expansion, or a conception of argument that admits diverse rhetorical traditions, especially the discourse practices of minority groups, as well as one that recognizes non-textual modalities, such as oral narrative, music, and dance. Should we see these as arguments, as means through which students propose and navigate human relationships, then we are once again returned to the realm of the ethical. Each of these new and expanded forms of argument, in other words, would equip their practitioners to argue in ways that have enabled them, paraphrasing Hursthouse, to act and react well, rightly, as they should—to get things right.

Similarly, the argumentative theory of reasoning can be read not as a nihilistic rejection of argument as a means for achieving consensus and searching for truth, but rather as a repudiation of the Cartesian view of reasoning in which the individual privately examines her beliefs for the purpose of discarding erroneous beliefs and finding more accurate ones. In place of the individual model of Cartesian reasoning, the argumentative theory offers a fundamentally social theory of reasoning. When individuals are left to their own devices or surrounded by like-minded believers, the cognitive scientists tell us, they will persist in their confirmation biases, motived reasoning, and other habits of mind that impede good decision-making. However, when opposing groups come together to argue, each presenting their own conceptions of what is right and true, the better arguments ultimately emerge.

If we are hard-wired to press ahead with our biases and motivated reasoning, in other words, we have equally evolved to listen for the better argument, and to adopt such arguments for our own benefit. "If the people who listen to argument were not better off on average," Mercier has written, "they would evolve to stop listening to arguments" (Mercier 2011a). For this reason, Mercier and Landemore contend that the argumentative theory of reasoning is compatible with practices of deliberative democracy, in which debates featuring diverse opinions ultimately produce better outcomes on questions that may be evaluated from "a factual, moral, or political point of view" (6).

And what of the realist objection to teaching an ethics of virtue? Is it chimerical to imagine that our classrooms might serve as locations for a transformative ethical discourse, one that might reform our toxic public argument and promote healthier forms of civic engagement? Is it another expression of the literacy myth and evidence of magical thinking? Perhaps. But let us consider, before we decide, the intellectual and structural state of Writing Studies in the twenty-first century.

Intellectually, we find ourselves as professional inheritors of the rhetorical tradition. This means, among other things, that we are charged with teaching the rhetorical knowledge that comprises the materials of academic and public argument. To that end, we have studied the structure of arguments, the relationship of argument and situation, and the delicate, sometimes murky interplay of argument and persuasion, belief and truth. We have at our disposal, moreover, a vocabulary for teaching students how to read, analyze, and write arguments. Nor do we limit ourselves to the study of argument in a single discipline—how arguments function in, say, philosophy or biology—but instead teach broader, transferrable principles that will enable our students to make effective arguments in venues as varied as a college essay, a county courthouse, or the editorial pages of the *New York Times* or *The National Review*. In short, while the field of Writing Studies is not defined by the teaching of argument, we have nonetheless been at such teaching for a long while. We know what good arguments look like, we know how to make them, and we know how teach them.

Structurally, there is nothing else quite like us. Our courses in writing and rhetoric are required at most postsecondary institutions in the United States, and the demand for enrollment is such that we typically lobby to reduce our class sizes, not increase them. In her 1998 essay, "Composition in the University," Sharon Crowley, citing data at the time indicating that more than twelve million students were enrolled in US colleges and universities, suggested that if just a quarter of those students were enrolled in freshman composition courses, enrollment in writing courses would exceed four million students (Crowley 1998, 1). Using Crowley's same calculations today, when the National Center of Education Statistics (NCES) reports that 20.2 million students were enrolled in US postsecondary education as of 2014, the number of students in our classes would exceed five million annually. Nor are the numbers likely to decrease anytime soon. The most recent NCES report predicts a 15 percent increase in postsecondary enrollment between 2015 and 2025, raising the number of students in our courses, using Crowley's thumbnail calculations, closer to six million annually (National Center of Education Statistics 2016). Of course, we do not know exactly how many of these students will take a first-year or other writing course, but even the most conservative estimates suggest the numbers will be substantial.

Who is better positioned, then, intellectually and structurally, to influence the future of public argument in the United States than teachers of college writing? Who is more qualified? Decades in the making, we have built in Writing Studies a dynamic enterprise, a powerful engine for shaping the way people speak, write, and argue. We have the capacity in our classes to engage hundreds of thousands and more likely millions of students each year in introductory conversations about the relationships of writing, rhetoric, argument, and ethical discourse. What have we done with this extraordinary opportunity? What could we do? What possibilities are available to us?

There are reasons to doubt the arguments of this book. We need not dismiss such doubts. Skepticism, too, is a virtue. I wrote this book, however, to offer my fellow writing teachers reasons to believe.

OVERVIEW OF THIS BOOK

In chapter 1, I discuss the construct of "toxic rhetoric," its features, causes, and effects. What is "toxic rhetoric"? How shall we define the term? What are its origins, and what forces work to sustain it in the twenty-first century? And why does it matter? What are its effects? What is so "toxic," finally, about toxic discourse? In addressing these questions, I consider the meanings of such terms as "incivility," "hate speech," "outrage discourse," and others. I examine specific language practices that comprise toxic discourse and review several of the explanations for its rise in US society. I conclude the chapter by reflecting upon the effects of toxic rhetoric upon our civic friendships and upon our students.

In chapter 2, "Imagining The Good Writer: Moral Theories in the Writing Class," I review the moral theories that have most influenced ethical decision-making in Western culture, deontology, consequentialism, and, more recently, postmodernism. I argue that each theory presents a conception of the "good writer," but that each of these conceptions is, for different reasons, inadequate as the basis of an ethical rhetoric in the twenty-first century writing classroom. I conclude the chapter by calling for an expanded ethical vocabulary, which I locate in the tradition of the virtues.

In chapters 3 through 5, I discuss the virtues and virtue ethics. In chapter 3, "Habits of the Heart: Virtue and Virtue Ethics," I provide an introduction to virtue and virtue ethics, reviewing ancient and contemporary treatments of each term. I provide an introduction to Aristotle's theories of virtue, briefly consider neo-Aristotelian virtue ethics, and offer summaries of alternative accounts of virtue, including sentimentalist, feminist, non-Western, and applied virtue ethics. In this chapter, too, I address the "vices of virtue," or the association of virtue with the subjugation of women, with neo-conservative ideology, and with an exclusively, and therefore exclusionary, Christian doctrine. I argue that while each of these associations informs the understanding of virtue, they neither define nor foreclose its possibilities for teachers of writing.

In chapter 4, "Rhetorical Virtues: Toward an Ethics of Practice," I look more closely at the relationship of argument and the rhetorical virtues. I contend that teaching the practices of making claims, presenting evidence, addressing counterarguments, teaching revision inevitably and necessarily involves teachers and students in questions of truthfulness, accountability, open-mindedness, intellectual courage, and other expressions of rhetorical virtue. I conclude by reflecting on how argument, typically conceived in terms of domination and control may be understood as an act of radical humility and community with others.

Chapter 5, "Teaching Rhetorical Virtues," offers strategies for discussing rhetorical virtue in the writing class. I offer the concepts of situation, naming, modeling, exemplars, and dissensus as means of stimulating ethical discussion in the writing class, and present examples of each for consideration. I emphasize in this chapter that discussions of rhetorical virtue can be accommodated within diverse approaches to teaching writing and do not require teachers to abandon closely held pedagogical commitments. Finally, I discuss the role of institutional culture in promoting ethical rhetoric in a writing program, concluding with a "thought experiment" in which I imagine what it might mean if writing programs across the nation were committed to the teaching of rhetorical virtue.

The conclusion of the book, "Revisiting the Q Question," is a meditation on Richard Lanham's brilliant essay titled, after Quintilian, the "Q Question" (Lanham 1993). Is there, asks Lanham, a demonstrable connection between "specific reading and writing practices and the moral life"? (173). To put it another way, do good writing and speaking skills help us, as Quintilian assumed, become good people? And might that lead to a better, healthier public discourse? I argue that while colleges and universities continue to pose contemporary versions of the Q Question, we are no better able to answer it today than Quintilian was in ancient Rome. I suggest that the Q Question is for us the wrong question, and propose instead a different kind of question, which I term the "P Question," the answers to which, I propose, may help students and teachers of writing begin to repair the toxic discourse of contemporary culture while gaining a better understanding what it means to be a Good Writer in the twenty-first century.

So much for preliminaries. Let's begin.

NOTES

1.   Who are "we"? "We" includes writing teachers, scholars, administrators, and anyone else reading this book.
2.   I use the term Writing Studies to stand in for all designations of the discipline: Rhetoric and Composition, Composition Studies, and others. I choose this term over others as it seems to me the most inclusive designation of the work of writing teachers, scholars, administrators, and others concerned with writing and writing instruction.
3.   See also, John Gage 2005. "In Pursuit of Rhetorical Virtue." *Lore.* 29–37.
4.   I am grateful to Norbert Elliot for suggesting this phrase to me.
5.   Of course, narrative and poems can also function as arguments.

1

TOXIC DISCOURSE
Character, Causes, and Consequences

"Founder of Civility Project Calls It Quits"
—Headline in *The Caucus*, the Politics and
Government blog of *The New York Times*,
January 12, 2011

On September 24, 2013 at 8:15 AM, the online editor at *Popular Science*, the monthly magazine that has been publishing articles on science and technology for the general reader since 1872, posted a brief announcement stating that the publication would no longer accept reader comments on its website. While Popular Science was "committed to fostering a lively intellectual debate" about the world of science, wrote editor Suzanne LaBarre in a post titled, "Why We're Shutting Off Our Comments" (LaBarre 2013), its website had become overwhelmed by "trolls and spambots," inhibiting the magazine's mission of informing the public about science and technology. Citing studies indicating that angry and *ad hominem* online comments, regardless of their source or credibility, skew readers' perceptions of an article and lead to polarized and negative interpretations of the text (Anderson et al. 2014), *Popular Science* felt "compelled" to shut down its online discussion section. The insults and epithets that passed for debate, wrote LaBarre in evident frustration, had the effect of undermining the mission of the magazine, and scientific knowledge generally:

> A politically motivated, decades-long war on expertise has eroded the popular consensus on a wide variety of scientifically validated topics. Everything, from evolution to the origins of climate change, is mistakenly up for grabs again. Scientific certainty is just another thing for two people to "debate" on television. And because comments sections tend to be a grotesque reflection of the media culture surrounding them, the cynical work of undermining bedrock scientific doctrine is now being done beneath our own stories, within a website devoted to championing science. (LaBarre 2013)

DOI: 10.7330/9781607328278.c001

Reasoning that reader comments shape public opinion, which influences public policy, which contributes to decisions about what kinds of research get funded, LaBarre declared, "Comments can be bad for science."

• • •

What is "toxic rhetoric"? How do we define the phrase? What are its features, its boundaries, its tropes? How has such rhetoric been characterized in popular and scholarly writing, and what reasons have been offered to explain its origins, growth, and influence? What are the consequences of toxic discourse? Why does it matter? What effects does it have upon our politics, our communications, our civic relations? How does it affect our students? Before we can articulate for Writing Studies an ethics responsive to conditions of contemporary public discourse, we should try to speak with some precision about the nature of that discourse to which we are responding. That is the aim of this chapter, in which I attempt to clarify the meaning, causes, and consequences of toxic discourse, or just what makes toxic discourse "toxic."

WHAT IS TOXIC RHETORIC?

The strident and confrontational nature of contemporary public argument in the United States has been characterized in different ways, with greater and lesser degrees of precision and partisanship, depending upon the purposes of those who would describe it. So, for example, toxic rhetoric may be defined as "incivility," a loosely defined term that can refer both to rude speech and boorish behavior (Forni 2008; Herbst 2010; Fritz 2013; Makau and Marty 2013), or it can be the subject to more exacting definitions, as in attempts to codify it as "hate speech" (Matsuda et al. 1993). Discussions of what I have termed toxic rhetoric can have frankly partisan overtones, as when those on the Right decry hypocrisy in Liberal appeals for civility (Hanson 2010), or they can be disinterested and scholarly, as in attempts by social scientists to provide empirical accounts of the features, appeal, and effects of toxic rhetoric (Berry and Sobieraj 2014). Let us now consider a few of these characterizations, drawing upon them in an effort to build a robust description of "toxic rhetoric."

INCIVILITY. Perhaps the most widely accepted characterization of angry and abusive discourse is "incivility," or rude speech, which is commonly represented in the discourse of crisis. So, for example, Stephen L. Carter laments the "crisis" of incivility exemplified by the negative character of political campaigns, the maliciousness of "public moral argument," and the bitterness of campus debate over curricula, but also by rude motorists, pornography, and offensive heavy metal music (Carter 1998, 9–10). Janie M. Harden Fritz writes of the "crisis of incivility" (Fritz 2013, 1) with reference to the workplace, characterized by "unthinking or deliberate rudeness, cutting remarks, lack of attentiveness, and violation of expectations for interpersonal interaction" (71). For their part, legal scholars Eli Wald and Russell G. Pearce argue that lawyers are responsible for what they term "the current incivility crisis" as a result of neglecting their obligation to the public good in favor of a self-interested understanding of the legal profession (Wald and Pearce 2011). Perhaps the central theme of incivility is disregard for others, which, P. M. Forni writes, is "to look elsewhere, to withdraw attention—and, with it, respect and consideration" (Forni 2008, 7).

HATE SPEECH. The concept of "hate speech" provides another, often controversial lens for characterizing abusive public discourse. While the boundaries of what is considered hate speech are often hazy, the term has been defined as "speech attacks based on race, ethnicity, religion, and sexual orientation or preference" (Walker 1994, 8, quoted in Gould 2005, 14 n5). Like incivility, hate speech can refer both to speech, such as racist jokes made at the expense of minority populations, as well as conduct, such as cross burning or spray-painting a swastika on the side of a synagogue. Abusive or uncivil speech is considered hate speech when directed at historically marginalized or persecuted groups or peoples, such as African Americans, Muslims, or Gays. Opponents of hate speech contend that it causes both emotional and physical damage to its victims, ranging from nightmares to post-traumatic stress syndrome to hypertension to suicide (Matsuda et al. 1993, 24). Legal scholar Patricia Williams has called hate speech a form of "spirit murder," given its effects on its targets (Williams 1987, 129; qtd. in Matsuda et al. 1993, 24).

In the 1980s and 1990s, US colleges and universities became testing grounds for the legal status of hate speech, as administrators attempted to respond to the increasing number of racially motivated incidents on campuses, which according to one study increased an astonishing 400 percent between 1985 and 1990 (Uelmen n.d.). In 1989, for example, The University of Wisconsin responded to a series of blatantly racist activities on campus by enacting, after much debate, a campus speech code prohibiting "Racist or discriminatory comments, epithets or other expressive behavior" that "intentionally demean" or "create an intimidating or hostile environment for education" (Siegel 1993). Other colleges and universities adopted similar policies to address "words that wound" (Matsuda et al. 1993), with the result that between 1987 and

1991 approximately one-third of all US colleges and universities had developed some form of hate speech codes (Gould 2005, 78).

Such codes have been repeatedly challenged in US courts by what scholar Jon B. Gould has describes as "an unusual mix of activists, including representatives from the civil libertarian left and the socially conservative right" (3). At issue is whether speech codes, however well intentioned, infringe upon the First Amendment right to free speech and so constitute a form of censorship. While the Supreme Court is not absolutist on the question of free speech—the 1942 decision *Chaplinsky v. New Hampshire* prohibited the use of "fighting words," or words that would provoke imminent physical harm—speech codes have been consistently overturned in the lower courts as "vague, over-broad, and ultimately illegal" (Gould 2005, 3). These decisions have not, however, settled the broader questions of what forms of speech are permissible in which social and institutional contexts, and what kinds of speech should be protected under the First Amendment. On such questions, writes Legal scholar David L. Hudson Jr. the courts have been "maddeningly inconsistent" (Hudson 2003).

Nor have these issues been resolved in the twenty-first century. Debates on college campuses about "free speech" frequently turn on the question of whether such professional provocateurs such as Milo Yiannopoulos or Ann Coulter, or controversial scholars such as Charles Murray or Ward Churchill, should be barred from speaking on the grounds that they are practicing forms of hate speech. Appearances by these and other controversial speakers have resulted in violent protests at Berkeley, Middlebury, and elsewhere.

ELIMINATIONIST RHETORIC. The journalist David Neiwert offers the concept of "eliminationist rhetoric" to describe the language of the violent, far-right wing of US politics—the white supremacists, neo-Nazis, radical militias, and similar groups (Neiwert 2009). "Eliminationism," Neiwert contends, describes, "a politics and culture that shuns dialogue and the democratic exchange of ideas in favor of the pursuit of outright elimination of the opposing side, either though suppression, exile and ejection, or extermination" (11). In such rhetoric, which is typically directed at "enemies" that include liberals, African Americans, Latinos, and Muslims, the targets are not merely objectionable, but "the embodiment of evil, unfit for participation in [the eliminationist vision of] society, and thus worthy of elimination" (11). Recurrent tropes in eliminationist rhetoric include the enemy as vermin or cancers that must be eradicated from the body politic. Neiwert argues that while such rhetoric has been a recurrent theme in US history, exemplified by the Ku Klux Klan among others, it has been amplified in recent years by mainstream media figures such as Bill O'Reilly, Glenn Beck, and Ann Coulter, who have profited by marketing fantastical conspiracy theories and other forms of misinformation derived from far-right sources.

VENOMOUS SPEECH. In his two-volume edited collection *Venomous Speech: Problems with American Political Discourse on the Right and Left,* Clarke Rountree offers an operational definition of venomous speech, characterizing it in terms of actions such as South Carolina Republican Representative Joe Wilson shouting "You Lie!" at President Obama during a speech to a joint session of Congress, and Florida Democratic Representative Alan Grayson claiming that the Republican plan for health care is for patients to "die quickly!" (Rountree 2013a). The essays in *Venomous Speech* illustrate, Rountree declares in his afterword, that we live in a "particular time in American political history where novel forces have converged into a perfect storm for spawning political gridlock, incivility, and demagoguery" (440).[1]

OUTRAGE DISCOURSE. Perhaps the most empirical account of what I am calling toxic discourse is to be found in Jeffrey M. Berry and Sarah Sobieraj's book, *The Outrage Industry: Political Opinion Media and the New Incivility* (Berry and Sobieraj 2014). Over a ten-week period in 2009, Berry and Sobieraj, a political scientist and sociologist, respectively, led a team of researchers in cataloging instances of what they call "outrage discourse," which they describe as discourse intended to provoke emotional responses such as anger, fear, and moral indignation through "the use of overgeneralizations, sensationalism, misleading or patently inaccurate information, ad hominem attacks, and belittling ridicule of opponents" (7). Such discourse, the authors contend, is "political theater with a scorecard," and offers a very different conception of the public sphere than that described in "normative theories of deliberation, which value political dialogue that is rational, inclusive, impartial, consensus oriented, and fact-based" (19). Given the vast and lucrative audiences for outrage discourse, the authors sought to understand its character and appeal.

To that end, Berry and Sobieraj coded the discourse of cable talk shows hosted by, among others, Bill O'Reilly and Sean Hannity of News Corp's Fox Cable Division, and Rachel Maddow and Keith Olberman of MSNBC. They tracked instances of outrage discourse on talk radio, following right-wing personalities Rush Limbaugh and Michael Savage, and those whom Berry and Sobieraj characterized as liberal-leaning hosts, Allan Colmes and Diane Rehm. They followed ten leading right-wing and ten leading left-wing blogs, among them *Townhall* and

Powerline on the right, and the *Huffington Post* and *Daily Kos* on the left. Finally, Berry and Sobieraj mapped outrage discourse as it appeared in syndicated newspaper columns by conservatives such as Charles Krauthammer and George Will of the *Washington Post*, and liberal columnists including Leonard Pitts of the *Miami Herald* and Eugene Robinson of the *Washington Post*. From these sources, Berry and Sobieraj identified thirteen types of recurring speech and behaviors that they contend constitutes outrage discourse:

> *insulting language, name-calling, emotional display, emotional language, verbal fighting/sparring, character assassination, misrepresentative exaggeration, mockery, conflagration, ideologically extremizing language, slippery slope argumentation, belittling,* and *obscene language.* (Berry and Sobieraj 2014, 36; emphasis in the original)[2]

• • •

Such characterizations—incivility, hate speech, eliminationist rhetoric, venomous speech, and outrage discourse—suggest commonalities and differences in the nature of toxic rhetoric. Both incivility and venomous discourse, for example, draw attention to rude and boorish speech and behavior, whether in everyday life or in political discourse. Eliminationist rhetoric is the frightening rhetoric of violence directed by white supremacists, neo-Nazis, and other such groups at minority populations. Outrage discourse emphasizes the hyperbole and sensationalism of political opinion media.

Drawing on all these, I define "toxic discourse" as language that is disrespectful to strangers, hostile to minorities, contemptuous of compromise, dismissive of adverse evidence, and intentionally untruthful. It is the use of language to harm, demean, or dominate others. Toxic rhetoric seeks to invoke a world of anger, fear, exclusion, violence, and unequivocal moral judgments on cultural and political questions. The rhetoric is "toxic" in the sense that it has the capacity, as do toxins in the body, to cause illness, psychological or physical, to the individuals and groups at which it is directed.

WHAT ARE THE FEATURES OF TOXIC RHETORIC?

Toxic discourse is the product of the specific language practices that generate and sustain it. While these practices and their purveyors are diverse, there are commonalities that, collectively, comprise the toxins in toxic discourse. To name them all would require another book, perhaps several, but some of the most frequent examples of toxic language practices include the following:

DISHONESTY. Dishonesty is the essential and encompassing practice in generating toxic discourse. Dishonest discourse involves the intentional use of language to deceive, dissemble, or manipulate by distorting or falsifying empirically verifiable facts, resulting in harm to others, either individuals or groups. So, for example, Donald Trump's claim that he personally witnessed thousands of people cheering as the World Trade Towers collapsed on September 11, 2001—"There were people over in New Jersey," said Trump, "that were watching it, a heavy Arab population, that were cheering as the buildings came down"—were repeatedly debunked by objective analysts, who could find no evidence that such an event ever took place (Carroll 2015). Mr. Trump's persistence in spreading this untruth was toxic in that it stigmatized Muslim Americans and aggravated racial tension.

UNACCOUNTABILITY. A form of dishonesty, unaccountability refers to the practice of making assertions without providing relevant and sufficient evidence to support the claim. When a man drove a car into a crowd of people protesting a white supremacist rally in Charlottesville, Virginia, killing one women and injuring nineteen, the notorious conspiracy theorist Alex Jones blamed Democrats for instigating the violence, claiming without evidence that the Southern Poverty Law Center had gone to "central casting" to hire actors to "dress up as White Supremacists" for the purpose of embarrassing President Trump (Sharockman 2017). Jones's assertion was echoed by California Republican Representative Dana Rohrabacher, who asserted, also without supplying evidence, that the violence in Charlottesville was "a total hoax" staged by liberals (Garofoli 2017). Unaccountability becomes toxic when claims potentially damaging to individuals or groups are made in the absence of credible evidence.

DEMONIZATION. Demonization is the rhetorical practice of representing individuals, groups, or ideas as evil, corrupt, cowardly, malevolent, or in some other manner as morally debased. President Obama is not only wrong about admitting Syrian refugees into the United States, according to right-wing polemicist David Horowitz, Obama is a "traitor" whose "heart is with the enemy" (Blue 2015). Former House Republican leaders John Boehner and Eric Cantor are not merely political opponents, Democratic Representative Maxine Waters said in a speech to a state party convention, they are "demons" intent on "destroying this country" (Fox News 2012). In the rhetoric of toxic discourse, one's political opponents must be understood as dictators (Donnelly 2014), Nazis (Selby 2015), or vermin (CAIR 2015). There is no middle ground or half-measures.

VIOLENCE. Given the proclivity for demonizing opponents in US public discourse, it can hardly be surprising that so much of our rhetoric is violent. By "violent," I do not mean the rhetorical practice of comparing public health campaigns to "war," as in "the war on drugs," "the war on cancer," "the science wars," and so forth. Rather, I am referring to calls for explicitly violent acts against individuals or groups or representations of violence against individuals or groups based on their political or cultural identities. Nevada Assemblywoman Michelle Fiore, for example, when asked to explain why she had not signed a petition circulated by her Republican colleagues opposing the resettlement of Syrian refugees in the state, said, "What, are you kidding me? I'm about to fly to Paris and shoot 'em in the head myself. I am not OK with Syrian refugees. I'm not OK with terrorists. I'm OK with putting them down, blacking them out, just put a piece of brass in their ocular cavity and end their miserable life. I'm good with that" (Lucas 2015).[3] The comedian Kathy Griffin provoked national outrage when she posted an online image of herself holding up a mask resembling the bloody, severed head of Donald Trump. She was subsequently fired as the host of CNN's New Year's Eve program (Bromwich 2017). These are similar examples of violent speech move us into the realm of toxic discourse.

DENIAL. By "denial," I mean the unwillingness to accept arguments based on empirical evidence when that evidence conflicts with one's interests or worldview. In discourses of denial, to recall *Popular Science* editor Suzanne Labarre's message to readers quoted at the start of this chapter, "Scientific certainty is just another thing for two people to 'debate' on television." Perhaps the most mainstream and consequential example of denial discourse is the refusal to acknowledge the role of human activity in climate change, even as multiple studies indicate that 97 percent or more of publishing scientists agree that the climate has warmed over that last century, and that it is "very likely" human activity has contributed to this trend (NASA 2017).

Denial discourses may be examples of "motivated reasoning," the human proclivity to accept or refuse propositions based on how they confirm or contradict our biases, or they may reflect political and economic interests. "Contrarian scientists, fossil fuels corporations, conservative think tanks, and various front groups have assaulted mainstream climate science and scientists for over two decades," write the sociologists Riley E. Dunlap and Aaron M. McCright (Dunlap and McCright 2011). The result has been the creation of a well-funded and relatively coordinated "denial machine" that "seeks to undermine the case for climate policy making by removing (in the eyes of the public and policy makers) the scientific basis for such policies" (144). Such efforts are consistent with other assaults on science, fronted by what Naomi Oreskes and Erik M. Conway term "Merchants of Doubt," referring to those scientists and lobbyists who sought to minimize or obscure the health risks associated with tobacco, asbestos, and certain pharmaceuticals (Oreskes and Conway 2010). Discourses of denial are toxic in the sense that they may degrade others, much as Holocaust Denial functions as a form of anti-Semitism, or when they result in actual physical harm to others, including illness, incapacity, and even death, as in the examples of the denial rhetoric of the tobacco and asbestos industries. In the case of climate-change denial, the harm done to others is of a global magnitude, threatening the very health of the planet.

POVERTY OF SPIRIT. Just as dishonesty may be understood as the essential and encompassing practice of toxic discourse, poverty of spirit, by which I mean public language devoid of generosity, charity, tolerance, and respect, is its prevailing temperament. Poverty of spirit is an attitude rather than a practice, and speaks to the inability—or worse, the refusal—to recognize that one's political or cultural opposites are not axiomatically evil, that there may be merit to their positions, and that the positions of one's own side might, in fact and finally, be misguided or simply wrong. Poverty of spirit exposes itself through a language of closing rather than opening, denouncing rather than exploring. It is dogmatism that mistakes itself for righteousness, meanness that confuses itself with conviction, myopia that congratulates itself for the expansiveness of its vision. Poverty of spirit is toxic in the sense that it poisons opportunities to find commonalities in conflicts among peoples of diverse values, and so is injurious to the communities in which it takes root.

What constitutes dishonesty, unaccountability, demonization, denial, and other practices of toxic discourse is never, of course, self-evident but is mediated by the particulars of the rhetorical context, including such variables as the topic of discussion, the purpose of the discourse, and the relative positions—ideological, economic, historical—of the interlocutors. To label a language practice "toxic" is not to determine its nature. However, utterances that can be judged harmful, demeaning, humiliating, or threatening to others are, in the language of this book, "toxic."

WHAT ARE THE CAUSES OF TOXIC RHETORIC?

Teachers of writing are well aware of the complexities, if not the treacheries, of making causal arguments. In formulating the causal argument, a correlation may be confused with the cause, the cause mistaken for the effect, the effect misunderstood as the cause. For good reason does Richard Fulkerson caution writing teachers that "Causal reasoning is probably the most complex of the various forms [of argument]" (Fulkerson 1996, 33).[4] So it is when attempting to discern the causes of toxic discourse, which has been variously explained in terms of the political and the historical, the structural and the ideological.

THE POLITICAL. For many journalists, pundits, and other members of the political intelligentsia, the origins of toxic discourse lie in the polarized state of contemporary politics. So, for example, does *The New York Times* columnist Joe Nocera argue, in an op-ed titled, "The Ugliness Started with Bork" (Nocera 2011) that the confirmation hearings on Robert Bork's nomination to the Supreme Court in 1987, in which Democrats blocked Bork's ascension to the court, is the event most responsible for poisoning US political discourse. "The Bork fight, in some ways," Nocera writes, "was the beginning of the end of civil discourse in politics." Nocera contends that Bork, while opinionated and conservative, was a qualified nominee, but that the tactics of the Democratic Left to defeat Bork's nomination relied on portraying him as a "right-wing loony," "an extreme ideological activist," and a judge whose vision of the United States, according to a speech delivered by Senator Ted Kennedy, was that of a country in which women would be forced to into "back-alley abortions," and "blacks would sit at segregated counters." These "truly despicable" tactics left conservatives seething at the demonization of Judge Bork, and laid the foundations of the present political dysfunction. In Nocera's view, "the line from Bork to today's ugly politics is a straight one."

Others point to the negative character of modern campaign advertisements, and particularly those adopted by Lee Atwater, who served as the campaign manager for George H. W. Bush in his 1988 presidential election contest against Massachusetts governor Michael Dukakis. The most infamous of these was the "Willie Horton" attack ad, which *Huffington Post* columnist David Sirota called "history's single most powerful symbol of incivility" (Sirota 2010). This ad effectively linked Dukakis to a rape and murder committed by convicted murderer Willie Horton, who had escaped from Massachusetts prison authorities while on a weekend furlough program Dukakis supported. The ad showed a menacing image of the African American Horton, followed by the words, "Kidnapping," "Stabbing," and "Raping," ending with a photograph of Dukakis. The racial overtones of the Willie Horton ad were not accidental, but part of what was known as the "Southern Strategy," in which Republicans sought to exploit the fears of white voters through racially coded language. Atwater explained in an interview:

> You start out in 1954 by saying, "Nigger, nigger, nigger." By 1968 you can't say "nigger"—that hurts you, backfires. So you say stuff like, uh, forced busing, states' rights, and all that stuff, and you're getting so abstract. Now, you're talking about cutting taxes, and all these things you're talking about are totally economic things and a byproduct of them is, blacks get hurt worse than whites. . . . "We want to cut this," is much more abstract than even the busing thing, uh, and a hell of a lot more abstract than "Nigger, nigger." (Perlstein 2012)

In a testimony to the effectiveness of such advertising, the Bush campaign overcame a seventeen-point deficit in midsummer polls to win the 1988 elections, and Atwater was rewarded by being named chair of the Republican National Committee (Oreskes 1991).

Still others point to the tactics of Georgia Representative Newt Gingrich, who engineered the Republican takeover of the House of Representatives in 1994. Known as "one of Washington's most aggressive practitioners of slash-and-burn politics," Sheryl Gay Stolberg wrote in *The New York Times*, "many fault [Gingrich] for erasing whatever civility once existed in the capital" (Stolberg 2012). Among Gingrich's machinations was the so-called "GOPAC Memo," titled "Language: A Key Mechanism for Control," which was sent to Republican candidates for office who wished to learn "to speak like Newt." (Information Clearing House n.d.). Candidates were advised to describe themselves and their candidacies using what the memo termed "Optimistic Positive Governing Words," such as "citizen," "courage," "family," "freedom," "prosperity," and "truth." Candidates were further advised to describe their opponents with language listed under the heading of "Contrasting Words," including "bizarre," "corrupt," "disgrace," "shame," "sick," and "traitors." The memo counseled candidates to apply such "contrasting" words "to the opponent, their record, proposals, and their party."

THE HISTORICAL. Those who adopt a historical perspective typically look askance at contemporary explanations of toxic discourse and are more broadly skeptical of the idea that public discourse today is somehow worse than in the past. Susan Herbst, for example, begins her study of civility and incivility in the modern era by recalling the 1856 attack on Massachusetts Senator Charles Sumner, an abolitionist, by pro-slavery South Carolina Congressman Preston Brooks on the floor of the United States Senate. "As historians know," Herbst writes in *Rude Democracy: Civility and Incivility in American Politics*, "our current period is not the first time we have seen incivility, name calling, and brutal rhetoric in politics" (Herbst 2010, ix).

Indeed, the history of US politics, and especially presidential politics, is rife with insults and slander. In the 1800 contest between Thomas Jefferson and John Adams, Jefferson's surrogates described Adams as a "hideous hermaphroditical character, which has neither the force and firmness of a man, nor the gentleness and sensibility of a woman." Adams's camp replied with racist discourse, calling Jefferson "a mean-spirited, low-lived fellow, the son of a half-breed Indian squaw, sired by a Virginia mulatto father" (PBS n.d.) When Abraham Lincoln ran for reelection against the Democrat George B. McClellan in 1864, one Wisconsin newspaper described Lincoln as "fungus from the corrupt womb of bigotry and fanaticism" and openly called for the president's assassination, asserting "the man who votes for Lincoln is now a traitor and a murderer . . . And if he is elected to misgovern for another four years, we trust some bold hand will pierce his heart with dagger point for the public good" (Fehrenbacher 1982).

The historical perspective offers a useful corrective to nostalgic longing for a golden age of rhetorical comity that never was. More, by demonstrating that much of the worst political rhetoric occurs at critical junctures in history, such as the onset of the US Civil War, the historical perspective makes a strong case for understanding toxic discourse as a symptom rather than a cause of political polarization. Finally, historical considerations of toxic discourse serve to reassure us that we are not in altogether uncharted waters. We have been here before, the historical perspective reminds us, and the nation has endured.

What the historical perspective cannot account for, however, is the dramatic increase in the reach and power of toxic discourse. Berry and Sobieraj argue that while the US media has historically reserved a place for "outrage discourse," such discourse today "is found in a far greater number of venues, circulates quickly, has vast audiences, and often gathers momentum from the attention of conventional news organizations and the synergistic coordination between media organizations, pundits, bloggers, and politicos" (12). To illustrate, Berry and Sobieraj note that the number of all-talk or all-news radio stations has tripled between 1999 and 2014, the development of cable and satellite technologies has allowed for more television stations devoted to opinionated political programming, and the Internet has resulted in the proliferation of blogs, Twitter accounts, and other venues for the expression of toxic rhetoric.

More, audiences for such rhetoric exceed anything we have known in the past. Approximately thirty-five million people listen to talk radio daily, Berry and Sobieraj report, the nightly opinion programs such as the Rachel Maddow Show and the since-cancelled *O'Reilly Factor* attract another ten million viewers, while two million people log onto one "outrage-based political blog" daily, meaning that the audience for toxic rhetoric in the United States totals some forty-five million people on any given day (Berry and Sobieraj 2014, 12–15). The interdependence of modern media, meanwhile, in which political blogs inform talk radio, which provides grist for cable news, which informs mainstream newspapers and television networks, ensures that personal attacks, scripted talking points, and other forms of toxic messaging are widely circulated and frequently repeated.

To say it another way, John Adams may have been called a "hideous hermaphroditical character," which is at least as noxious as anything in our present public discourse, but the accusations were not broadcast to millions on Fox News, shared with thousands of "friends" on Facebook, or tweeted to hundreds of thousands, if not millions, of followers. Toxic discourse today can be heard on more platforms, moves more quickly, and reaches infinitely more people than at any time previously. To understand such developments we must look, Berry and Sobieraj write, to structural changes in the modern media landscape, specifically to the regulatory and technological changes that have made toxic discourse a highly profitable industry.

THE STRUCTURAL. Berry and Sobieraj argue that the landscape of modern mass media has been transformed over the last three decades by two seemingly incompatible trends. The first is deregulation and concentration of ownership, as the industry has moved from what the authors call "a relative diversity of ownership" toward an almost complete control of the industry by five mass media conglomerates: Viacom, Bertelsmann AG, News Corp, Time Warner, and Disney (75). The second trend is the democratization of the media space for individual user, whose participation in media has been enabled by personal computers, smart phones, and other technological developments. Both trends, the authors argue, underwrite the growth of toxic discourse.

Regarding ownership, Berry and Sobieraj argue that beginning in the 1930s the relationship of the US government to radio and television broadcasting might best be described as "protectionist" (75). The public airwaves were regarded as a vital public interest, essential for communicating with citizens in times of emergency and promoting attitudes and viewpoints thought to be essential for a healthy, functioning democracy. To ensure against dangerous private monopolization of the airwaves, the Federal Communications Commission (FCC) regulated both ownership, limiting the number of stations a single corporate entity could control, and programming, requiring that a percentage of broadcast hours be set aside for news and public affairs programs (76).

The conception of the radio and television as a public trust began to shift in the 1970s and 1980s, replaced by what Berry and Sobieraj call a "corporatist" approach, which favored deregulation, concentration of ownership, and emphasis on profit. As other industries, including transportation, energy, and telecommunications, were deregulated during the presidency of Ronald Reagan, so, too, were restrictions on ownership and guidelines for programming in mass media steadily relaxed. Advocates of deregulation argued that the public interest was best served not by government regulation but by the unfettered operation of the free market. "The perception of broadcasters as community trustees should be replaced," wrote Mark Fowler, FCC Chairman under President Reagan, "by a view of broadcasters as marketplace participants" (Brainard 2004, quoted in Berry and Sobieraj 2014, 78).

The concentration of ownership and emphasis on profit, Berry and Sobieraj contend, changed the way news is gathered and reported. As news production has become centralized to reduce costs, and "nonessential" bureaus such as international and rural are downsized or closed, the "product" offered by the major networks, Berry and Sobieraj explain, has become increasingly homogenized. News on the major broadcast networks programs is largely indistinguishable from one network to another. To set themselves apart themselves from their competitors, and maximize profitability, the networks have progressively blurred the line between news and entertainment, thus opening the door for opinion-driven programming that relies upon practices of toxic discourse to generate ratings.

The deregulation of the 1980s led to transformations, Berry and Sobieraj further contend, of programming content as well as ownership (79). The elimination in 1987 of the Fairness Doctrine, which required that a percentage of broadcast hours be set aside for public affairs programs, and that controversial public issues be presented in an even-handed manner, resulted in fewer hours of news programming, an imbalanced media landscape—conservative talk radio programs have ten times as many minutes of airtime as progressive stations—and increasingly toxic programming featuring personal attacks and insults (79–80).

The democratization of the media space, the result of new technologies that make it possible for every individual to create a blog, establish a Twitter account, or upload content to YouTube, has additionally contributed to the increase in outrage discourse as the technical and financial barriers to self-publishing have largely come down. Berry and Sobieraj cite data indicating that the number of blogs has increased from 50 million in July 2006 to 181 million in March 2012, and that the research engine *BlogPulse*, which tracks and monitors blog activity, indicates that since the late 2000s more than one hundred thousand new blogs are created every twenty-four hours (84). While some online sites boast of audiences in the millions—*The Drudge Report* attracts 5 million visitors a month, the *Daily Kos*, 1.4 million (83)—the vast majority of bloggers and others distributing political content must compete in an oversaturated market for web traffic. To attract and maintain an audience, particularly one that will make a website appealing to potential advertisers, bloggers, and other web-based entrepreneurs must distinguish themselves from the competition. One way to do so is to trade in toxic discourse, the more outrageous the better—at least for drawing attention to one's website.

In sum, Berry and Sobieraj argue that the increasingly vitriolic state of public argument is a product of structural conditions, specifically the regulatory, technological, and economic developments that work to enable and sustain toxic rhetoric.

THE IDEOLOGICAL. Rhetorical scholar Clarke Rountree offers what he describes as a "pessimistic view" of political and public discourse, which he regards as rancorous and resistant to change. As have others, Rountree (2013b) references recent developments in media and politics as sources of "the lowly state of our political discourse." However, Rountree suggests another cause: the "culture of fear" that infected life and politics in the United States after 9/11. Rountree argues that following the attacks of September 11, the US government and many Americans abandoned long-held values and practices that had formerly distinguished the United States from its enemies (Rountree 2013b, xxxiii). The Bush administration's use of waterboarding, extraordinary rendition, indefinite detention, and other practices did not generate, Rountree writes, a widespread outcry but were instead tacitly accepted by much of the US public, which was rendered fearful in the aftermath of 9/11. Rountree argues that President George W. Bush and Vice President Dick Cheney exploited such fears to push through controversial legislation and policies, such as the Patriot Act and the decision to preemptively attack Iraq. More, pundits and politicians used the language of fear to undermine their rivals, Rountree writes, as when Vice President Cheney stated that a vote for Democratic presidential candidate John Kerry might encourage a terrorist attack upon the

United States. The culture and language of fear Rountree identifies have not lessened but continue to resonate in US politics and influence political discourse. In the 2016 presidential election, for example, then candidate Donald Trump, stoked fears of Mexicans, Muslims, African Americans, and others (Kopan 2015).

• • •

Each of the accounts we have considered—the political, historical, structural, and ideological—tells a particular story about the causes of toxic rhetoric in US public argument. We need not choose among these stories, but we may read them instead as complementary, each account revealing part of a whole, providing part of an answer to the question of why our public discourse has become so corrosive. Neither should we regard these accounts, recalling the complexities of the causal argument, as definitive. There are no doubt other, perhaps equally compelling narratives to explain dysfunctions of our public arguments. What does seem clear, however, is that while toxic discourse has long been part of the US rhetorical tradition, it is no exaggeration to say that it now comes from more sources, is more incessant, and reaches wider audiences than at any other time in human history. And this means that its effects are quite likely more consequential than in the past.

WHAT ARE THE EFFECTS OF TOXIC DISCOURSE?

What effects does toxic rhetoric have on our politics, our communications, our civic relations? What are its effects upon our students? Some would say: not so much. While the conventional wisdom holds that toxic rhetoric, as noted previously, undermines the political process by lowering political trust, promoting negativity toward political leaders, and increasing suspicion among Americans of one another, there is a small but suggestive body of counter-arguments from the social sciences suggesting that such claims may be overstated, or at least that the research is inconclusive.

So, for example, Deborah Jordan Brooks and John G. Geer argue in their essay, "Beyond Negativity: The Effects of Incivility on the Electorate" (Brooks and Geer 2007), that there is little evidence to support the belief that "uncivil messages" are detrimental to the political process. "Upon close examination," the authors write, "we see no evidence that even the most despised of candidate messages—negative, uncivil, trait-based messages—are harmful to the democratic engagement of the polity" (Brooks and Geer 2007, 12). Indeed, the authors aver, negative campaign advertisements "may modestly stimulate two things we tend to care a great deal about improving as a society: political interest and likelihood to vote" (ibid.). Lee Sigelman and Mark Kugler agree, stating the despite the "shrillness and incivility of political campaigns," research does not support the negative effects so commonly presumed. "Indeed," the authors write, "for every finding about the consequences of negative campaigning, there is an equal and opposite finding . . . and many studies have uncovered no significant effect one way or the other" (Sigelman and Kugler 2003, 142). For their part, Berry and Sobieraj concede that "outrage media" can offer "entertainment, information, a sense of community, and validation," while perhaps inspiring "more consumption of political information" (Berry and Sobieraj 2014, 21).

Such studies provide an important corrective to casual, unspecified assertions about the effects of toxic discourse. However, what such studies generally do not attempt to capture, are indeed not intended to capture, is a more elusive measure, one not easily rendered through statistical or survey data. In her eloquent book, *Talking to Strangers: Anxieties of Citizenship Since Brown v. Board of Education*, Danielle S. Allen (2014) explores the meanings of two related concepts: political trust and civic friendship. Allen is interested in how these condition the conflicting desires and interests of citizens and non-citizens in diverse communities.

Political trust, according to Allen, is belief that the democratic process of electing strangers to rule over us, as it were, can be entrusted to fellow citizens with whom one can participate in meaningful civic activity. Trust in one's fellow citizens," Allen writes, "consists in the belief, simply, that one is safe with them" (Allen 2014, xvi). Trust in one's fellow citizens, in turn, leads to what Allen calls "civic friendship." By "friendship," Allen does not mean easy comradeship or fleeting emotional attachments. Rather, friendship is "a practice, a set of hard-won, complicated habits that are used to bridge trouble, difficulty, and differences of personality, experience, and aspiration" (xxi). Friendship begins with the recognition that friends have a "*shared* life" (emphasis in the original), and civic friendship in a democracy begins with the recognition of what citizens and non-citizens have in common. As friends, we recognize what we share and, critically, where we differ and how we disagree. For civic friendship to thrive in a democracy, we must trust one another, but we must also acknowledge and understand the reasons why, in diverse, multicultural societies, we will also distrust one another. "The politics of friendship, Allen writes, "requires of citizens a capacity to attend to the dark side of the democratic soul" (xxii), by which I take Allen to mean that skepticism, indignation, and justified anger have a place in developing trust and maintaining civic friendships.

Expressions of toxic rhetoric, however—the discursive practices of dishonesty, unaccountability, demonization, violence, denial, and poverty of spirit—damage the capacity of citizens and non-citizens to develop trust and establish civic friendships. How can there be trust between us if you perceive that I am willing to lie to you, make unsupported assertions, represent you or those in your community as evil, corrupt, or morally debased? How can we develop those "hard-won, complicated habits that are used to bridge trouble, difficulty, and differences" if my language about you or those whom you love is devoid of generosity, charity, and respectfulness?

Toxic rhetoric ultimately is more than persuasive; it is constitutive. It invites us not simply to affirm or deny a given rhetorical argument but, more, to define ourselves within the terms and tropes of the rhetoric. We are invited by the discourse, as the rhetorical critic Edwin Black wrote so perceptively years ago, "not simply to believe something, but to *be* something. We are solicited by the discourse to fulfill its blandishments with our very selves" (Black 1970, in Burgchardt, 76). Toxic rhetoric offers us an identity to assume, a role to play, and in some cases a tribe or community with which to identify. Given the dishonesty, violence, and poverty of spirit that characterizes the kinds of identities and communities solicited by toxic rhetoric, is it any wonder the Pew Research Center finds greater partisan antipathy than at any point in the last two decades?

Nor can we assume that our students are unaffected by toxic discourse. A 2017 study of 137,400 full-time first-year students at 184 four-year colleges and universities reported that the fall 2016 cohort of incoming freshmen "has the distinction of being the most polarized cohort in the 51-year history of the Freshman Survey" (Eagan et al. 2017, 4). Fewer students than ever before identified as "middle of the road" (42%), while the number of students identifying as "liberal" or "far left" (35%) and "conservative" or "far right" (22%) increased. Gender played a role in polarization, with approximately 41 percent of women self-identifying as "liberal" or "far left" compared to approximately 30 percent of men, which the authors of the study termed "the largest gender gap in self-reported liberalism to date." Attitudes of tolerance and empathy appeared to break along lines of partisan identification, with students identifying as "left-leaning" self-reporting higher degrees of tolerance (86.6%) and an ability to see the world from another's point of view (83.6%) compared with their conservative classmates' self-reported capacities for tolerance (68.1%) and seeing the world through the eyes of others (68.8%). While we cannot definitively attribute these differences to the effects of toxic rhetoric—the report notes that the survey was conducted during an especially contentious US presidential election—neither can we dismiss the correlation between the polarization of students and that of the broader US population.

Based on the findings, the authors of the report recommend that institutions of higher learning consider sponsoring or expanding activities that promote dialogue for the purpose of helping students "develop their ability to engage in productive conversations about their political views with peers or others who might hold dissimilar views or values" (6).

Set in the context of our work, the authors' recommendation suggests that we make our classrooms into spaces where students might examine, in their speech and writing, what they hold in common, where they depart from one another, and how they might begin to bridge the differences that divide them. And this will call for students to engage in the kind of reflection typically associated with ethics and ethical discourse. What kind of person do I want to be? What is my relationship to those who think differently than I do? What principles, systems, or habits will guide my decisions and my actions? In short, the authors of the freshman survey are inviting us to make our classrooms into centers of ethical language reasoning and practice. If we are to take up this invitation, however, we need to clarify for ourselves the different meanings of the term, "ethics," and how these have historically been enacted in the writing classroom. That is the subject of the next chapter.

NOTES

1. The line between "hate speech" and "venomous speech" is hazy, as an anonymous reader pointed out. The former is a legal designation, while the latter involves a critical judgment.
2. For coding methods and summaries of each category, see Berry and Sobieraj, "Methods Appendix" (241–255).
3. Fiore later issued a clarification, stating she meant to say she wanted to shoot terrorists, not refugees, in the head (Chokshi 2015).
4. "Yet," Fulkerson adds, "it [causal argument] is absolutely necessary" (33).

2

IMAGINING THE GOOD WRITER
Moral Theories in the Writing Class

"All writing practices, including writing pedagogy, involve the trans-mission of value systems. All writing practices are embedded in ideology. For these and other reasons, even skills and drills writing practices and pedagogy derive from and in turn promote value systems, or ethics"
—Kathleen Ethel Welch 1999, 137

THREE VIGNETTES

Lindsay is a first-year student planning to major in political science. In recent months, she has become increasingly distressed by the killings of African Americans by police. In a paper for her first-year writing class, an essay she hopes to publish in her college newspaper, she cites statistics on the number of police killings, contrasts the degree of police violence in the United States with other industrialized countries, and recommends specific actions to reduce police violence in predomi-nantly African American communities. Reviewing the draft of her essay, however, Lindsay is dissatisfied. The essay fails to convey what she feels is the enormity of racial violence, nor does it express the anger she wants her readers to feel. She decides to revise using a comparison she has come across in her research. The police killings of African Americans in cities across the United States, she writes in her revised introduction, is the twenty-first century equivalent of the lynchings that took place in the American South. Steve, a member of Lindsay's writing group, is deeply offended by the comparison and objects to it strenuously. Steve is from a police family, he tells Lindsay, and he knows firsthand that most police are decent men and women. Steve urges Lindsay to strike the analogy from her essay.

• • •

VJ is an evangelical Christian who strives to live his life according to the tenets of his faith. He believes Jesus provided an example of how society should treat the less fortunate, so he argues, in an essay for his

DOI: 10.7330/9781607328278.c002

first-year writing class, that the United States has an obligation to accept and resettle Syrian and other refugees from the Mideast. To support his argument, he cites Matthew, 25:35–40: "For I was hungry and you gave me food, I was thirsty and you gave me drink, I was a stranger and you welcomed me . . ." Taya, VJ's classmate, rejects his argument. She cites news reports indicating that members of ISIS are entering Europe posing as refugees, and argues that the United States cannot afford the security risks of bringing potential terrorists into the country. What's more, Taya tells VJ, biblical quotations are unsuitable sources of evidence in an academic essay about national security. She recommends VJ use more appropriate sources in making arguments about public policy.

• • •

The assignment calls for students to write a response to the Michael Moore (2003) documentary, *Bowling for Columbine,* Moore's polemic on American gun culture. Austin knows exactly where he stands and what he wants to write. Austin believes laws restricting the sale of guns in the United States are ineffective and he is repulsed by what he regards as the opportunism of cynical politicians seeking to exploit tragedies such as the Sandy Hook elementary school shootings. However, Austin is unsure how his essay will be read. In a classroom discussion on the topic a day earlier, the course instructor made his own views clear when he described gun rights in the United States as "a kind of cultural sickness." Austin wonders how his essay will be evaluated if he expresses his views honestly, and whether his grade in the course will suffer. After a few false starts, he decides not to hold back. He will write an essay calling out *Bowling for Columbine* as deceptive and hypocritical.

• • •

To write is to make choices, and to teach writing is to teach rationales for making such choices. We tend to think of these choices, those of us who write and teach writing, as belonging to certain categories, or domains, such as the rhetorical, the linguistic, or the aesthetic. These are not airtight compartments, independent of one another, but are mutually informing, each having a part in the development of a given text. So, for example, the writer makes rhetorical decisions about topic, evidence, and organization in response to the constraints and opportunities of particular audiences, purposes, and occasions. The writer's linguistic choices, which are also rhetorical, may involve the degree of formality or informality in the text, or what sociolinguists call the linguistic register (Fairclough 1992, 70). The aesthetic choices of the writer, both linguistic and rhetorical in their own right, may call for decisions about sentence variation or word choice, with one word selected over another based on the writer's ear for patterns of rhythm and sound.

We understand these categories, the rhetorical, linguistic, and aesthetic, and we are skilled at teaching them. However, there is another category, another domain, one that is perhaps less discussed in our classes but nonetheless calls for decisions on the part of the writer. When students deliberate, as in the vignettes above, on whether to use an incendiary comparison, or cite a contested source, or risk troubling those in authority, they are deliberating on ethical questions, on the ethics of a rhetorical activity. They are deliberating on ethical questions because to write, as I have suggested previously, is to propose a relationship with another, the reader. As James E. Porter writes, "all writing entails ethical obligations because writing always involves social relations between readers and writers, which presuppose some understanding of how those social relations are to be constituted" (Porter 1998, 30). Defining the nature of those social relations invariably entangles readers and writers in those questions of values and virtues that are traditionally the domains of ethics and ethical choices.

The purpose of an ethical theory is to offer a set of principles for making such choices and to provide support for those principles with sound and consistent reasons. Indeed, one way to read the history of Western ethics is to understand it as a series of conversations about the best principles by which to live. For the ancient Greeks, the supreme principle for deciding moral questions was to be found in the concept of *eudaimonia*, commonly translated as "happiness," or "flourishing," or a "good human life" (Van Zyl 2015, 183). An action counted as good, as a virtue, to the extent it contributed to the achievement of *eudaimonia*, and counted as a vice to the degree it inhibited the attainment of a good life. Christianity, in turn, located moral principles in God's commands, which if followed could lead to the highest good of salvation. And the intellectual, political, and religious turmoil of seventeenth and eighteenth century Europe called for revised conceptions of moral order, resulting in a proliferation of new and original ethical theories (Schneewind 2003).

The most significant moral theories to emerge from modern Western moral philosophy, however, have been deontology, the ethics of rules, and consequentialism, the ethics of outcomes. Both normative traditions have had an enormous influence on ethical thinking in the West, touching not only upon individual morality but upon such diverse areas as health care (Wu et al. 1997), human rights (Talbott 2013; Blackburn 2015), legal theory (Alexander 2000), international relations (Donaldson 1992; Ellis 1992), and others. In recent years, these theories have been challenged, especially in the humanities, by the emergence of postmodern ethics, which offers a radical critique of modern moral philosophy, and which posits an ethics grounded in conditions of contingency, difference, and relativity.

Implicit in each of these theories, deontology, consequentialism, and postmodernism, are principles and reasons for making ethical choices when composing or evaluating texts. Each of the major ethical theories, that is, offers students and teachers of writing a set of reasons for making one choice over another—for using or not using an incendiary analogy, for citing or not citing a contested source, for choosing or not choosing to make a provocative argument. Each of the major theories, in this view, provides writers and teachers of writing with principles for determining what Don J. Kraemer would term, "The Good, the Right, and the Decent" (Kraemer 2017). More, each of the major theories presents writers and teachers with a particular moral identity, a conception of what it means to be a "good writer," or one who makes, in the ethical sense, good choices instead of bad, right choices instead of wrong, when composing or evaluating texts.

I do not mean by this that students and teachers of writing consciously reflect on, say, deontological ethics as they write, or that they review consequentialist or postmodern theories at critical moments in the composing process. I mean rather that the major moral theories have shaped to varying degrees the cultures of Western institutions and peoples, that they are ingrained in much of Western moral reasoning, and that they have therefore influenced and continue to influence how we understand the notions of "the good," "the right," and "the decent."[1] And so when writers come to an ethical crossroads in a text, the choices they make reflect, consciously or unconsciously, a moral framework of some kind, from which writers derive a set of principles and reasons for their decisions. And when we teachers of writing evaluate the choices students make, we, too, are influenced by principles and reasons grounded in moral theories that suggest to us some notion of "the good" and what it means to be a "good writer."

In this chapter, I argue that each of the major moral theories—the deontological, consequentialist, and postmodern—offers a conception of rhetorical ethics that is in different ways and to varying degrees inadequate for addressing the needs of students and teachers of writing in the twenty-first century. None of the major theories, in other words, provides an entirely satisfactory account of "the good writer" in the present cultural moment. I will not in this chapter attempt to provide a complete chronicle of each theory, which would be well beyond the scope of this book. I am interested, rather, how the principles and reasons derived from each theory—mostly implicitly in the cases of deontology and consequentialism, often explicitly in the case of postmodernism—have influenced ethical decision making in the writing classroom. Let us begin with deontological ethics, in which the good writer is construed as one who adheres to rules and observes constraints.

DEONTOLOGICAL ETHICS: THE RHETORIC OF ABSOLUTES

*Deontologists believe that certain actions are
intrinsically morally right or wrong.*
—Shafer-Landau (2007, 521)

In deontological ethics, from the Greek *deon*, "obligation" and *logos*, meaning "speaking" or "study," moral decisions are grounded in foundational and absolute principles of obligation, rules, and constraints. These principles are considered *a priori*, or outside the particulars of human experience, and apply to all moral agents in all situations, transcending specific social and historical contexts (van Hooft 2006, 30). To say it another way, deontologists hold that certain actions are morally right or morally wrong, inherently good or inherently bad, regardless of the circumstances. It is absolutely and unconditionally wrong, for example, to murder, rape, torture, or enslave another human being. It is absolutely and unconditionally wrong to lie, steal, or humiliate another person. "At the heart of deontologists' insistence on the importance of moral rule or constraints," writes Nancy (Ann) Davis, "lies the belief that the avoidance of wrongdoing is the principal—if not the only—task of the moral agent" (Davis 1993, 216). And wrong actions are wrong even if they might lead, through some particular set of circumstances, to a greater good. So, for example, it would be wrong to torture a terrorist even if torture might result in gaining information that would save many lives. For the deontologist, morality is not dependent on consequences, no matter how desirable or undesirable these might seem.

Deontology in this sense is a morality of constraints on human behavior, most of which, Davis asserts, are "negatively formulated," meaning they take the form of "thou shalt nots" (208). A typical list of such constraints would include "Never lie," "Never steal," "Never harm an innocent," and so forth. Davis argues that deontological constraints are "fundamental" and provide the basis for knowing which rules we should follow: if we are morally prohibited from telling a lie, then it follows that we have a categorical obligation always to tell the truth. We derive the moral rules we must follow, in other words, by determining those actions that are forbidden. Though deontologists may differ on what rules one is obliged to follow, they agree that moral obligations, once these are realized, are grounded in principles that are universally binding upon the moral agent.

Where do such principles come from? By what authority are they sanctioned? While deontological thinkers have located the source of morally obligatory principles in divine command, such as the Ten Commandments; in human authority, that of kings and emperors; and in institutions of various kinds, Immanuel Kant (1724–1804), the most famous proponent of deontological ethics, located them in human reason (O'Neill 1993, 176). Since we are incapable of understanding transcendent reality to which we have no access, Kant argued, the source of our moral principles must come within ourselves, from our status as rational agents possessed of free will. These principles of reason, once we have established them, are binding and absolute on all people in all circumstances. Kant called such principles "categorical imperatives," which represent the supreme principles of morality.

Kant formulated several expressions of the categorical imperative, the most famous of which is the Principle of Universalizability, which holds that that we should act only on those maxims, or principles for action, that we would will into universal law (Shafer-Landau 2007, 521). An action is considered a categorical imperative, in other words, if it articulates an objective principle that can be made universal, applied to all people in every conceivable context. Once the categorical imperative is established, there are no contingent conditions or moral ambiguities by which it may be transgressed. Hence the famous, and notorious, example in Kant's (1797/1996) "On a Supposed Right to Lie from Philanthropy," in which Kant declares it would be wrong to lie to a murderer who is seeking a person we have hidden in our home. One must do one's duty, Kant argued, whatever that duty may be—in this case telling the murderer where his intended victim is hiding. "To be *truthful* (honest) in all declarations," wrote Kant, "is therefore a sacred command of reason prescribing unconditionally, one not to be restricted by any inconveniences" (613). Following World War II, the "murderer at the door" example repulsed many Western readers who took Kant to be saying that it would be immoral to lie to Nazis seeking Jews hiding during the Holocaust.[2] However, the Principle of Universalizability, Thomas E. Hill Jr. has argued, is essentially an attempt to provide a formula, given our limited understanding of the human condition, for applying universal moral principles in diverse cultural and social contexts (Hill 2000, 234).

While Kantian ethics is vastly more complex than this summary admits, and while it is not without its share of internal debates and controversies (see, for discussions, O'Neill 1992; Hill 2000), I am interested here primarily in the idea of an ethics in which in which moral obligations are absolute, and in which the primary task of the moral agent is the avoidance of wrongdoing. Can such a theory provide the basis for an ethics of writing—for helping students realize what it means to be a good writer?

For many years, the answer to that question was an unequivocal "yes." Prescriptivist grammar and usage manuals such as H. W. Fowler's ([1926] 1965) *Modern English Usage* and Strunk and White's *Elements of Style* posited linguistic forms and rules that were said to be correct, proper, and universally binding upon good writers. Such manuals were essentially arguments from authority, in which prominent writers, editors, or educators rendered judgments on what constituted acceptable prose style. "Do not affect a breezy manner," Strunk and White (1999, 70) commanded. "Avoid fancy words" (ibid., 73). Such injunctions were often more than innocuous recommendations about syntax and style. Rather, they expressed implicit (and sometimes explicit) value judgments about the "right" and "wrong" of rhetorical choices. Fowler, for example, was described by his contemporary Otto Jesperson as "an instinctive grammatical moralizer," a description Fowler apparently welcomed (in Gowers 1965, viii). The introduction to the Fourth Edition of *Elements of Style*, meanwhile, conveyed the "scorn," "revulsion," and "gloom" the authors felt about constructions that "violated" their prescribed principles (Strunk and White 1999, 8–12).

The admonitions of usage and style manuals are not, of course, the equivalent of teaching writing. However, the composition classrooms of the nineteenth- and twentieth-century United States were also scenes of unconditional judgments about what constituted good writing and good writers. In what we have come to call current-traditional rhetoric, writers were taught strict rules and principles governing the structure of the sentence, the coherence of the paragraph, the arrangement of the essay, and the use of figurative language (Berlin 1984). The rhetoric textbooks of A. S. Hill, who held the Boylston Chair of Rhetoric at Harvard from 1876 to 1904, for example, assumed "an overall tone of dogmatism," and "reduced rhetoric to lists of principles and rules, set forth *ex cathedra*" (Reid 1959, 257, quoted in Crowley 1998, 338).

S. Michael Halloran argues that the rise of the middle class in the first half of the nineteenth century had "profound consequences" for the teaching of writing in American colleges, as the increasingly competitive social and economic climate imposed a "credentialing" function upon schools, resulting in a new emphasis on correct grammar and usage as signs of membership in the desired social class (Halloran 1990, 165–166). Writing became a medium through which one was evaluated, and current-traditional rhetoricians including John Franklin Genung, Barrett Wendell, and A. S. Hill developed "hyper-correct" standards for written discourse (ibid., 167). By the 1870s, Robert J. Connors notes, the perceived "illiteracy of American boys" was causing much public anxiety, the relief for which was "the collection of form-based mechanical lessons that came to be known as 'grammar'" (Connors 1997, 129). College level writing instruction of the era became increasingly defined by error avoidance and mechanical correctness—forms of constraint—rather than by any sort of genuine communicative practices or goals. The nineteenth century rhetorics of dogmatism and hyper-correctness, in other words, conceived of writing and writing instruction as fundamentally deontological: a striving to fulfill obligations and observe constraints that were foundational and absolute.

Nor can we regard these rhetorics as a faded memory of some bygone era. Mina Shaughnessy's celebrated *Errors and Expectations: A Guide for the Teacher of Basic Writing*, published in 1977, begins by noting the "obsession with error" in the minds of many students new to college, which was the result, according to Shaughnessy, of "the fact that most college teachers have little tolerance for the kinds of errors [basic writing] students make" (Shaughnessy 1977, 8). Building upon Shaughnessy's work, David Bartholomae's 1980 essay, "The Study of Error," critiqued mechanistic basic writing pedagogies that were based not on studies of successful writers, but "on old text-book models that disregard what writers actually do . . . and break writing conveniently into constituent skills like 'word power,' 'sentence power,' and 'paragraph power'" (Bartholomae 1980, 253). And Mike Rose has written poignantly of how students described as "basic" can be isolated in "developmental centers" where they are given worksheets and atomistic grammatical exercises in place of assignments that call for extended discourse and critical analysis (Rose 1989, 205–212). Well into the twentieth century, then, good writers could be defined as those who had learned the rules and did not deviate from them, while bad writers were defined as those who had not learned the rules, or who deviated from them.

Applied to the contemporary writing classroom, deontological theory calls upon writers and teachers of writing to determine what counts as appropriate rules and principles, to recognize these as binding, and to derive from them a list of constraints, a rhetorical catalog of negatively formulated "thou shalt nots." And this suggests that questions of what is good, right, and decent are *a priori*, independent of social context and the messy particulars of human experience. Should we embrace the ethics of deontology in our courses, we would in effect be telling students that whatever moral ambiguities they may encounter when writing or evaluating texts can be resolved by appealing to inviolate rules, that such rules eclipse the situational variables of topic, occasion, purpose, and audience, and that the good writer is one who adheres to those rules, categorically.

The strengths of a deontological approach to rhetorical ethics are the strengths of deontology more broadly: the clarity of principles, in which, applied to the writing class, lexical choices, grammatical constructions, and syntactical arrangements are unconditionally right or wrong; the stoic indifference to consequences, in which the right words must be spoken or written, regardless of the outcome; and the inherent justice of its moral framework, in which rules and imperatives are universal and apply to writers regardless of class, gender, ethnicity or other identity markers. Moreover, the teaching of absolute rules and principles, even if taught *ex cathedra*, does not negate the capacity for ethical reflection and discernment. Instead, teachers and students of writing in the deontological classroom are faced with the problem of choosing among competing rules and constraints to determine the "intrinsically morally right or wrong" when writing or discussing texts.

Yet if we have learned anything from our postmodern era, it is that both the "intrinsically right" and "intrinsically wrong" are not always apparent, are often rife with contradictions, and can be stubbornly resistant to the application of universal moral principles. We have learned that the seemingly foundational and absolute are often chimerical, subject to qualifications, protestations, and historical revisions. And while a rhetoric informed by a deontological moral theory promises to resolve, categorically, seemingly unresolvable moral ambiguities, teachers of writing know that moral ambiguities are very often the impetus for rhetorical activity, and that we most require rhetoric when we can discern no clear rules or certain paths to follow. In sum, deontological ethics seems for our purposes less a framework for guiding ethical decision-making than a principled effort to banish ambiguity, error, and risk from the acts of writing and the teaching of writing. We require, it would appear, a different kind of moral theory for making ethical decisions in the writing classroom and for determining what constitutes the good writer in the twenty-first century.

CONSEQUENTIALIST ETHICS: THE RHETORIC OF OUTCOMES

*"Consequentialist ethical theories maintain that right and wrong are a
function of the consequences of our actions—more precisely, that our actions
are right or wrong because, and only because, of their consequences."*

—William Shaw (2007, 463)

If the deontological does not adequately serve in a world of conflicting
claims and uncertain knowledge, what conceptions of the good and the
good writer are offered by an ethics of consequences? The term "consequentialism," Shafer-Landau writes, describes not a single moral theory
but "a family of theories" that are united by the idea that the morality
of an act is measured by "how much good such things produce, or how
much bad they allow us to avoid" (453). What will happen if I tell this
lie? Who will be hurt, or spared from hurt? What harms will I cause by
lying, and which will I prevent? Consequentialist ethical theories hold
that an action is right or wrong, R. G. Frey writes, "solely in virtue of the
goodness or badness of their actual consequences" (Frey 2000, 165).
Consequentialism represents a sharp departure from ethical theories
grounded in obligation, natural law, conceptions of God, or other
presumed sources of authority. Instead, the morality of an action is to
be found in a kind of cost-benefit analysis, in which the good of possible
outcomes is weighed against the possible wrongs it produces. In the most
developed of the various consequentialist theories, Utilitarianism, the
good is defined in terms of happiness, or well being, and actions are
considered good if their outcomes promote greater happiness and so
reduce the quotient of unhappiness (Shaw 2007, 467).

In consequentialist ethics, in direct contrast to deontological ethics, nothing is inherently good or bad independent of consequences.
Murder, rape, torture, slavery are not immoral in and of themselves but
obtain their moral status through the assessment of their consequences
(Shafer-Landau 2007, 454). To revisit the example considered above,
the torture of a suspected terrorist would not be considered immoral
if the results of waterboarding or sleep deprivation were deemed sufficiently beneficial. Indeed, torturing a suspected terrorist believed to
be planning to detonate a nuclear weapon in a populated city could be
considered morally *essential* in a consequentialist ethic, given how many
lives would be saved if the torture compelled the suspect to reveal the
location of the device so that it might be disarmed before catastrophe
strikes. In the same way could murder be morally justified, if we imagine a case in which the assassination of a tyrant might spare the suffering
of the tyrant's subjects. Would it have been immoral, for example, to
have assassinated Hitler or Pol Pot?

Consequentialism has been criticized for its seeming lack of a moral firmament, in which even objectively terrible things can be justified, and for its insistence on the impartial assessment of consequences, which can lead to moral choices that are contrary to most people's moral instincts. Shafer-Landau gives the example of choosing whether to spend our money to feed and educate our children, or to spend the same money feeding and educating total strangers (454). Most people, faced with such a choice, would choose to feed their family members. But if our money would go further in another country, feeding and educating a greater number of equally worthy people, then consequentialist ethics would compel us to act impartially for the greater good, forsaking our own children to help strangers.

In response to critiques of the unrealistic impartiality called for in "act-consequentialism," in which an action is considered morally right "if and only if the actual (or expected) good produced *by that particular act* would be at least as great as that of any other act open to the agent" (Hooker 2000, 188), some consequentialists have proposed "rule-consequentialism," in which the morality of an action is based on following a code or set of rules that will, if followed, produce an actual or expected good greater than would result from adhering to any other code or set of rules. So, for example, rule-consequentialism might stipulate that when faced with an absolute choice between caring for loved ones or for strangers, our loved ones take precedence. And this would be morally justified, in the version of rule-consequentialism we are imagining, on the premise that we agree to a code stipulating that the greatest good is likely to be achieved in societies that place the interests of loved ones over those of strangers.

Consequentialism is frequently invoked in debates over social and economic policy. How will a proposed law or recommended policy, for example, achieve the maximum good for the greatest number of people? Given that two of the earliest and most influential consequentialists, Jeremy Bentham (1748–1832) and John Stuart Mill (1806–1873), were both reformers who saw consequentialism as a critical tool for analyzing and addressing social ills such as slavery and the oppression of women, perhaps it is not surprising that echoes of consequentialism continue to be heard in contemporary public argument.[3]

As is true of deontology, consequentialist moral theories are not without their complications and internecine debates. And while these are deserving of more discussion than this review allows, I am principally interested in considering what consequentialism offers teachers and students of writing. How does an ethical framework grounded in consequences and outcomes inform conceptions of the good, and of the good writer?

In a sense, we teachers of writing have already answered this question. Every time we put a grade on a student paper, we are sending the message, implicitly but nonetheless clearly, that good writing is writing that results in receiving a good grade, while poor writing results in that which results in a substandard or failing grade. So long as we teach in institutions that call upon us to evaluate and rank our students, we are practicing, and our students are learning—indeed, most have already learned—an ethics of writing defined at least partly by outcomes and consequences. And this suggests that when students come to ethical crossroads in writing their papers, choices of whether to use an incendiary metaphor, cite a contested source, or risk troubling those in authority, their decisions about what is good, right, and decent may be guided by cost-benefit analysis that is, given the institutional context in which they are writing, utterly rational. How will this metaphor, this source, or this argument affect my grade? What consequences—for my GPA, my financial aid, for my chances of getting into medical school—might follow?

Perhaps I am thinking too narrowly about outcomes and consequences. Certainly, there are outcomes that go beyond grades. As teachers of writing, we strive to help our students achieve successful outcomes on application essays, job letters, and the like. Consequentialism provides certain advantages to these ends. A consequentialist ethic provides a cogent rationale for making rhetorical decisions, as students and teachers consider what strategies will lead to the best outcome for such texts. A consequentialist ethic, too, can lead student writers to greater awareness of audience, as writers contemplate the effects of their writing: What consequences will come of making this argument with this audience? How will this metaphor, simile, or punctuation mark effect my readers? What attitudes, emotions, or actions are likely to follow? A consequentialist ethic focuses the writer on such questions, which can lead to more self-aware, responsible, and sophisticated writing.

However, how satisfied are we, as teachers of writing, that outcomes and results are sufficient measures of what constitutes the good or and the good writer? If outcomes are the ultimate measure of a good text, how confident are we, beyond our capacity to assign grades, that we can predict or even understand these? Let us consider as a cautionary tale the case of one John Jay Chapman, which is related by Edwin Black in his book, *Rhetorical Criticism: A Study in Method* (Black 1965), and which may serve as an example of what Kenneth Burke called a "representative anecdote."

In 1911, the American essayist John Jay Chapman read an account of "a particularly brutal lynching" of a black man by a white mob in Coatesville, Pennsylvania (Chapman 1911, in Black 1970, 78). Chapman had no connection to the victim or to Coatesville, but the account so disturbed him that as the first anniversary of the murder approached, Chapman announced to his family that he was going to Coatesville to hold a prayer meeting and deliver a public address to commemorate the terrible event. He was not welcomed in the town, and had trouble finding a location from which to speak. Eventually, he rented a storefront and delivered his address to exactly three people: a woman who had accompanied him to Coatesville, an elderly African American woman, and a third, unidentified person believed to be a local spy. In terms of immediate outcomes, writes Black, the speech was a failure: the audience was tiny, the critical response negligible, and the social and political effects of the oration virtually nil.

Yet the speech should not be judged, Black concludes, by its immediate effects. Rather, Chapman's speech should be understood as part of a broader cultural dialogue, one conducted over the time and space of the American moral landscape, and one that was joined at different moments, Black asserts, by such luminaries as Thomas Jefferson, Abraham Lincoln, Herman Melville, and William Faulkner. In this sense, the audience for Chapman's speech was not those few gathered at the Coatesville storefront, but rather all those "interested in a meaningful interpretation of history and moral status of this country" (84). Chapman's speech was later published, and continues to be read to this day, meaning its audience continues to grow, and its transformative potential continues to unfold.

While the circumstances of John Jay Chapman's speech are far removed from those of the typical first-year classroom, Black's narrative reminds us that the outcomes of a rhetorical act may not be immediately apparent but may unfold over time, in unforeseeable ways. Judgments we might make about a text or rhetorical performance may be at best premature, at worst simply wrong. What is good, right, and decent about a given text may ultimately transcend the cost-benefit calculus of the consequentialist ethic.

So it is with the writing of our students, some of whom may one day write, if they are not doing so already, for outcomes and results that may not be immediately realized. They may write, whether as citizens, scientists, soldiers, activists, or parents, in support of unpopular ideas, improbable purposes, and lost causes. They may write with the knowledge that their letters, essays, proposals, and petitions will go unread, effecting no change. Yet they may write regardless, compelled by motives beyond outcomes and consequences. In such instances, the worth of their writing should be judged not by what it brings about, the consequentialist ethic, but by such qualities as the conviction and courage of their written words. A framework for making ethical decisions in the writing class, I mean to suggest, should account for more than outcomes and consequences.

POSTMODERN ETHICS: THE RHETORIC OF THE CRITICAL AND CONTINGENT

> *"Postmodernism challenges the foundationalist assumptions that reside at the center of most ethical discussions."*
>
> —James E. Porter (1993, 49)

The argument in the previous sections has been that deontology and consequentialism have long provided students and teachers of writing with implicit principles and reasons for making ethical choices in the writing course. Not so with postmodern ethics. If other moral theories have affected the teaching of writing in ways that are largely undeclared and under-theorized, the principles and reasons of postmodern ethics have been made thoroughly explicit, and their influence on modern writing pedagogy has been profound. Indeed, one could plausibly argue that postmodernism has provided Writing Studies with its most complete and comprehensive statement on the ethics of writing.

Well into the 1990s, Sheryl I. Fontaine and Susan M. Hunter argue in their insightful essay, "Ethical Awareness: A Process of Inquiry," Writing Studies narrowly construed ethics in one of two ways: as a set of established codes intended to regulate professional behavior, or as the basis for creating environments for reflection and moral action (Fontaine and Hunter 1998). In the first conception, ethics is understood as a set of norms to be applied in the context of professional organizations for regulating members' conduct. Fontaine and Hunter reference as examples "The Statement of Professional Ethics" promulgated by the Modern Language Association in 1992, and the series of columns on writing center ethics that appeared in *The Writing Lab* Newsletter from 1993 to 1997. Student behavior, too, was subject to codes of conduct, according to Fontaine and Hunter. Sandra Stotsky's 1992 essay "Writing as Moral and Civic Thinking," for example, sought to establish an ethical framework that would "help scholars explore the moral dimensions of academic writing and assist teachers in fostering their students' responsibilities as writers" (Stotsky 1992, 799, quoted in Fontaine and Hunter 1998, 2).

The second commonly understood approach to approach to ethics in the discipline, according to Hunter and Fontaine, was as a basis for creating environments for reflection and moral action. Fontaine and Hunter provide as examples writing assignments that were used to promote ethical responses to issues surrounding death (Friend 1994), the use of computers (Selfe and Selfe 1994), and corporate responsibility (Jacobi 1996). Professional organizations also attempted to create environments in which members might be encouraged to reflect and act upon ethical issues. Hunter and Fontaine cite the examples of the 1996 Bard Conference on "Teaching Ethics" and the NCTE 1997 convention theme of "Language as Moral Action" (3). As before, the focus is not on ethics as a subject in its own right but rather as a means for addressing other concerns.[4]

The advent of postmodernism, however, led by the end of the 1990s to a "conceptual shift" that brought a greater exigency to ethical awareness within the discipline. And so we see Kathleen Ethel Welch arguing in the 1992 collection, *Ethical Issues in College Writing* (Gale, Siporia, and Kinneavy) that since all writing practices, including writing pedagogy, involve the transmission of values, that "writing programs and teachers are in fact teaching ethics" (Welch 1999, 137). And we find James L. Kinneavy declaring in that same collection that we are living through an ethical "catastrophe" (3) and challenging teachers of writing and rhetoric to establish "a modern moral language" (13) in which students might discuss questions of morality and politics (Kinneavy 1999). "Ethical awareness has moved to the foreground in Composition and English studies," Hunter and Fontaine write, ". . . because the postmodern, epistemological climate gives rise to both disciplinary reassessment and context-sensitive judgment" (7).

Postmodern ethics, Hunter and Fontaine appear to be saying, offers the discipline a broader, more comprehensive, more urgent conception of ethics for the writing classroom. But what do we mean by "postmodern ethics"? If the ethics of deontology and consequentialism resist abridgment, the ethics of postmodernism is even less amenable to reductive summary. "A postmodern ethics," writes James E. Porter, one of the most cogent and able guides to the postmodern ethical terrain, "differs from traditional ethics primarily in its contingent nature; it sees ethics as grounded in fluctuating criteria, in difference, or in community or local practices. It does not rely on, nor would it attempt to seek, a universal common ground for ethical action" (50). The ethics of postmodernism reflect, Zygmunt Bauman writes, a vision of modern life grounded in "postmodern wisdom," which consists of the recognition:

that there are problems in human and social life with no good solutions, twisted trajectories that cannot be straightened up, ambivalences that are more than linguistic blunders yelling to be corrected, doubts which cannot be legislated out of existence, moral agonies which no reason-dictated recipes can soothe, let alone cure. (Bauman 1993, 245)

Central to Bauman's vision of postmodern wisdom is the repudiation of what he calls "the twin banners" of "universality" and "foundation" (8) in favor of an ethics that acknowledges moral uncertainties, persistent ambiguities, and "'messiness' of the human world" (32).

One does not pull down such long-billowing banners without a vigorous language of critique, and postmodern ethics has provided that vocabulary. The language of "truth," "universal," and "foundational," has been supplanted in the postmodern idiom by "contingent," "subjective," and "ideological." The vocabulary of "reason," "rational," and "systemic," has given way to the vernacular of "difference," "negotiated," and "hermeneutic." In the postmodern view, ethics is no longer seen as a disinterested set of fixed principles but is viewed instead as a process of negotiation among competing political and ideological interests.

Nor is the postmodern ethos sanguine about resolving these competing interests. In the postmodern worldview, write Lucaites and Condit (1999), disagreement is the "natural" result of different social, political, and ethnic groups, each with their own logic, interests and values, living together and competing for the same limited resources. In this view, "struggle, not consensus, is the defining condition of social life [and] social discord is not a pathology to be cured but a condition to be productively managed" (Lucaites and Condit 1999, 11). How we might productively manage such struggles and social discords, however, is for the most part unaddressed in postmodern writing. While it is not accurate to say that postmodernism offers an entirely critical hermeneutic—the ethical vision of Emmanuel Levinas offers a profoundly humane view of engagement with The Other (Levinas 1969)—the postmodern ethos is primarily one of fragmentation, irony, positionality, and contingency. One does not repair the fractures and fissures of the modern world, but learns to navigate among them.

Some in Writing Studies have argued that postmodernism meant the end of ethics, at least as it was previously understood. James Berlin, for example, rejected "elevating an historically specific mode of thought to a universal standard" (Berlin 1990, 170) in histories of rhetoric, while Gary A. Olson noted that the advent of the postmodern age led certain theorists to declare that "ethics is dead, that no system or code of moral values can universally regulate human behavior" (Olson 1999, 71). Yet if some questioned the possibility of ethics, others, including Olson, worked at the project of defining a rhetorical ethics for the postmodern age. One of the most trenchant statements was provided by Porter:

> Ethics in the postmodern sense, then, does not refer to a static body of foundational principles, laws, or procedures; it is not to be confused with particular moral codes or particular sets of statements about what is appropriate or inappropriate behavior or practice. Ethics is not a set of answers but a mode of questioning and a manner of positioning. That questioning certainly involves principles—but it always involves mediating between competing principles and judging those principles in light of particular circumstances. (Porter 1993, 223)

The influence of postmodern ethics on the teaching of writing has been largely invigorating, providing students and teachers with an expanded and expansive framework for making ethical decisions. In her excellent *JAC* essay, "'Just Multiculturalism': Teaching Writing as Critical and Ethical Practice," Laurie Grobman argued that postmodernism has "exposed the oppressiveness of foundational claims; led to a reconsideration (and some redress) of injustices based on race, class, and gender; recovered previously silenced voices and discourses; and led to a committed effort to respect cultural differences and to refrain from imposing privileged views on the colonized" (Grobman 2002, 817). In recent years, the postmodern conception of rhetorical ethics has been complicated and enriched by perspectives in feminism (Powell and Takayoshi 2003), digital writing, (Pandey 2007), discourse analysis (Barton 2008) and others. Each of these has in different ways shifted the theoretical and ethical ground, providing nuance, elaboration, or new insights.

In general, then, let us posit that postmodern ethics provides a set of rhetorical and strategic practices that collectively offer a sustained critique of Western ethical codes, systems, and narratives. In a postmodern ethics, there is an emphasis on the salience of the writer's position, the contingency of received doctrines, the role of ideology in framing moral choices, and the workings of power in shaping rhetorical and social interactions. Taken together, these represent, we may say, the postmodern conception of the good, with the good writer construed as one who can absorb and articulate the fragmented moral landscape.

However, if ethical principles are, as the postmodern move would have it, grounded in the "particular circumstances" of the contingent and the positioned, if they are a product of prevailing social and cultural discourses, perhaps the time has come to ask whether an ethics of postmodernism is adequate for addressing the circumstances of the current prevailing cultural moment, one in which democratic commitments and conceptions of civic good have been undermined by a corrosive, post-truth, market-driven public discourse that disdains evidence and fact-based argument generally. Perhaps we need to provide students with another kind of ethics and another language for deliberating over ethical choices—a language that expresses not only the values of contingency, difference, and critique, but one that can speak beyond these to the values of connections, reciprocities, and interdependencies among peoples of diverse and often conflicting ideologies and values.

No less a postmodern stalwart than Bruno Latour has expressed misgivings about the postmodern critique (Latour 2004). Latour is dismayed by how the postmodern project of unmasking of ideology posturing as unvarnished fact has been hijacked, for lack of a better term, by those seeking to cast doubts on the scientific evidence for global warming, or by the conspiracy-minded claiming 9/11 was a hoax. "What has become of critique," Latour asks, "when there is a whole industry denying that the Apollo Program landed on the moon?" (228). Latour worries that the postmodern critique has "run out of steam" while extremists use the tools of social construction, the critical and methodological tools Latour has spent his career developing, to undermine and overthrow scientific evidence that might well be necessary to save the planet.

Latour is not ready to disavow postmodern commitments, however, but is instead seeking to re-imagine, reorient, and remake them. "Is it really asking too much," he muses, "from our collective intellectual life to devise, at least once a century, some *new* critical tools?" (243). Such tools, he writes, might lead to critical attitudes in which critics would practice the arts not of debunking, but of assembling; not of exposing, but of gathering; not of moving away, but of moving toward. This re-imagined critique would necessitate, Latour writes, "a whole set of new positive metaphors, gestures, attitudes, habits of thoughts" (244) that would be associated "with *more*, not with *less*, with *multiplication*, not with *subtraction*" (248).

We have learned in our discipline, and, indeed, throughout the humanities, how to deconstruct, unmask, destabilize, and distance. We have become skilled, and we have helped our students to become skilled, in the postmodern arts of interrogation and irony. But has the moment arrived for us to speak a different language with our students, one that emphasizes not just debunking but also assembling, not simply exposing but also gathering, not only moving away but also moving toward? Can we offer our students a language that will enable them to express necessary critical commitments but can equally articulate the ethical discourses of affinity, solidarity, and empathy?

I do not mean to suggest that we can return to Platonic ideals of foundational truths, or that we should seek to recover Enlightenment narratives of the autonomous individual. Even if such things were possible, they would hardly be desirable. The violence wreaked upon individuals and peoples by grand narratives and essentializing discourses has been well documented. However, to say there are no universal truths does not mean there can be no shared values; to acknowledge there are no absolute principles does not mean there are no mutual aspirations; to accept that there can be no transcendent ethical systems does not mean we cannot search for reciprocal moral standpoints through which we may begin to breach our deepening and increasingly bitter divides. Our cultural moment, I submit, calls for an ethical language that can help us speak—and help our students speak—to the possibilities of this search. And this means we require a moral theory that takes us beyond the language and practices of postmodern ethics.

RE-IMAGINING THE GOOD WRITER

The purpose of a moral theory is to guide the choices we make, to provide principles and reasons for those choices, and to help us realize the social vision we would communicate. More, I have suggested, the purpose of a moral theory is to offer us, writers and teachers of writing, an identity, a way of understanding ourselves relative to some particular understanding, recalling Kraemer, of the good, the right, and the decent. In the context of the writing class, each of the moral theories we have considered proposes a particular account of the "good writer," if we are willing to understand "good" in the ethical sense of a one who makes good choices instead on bad ones, right choices instead of wrong, when composing or evaluating a text.

The deontological writer, as we have seen, locates the good in principles of obligation, rules, and constraints that are absolute and binding upon all moral agents. Having established through reason and the exercise of free will what is universal and therefore categorical, one chooses a topic, a source, or a word because one must, because to do otherwise would wrong, absolutely. For the consequentialist writer, the good is approached through the calculation of intended results. One makes decisions when composing based on the outcomes and consequences those decisions are likely to effect. The postmodern writer complicates and critiques these previous conceptions of the good, which is to be found, if it can be said to exist at all, in the entanglements of contingency, difference, position, power, and ideological struggle. The good postmodern writer is one who can recognize and negotiate these conditions, leaving behind the illusions of the universal and the foundational.

I have suggested that while each of these moral theories, each of these ethical identities, has advantages and insights that recommend it to teachers and students of writing, none offers an adequate account of rhetorical ethics for the twenty-first century writing classroom. In place of these, I propose in this book an alternative moral theory, one grounded neither in terms of rules or consequences, nor in contingencies or differences, but in the qualities of truthfulness, accountability, open-mindedness, and others such qualities that the ancients called "virtues," and that today are the subject of that branch of moral philosophy known as "virtue ethics." In the discursive enactment of the virtues, we find principles for action for making moral decisions in the writing class. We find a vocabulary for helping Lindsay decide on her metaphor, VJ on his selection of evidence, Austin on the topic of his paper. In virtue and virtue ethics, we are offered, writers and teachers, a language for re-imagining what it means in to be a "good writer" in the twenty-first century.

Perhaps as should be expected of a word with so long a lineage, however, the meaning of "virtue" is neither timeless nor stable, but is instead variable, protean, and culturally inflected. Nested within it are multiple commitments, histories, and narratives that express diverse and sometimes contrary understandings of "the good" and the "good person." In the following chapter, I attempt to sort out some of this complicated story, considering the questions, "What do we mean by virtue?" and "What is virtue ethics?" If we are to ground our conceptions of the good writer in an ethics of virtue, we need to sort out some of this complicated story by considering the questions, "What do we mean by virtue?' and "What is virtue ethics?" I take up these questions in the following chapter.

NOTES

1. I discuss certain non-Western approaches to ethics in chapter 3.
2. The "murderer at the door" has been debated as to Kant's meaning. See, for example, Wood (2011).
3. That said, deontology, too, continues to exercise a potent influence on public debate, as issues of immigration, gun control affirmative action, and other are debated in *moral terms*, or on the basis of what is inherently right and wrong—the deontological ethic.
4. For a competing view, see Porter, who argues that rhetoric and writing scholars, including Carolyn Miller, James Kinneavy, Louise Weatherbee Phelps, Lester Faigley, John Schilb, and others were vigorously exploring what Faigley (1992) called "a missing ethics throughout the activities of composing" (239, quoted in Porter 1993, 25).

3
HABITS OF THE HEART
Virtue and Virtue Ethics

"Considerations of justice, charity and the like have a strange and powerful appeal to the human heart."
—Philippa Foot, *What Are the Virtues?* (xvi)

In her painful and extraordinary 1988 essay, "Nobody Mean More to Me than You and the Future Life of Willie Jordan," poet and essayist June Jordan tells the story of how students in her college course, "The Art of Black English," decide to write a letter to the editor of a local newspaper after learning that one of their classmates' siblings has been shot and killed by the police (Jordan 1988). Many of the students, Jordan writes, came from the Brooklyn neighborhood where the shooting took place. Many had known someone close to them who had been killed by police. Many had had their own frightening encounters with police. The students wanted their letter to speak on behalf of Reggie Jordan, the victim. The crucial decision before them, Jordan relates, was whether to write the letter in Standard English or in the Black English they had been studying throughout the semester, and in which they expressed their deepest values and worldview. Jordan writes:

> I have seldom been privy to a discussion with so much heart at the dead beat of it. I will never forget the eloquence, the sudden haltings of speech, the fierce struggle against tears, the furious throwaway, and useless explosions that this question elicited.
>
> That one question contained several others, each of them extraordinarily painful to even contemplate. How best to serve the memory of Reggie Jordan? Should we use the language of the killer—Standard English—in order to make our ideas acceptable to those controlling the killers? But wouldn't what we had to say be rejected, summarily, if we said it in our own language, the language of the victim, Reggie Jordan? But if we sought to express ourselves by abandoning our language wouldn't that mean our suicide on top of Reggie's murder? (Jordan 1988, 371–372)

DOI: 10.7330/9781607328278.c003

Ultimately, the students decide unanimously to write in Black English: *"At least we don't give up nothing else. At least we stick to the truth: Be who we been. And stay all the way with Reggie"* (372; emphases in original). Everything from this point forward is "heartbreaking" because the students understand that their decision has doomed the letter's chances at publication, "even as the distinctive reality of our Black lives," Jordan writes, "has doomed our efforts to 'be who we been' in this country" (ibid.). In the end, the letter is never published in any newspaper, no media outlets take up the case of Reggie Jordan, no money is raised to secure legal counsel for the victim's family, and "Reggie Jordan is really dead" (373).

Here is the letter the students produced, as it was dictated in class to June Jordan:

> YOU COPS! WE THE BROTHER AND SISTER OF WILLIE JORDAN, A FELLOW STONY BROOK STUDENT WHO THE BROTHER OF THE DEAD REGGIE JORDAN. REGGIE, LIKE MANY BROTHER AND SISTER, HE A VICTIM OF BRUTAL RACIST POLICE, OCTOBER 25, 1984. US APPALL, FED UP, BECAUSE THAT ANOTHER SENSELESS DEATH WHAT OCCUR IN OUR COMMUNITY. THIS WHAT WE FEEL, THIS, FROM OUR HEART, FOR WE AIN'T STAYIN' SILENT NO MORE

• • •

Reading the letter even decades after it appeared in Jordan's essay, it is difficult not to feel the outrage and grief that engendered it. One feels, as well, the intensity of the students' righteous anger, their solidarity with their classmate, Willie Jordan, their courage in speaking out against established power, and their resolve to continue the struggle for justice. Righteous anger, solidarity, courage, resolve, justice: these are instances of what moral philosophers call virtues. The students' letter, in turn, is an illustration of virtuous discourse, the rhetorical enactment of those qualities or traits that in this particular case, as Lisa Tessman writes in her study of virtue ethics in liberatory struggles, "are consistent with bringing about and living lives free from oppression and domination" (Tessman 2005, 19n8).

Perhaps this seems an unlikely pairing: virtue, which in contemporary discourse is often associated with musty moralizing and sexual priggishness; and the scalding language of a letter that presages by decades the Black Lives Matter movement. But if this pairing gives us pause, perhaps it also serves as reason to re-examine the concept of virtue and the ethical tradition that places virtue at its core. What is virtue? What do we mean when we speak of "the virtues"? What is "virtue ethics," and what does it have to offer teachers of writing and rhetoric? Let us begin with the question of what we mean when we speak of "virtue."

WHAT IS VIRTUE?

Many discussions of virtue begin with the concept of "excellence." This is at least partly due to the etymology of the word, which, as van Hooft reminds us, comes to us from the Latin *virtus*, which was the Roman translation of the Greek *arête*. What we call "virtue," in other words, should more properly be translated into English as "excellence" (Steutel and Carr 1999, 8; van Hooft 2006, 1).[1] When feminist scholars object to the sexist associations of the word, however, they have both history and etymology on their side. Derived from the Latin *vir*, for "man," virtue in ancient Rome was personified as *Virtus*, the Roman god of bravery and military strength, and was associated with qualities the Romans regarded as masculine, such as valor, while a woman's virtue, Deidre N. McCloskey points out, was *pudicitia*, or "modesty, purity" (McCloskey 2006, 201). The Greek word *arête*, meanwhile, is derived from *aner*, which means "man," and about which feminist philosopher Susan Okin writes, "Only qualified and inferior forms of *arête* . . . attach to women, slaves, and those free males who are unsuited, for whatever reason, to be heroes" (Okin 1996, 212). Nor did such associations perish with the classical societies. Well into the Renaissance and beyond, McCloskey notes, "the Latin word and its Romance derivatives kept this whiff of the men's locker room" (McCloskey 2006, 201). We will revisit this dolorous history in more detail when we consider, below, the development of feminist virtue ethics, but for now let us acknowledge the problematic origins of the term.

Philosophers and other scholars of virtue typically retain the association of the word, whether in the singular or the plural form, with qualities of moral excellence inherent in individual character. Daniel C. Russell, for example, describes virtues as "excellences of character that consist in both caring about the right sorts of things and having the wisdom and practical skills to judge and act successfully in respect to those things" (Russell 2013, 7). Heather Battaly asserts that virtues "*are qualities that make one an excellent person*" (Battaly 2015, 5; emphasis in original), while George Sher writes simply that a virtue is "a character trait that is for some important reason desirable or worth having" (Sher 1992, 94, quoted in Steutel and Carr 1999, 4). Virtues are not regarded as hard and fast principles or rules, but rather as "general patterns or tendencies of conduct which require reasonable and cautious adjustment to particular and changing circumstances and which may even, in some situations, compete with each other for preference and priority" (Carr 1991, 5, quoted in Lapsley and Narvaez 2006, 256).

For a quality to count as a virtue, it must be "settled," consistent in our character, a reliable disposition to act in a predictable way. The virtue theorist Julia Annas, for example, argues that a virtue is "a deep feature" of a person, "a disposition which is central to the person, to whom he or she is, a way we standardly think of character" (Annas 2011, 9). Russell similarly describes the virtues as deep, "insofar as they are steady, reliable, and intelligent dispositions, rather than mere habits" (17). Suppose that late one night after two glasses of wine I am moved by a television commercial depicting the suffering of refugees in a far-away land. I respond by making a generous online to donation to the charity helping the refugees. Do I possess the virtue of generosity? Not according to Annas or Russell, whose conceptions of virtue require that my actions be characteristic and reliable. If I am not as generous in the glare of day, or when drinking water, then my disposition to generosity is neither steady, predictable, nor settled. I have not fully acquired the virtue of generosity, despite the occasional impulse to act generously.

To say that virtues have or have not been "acquired" suggests they are not innate but must be learned and developed. Aristotle believed that we acquire virtue in two distinct ways. What he called "moral virtues," such as kindness, self-control, and generosity, are developed through practice and habituation. The more I make a practice of giving, the more likely I am to become a generous person. In contrast, what Aristotle called "intellectual virtues," such as wisdom, are acquired through formal training and experience.

Annas argues that virtues are developed in much the same way we would develop a practical skill, such as piano playing or tennis: through repetition and practice. However, Annas distinguishes a "skill" from a mere "knack" or "routine," both of which are formulaic and repetitive. Practical skills and virtues, in contrast, "require more than a predictably similar reaction; they require a response which is appropriate to the situation . . . [and which] enable us to respond in creative and imaginative ways to new challenges" (15). Such skills are not learned independently, according to Annas, but through our interactions with others: "We always learn to be virtuous in a given context; there is no such thing as just learning to be generous or loyal in the abstract" (21). Annas represents the virtues as embedded in social contexts that "stand in various relations, from overlapping to conflicting: family, school, church, employment, siblings, friends, neighbourhoods, the internet" (ibid.) All of which is to say that virtues are not isolated and autonomous traits but are rather contextual and communal, "discovered in the rough and tumble of human interpersonal relations and conduct" (Carr 1991, 4, quoted in Lapsley and Narvaez 2006, 256). Virtues in this sense reflect the values, traditions, memories, and narratives of the cultures and communities from which they emerge. And while different communities may recognize different virtues, or interpret the meanings of individual virtues, such as truthfulness, generosity, or courage, in culturally specific ways, "it is hard to envision a human community in which these qualities are not needed, or recognized, held to be of any value at all" (Carr 1991, 6, quoted in Lapsley and Narvaez 2006, 256.)

Where does this leave us? Virtues, we have said, are those excellences of character, such as empathy, open-mindedness, and courage, as well as solidarity, resolve, and righteous anger, that enable us to make good choices, to act and react rightly, and to live as good people. Virtues are not hard and fast rules of conduct, but rather should be understood patterns or tendencies that call for, much like rhetoric, adjustment to particular and changing circumstances. Neither are virtues ephemeral or fleeting impulses but are instead deep features of our character, central to the kind of person we are, or are striving to become. Finally, virtues are learned in social contexts, the product of our relations with family, friends, teachers, community members, and others that influence us to greater or lesser degrees. Deidre N. McCloskey (2006) summarizes gracefully: "A 'virtue' is a habit of the heart, a stable disposition, a settled state of character, a durable, educated, characteristic of someone to exercise her will to be good" (64). If we are willing to accept McCloskey's characterization, we may proceed to the moral theory that places virtue at its very core: virtue ethics.

WHAT IS VIRTUE ETHICS?

For many centuries, moral philosophers regarded the concept of virtue as a historical artifact, a relic of pre-enlightenment philosophy long eclipsed by moral theories grounded in concepts of God and duty. In recent decades, however, the study of virtue-based ethical theories has been ascendant, and the "aretaic turn" has led to new insights into problems unresolved by traditional Western approaches to moral theory (Aberdein 2007). In what has become known as virtue ethics, which Steutel and Carr characterize as "a systematic and coherent account of the virtues" (4), the emphasis is on the character of the moral agent and the traits, dispositions, and attitudes that we typically associate with a good person, living a good life.

The modern revival of a virtue-based ethical theory is generally credited to the publication in 1958 of Elizabeth Anscombe's essay, "Modern Moral Philosophy," in which Anscombe critiqued ethical theories grounded in concepts of duty and obligation, the ethics of "should" and "ought" (Anscombe 1958). Anscombe argued that such theories historically derived their authority from God as a lawgiver, a conception that modern moral philosophy no longer assumed, thus rendering doctrines of obligation unintelligible. Anscombe recommended that philosophers discard the language of obligations and duties, and return to Aristotle and the concepts of character and virtue for guidance on how to do ethical theory.

Alasdair MacIntyre, writing some two decades after Anscombe, made a similar critique, arguing in his celebrated book, *After Virtue*, that modern societies, having rejected the rational morality of Aristotelian ethics, were incoherent, borrowing from multiple ethical theories without having any shared means of deciding among incommensurable moral claims (MacIntyre 2007, 8). To illustrate, MacIntyre begins *After Virtue* with what he calls a "disquieting suggestion." Imagine, he asks readers, that the natural sciences were to suffer a "catastrophe":

> A series of environmental disasters are blamed by the general public on the scientists. Widespread riots occur, laboratories are burnt down, physicists are lynched, books and instruments are destroyed. Finally a Know-Nothing political movement takes power and successfully abolishes science teaching in schools and universities, imprisoning and executing the remaining scientists. (MacIntyre 2007, 1)

Eventually there is a backlash and a few "enlightened people" begin to pick up the pieces, collecting "instruments whose use has been forgotten; half-chapters from books, single pages from articles, not always fully legible because torn and charred." The idea of science is revived, but what is revived is fragmentary and incomplete, leading to theories and practices of a kind pseudoscience, a simulacrum of science, and not science as it had been. However, no one practicing or teaching pseudoscience is capable of understanding "the grave state of disorder" of their theories and practices. Instead, they carry on as though they are doing science proper.

The state of modern ethics, MacIntyre argued, is analogous to the state of science in this fictional society. The catastrophe that has befallen modern ethics, and modern society more broadly according to MacIntyre, has been the rejection by Enlightenment philosophers of the Aristotelian teleological tradition, in which all things, human and non-human, have an apparent purpose, and in which purpose individuals find their social and moral identities. When Enlightenment philosophers, Kierkegaard, Kant, and others, repudiated teleological morality, MacIntyre avers, positing in its place a conception of the individual as a sovereign moral authority, they removed the basis for objective social judgments about morality. Ethics became an expression of individual preferences and assertions, what MacIntyre calls "emotivism," while moral concepts such as justice were separated from the traditions that made them intelligible.

Moral philosophers since the Enlightenment, contends MacIntyre, have been like those pseudo-scientists, making arguments based on concepts whose meanings are fragmentary and divorced from the philosophical contexts that once gave them meaning. "The rhetoric of shared values is of great ideological importance," MacIntyre writes in "The Privatization of Good," "but it disguises the truth about how action is guided and directed. For what we genuinely share in the way of moral maxims, precepts and principles is insufficiently determinate to guide action and what is sufficiently determinate to guide action is not shared" (MacIntyre 1990, 349). MacIntyre's response to this disorder is to reaffirm the centrality of the virtues in moral life, and *After Virtue* is his attempt to justify that project.

Many discussions of virtue ethics since Anscombe and MacIntyre begin, as those philosophers did, by contrasting it with other moral theories, specifically deontology and consequentialism. Hursthouse's *On Virtue Ethics* begins, for example, by describing virtue ethics as "an approach to normative ethics which emphasizes the virtues, or moral character, in contrast to an approach which emphasizes duties or rules (deontology) or one which emphasizes the consequences of actions (utilitarianism)" (1). Similarly, Christine Swanton begins *Virtue Ethics: A Pluralistic View* by observing that the modern context of virtue ethics "has largely been its opposition to the two kinds of moral theory [i.e., those grounded in rules and consequences] that have dominated moral philosophy in recent times" (Swanton 2003, 1). And Steven M. Gardiner observes that "much of the relevant early work in ethical theory in the twentieth century was essentially negative: it was focused around a critical reaction to the existing utilitarian and Kantian orthodoxies" (Gardiner 2005, 2).

In contrast to deontology and consequentialism, writes Hursthouse, virtue ethics offers a broader landscape of moral inquiry, one that makes a place for addressing "motives and moral character, moral wisdom and discernment, friendship and family relationships, a deep concept of happiness, the role of emotions in our moral life, and the questions of what sort of person I should be, and of how we should live" (3). Russell argues that what distinguishes virtue ethics from such rival moral theories is its concern with the whole of one's life, in which the focus "is not so much on what to do in morally difficult cases as on how to approach all of one's choices with such personal qualities as kindness, courage, wisdom, and integrity" (2). Virtue ethics, in this understanding, is a theory for attending to those traits of character that ought to guide our most consequential decisions: whether and whom to marry, whether to have children, what career to pursue, how to choose friends, and other life-shaping choices (Pence 1993, 257).

The theologian William Mattison has argued that what most distinguishes virtue ethics from rival moral theories is it attention to a final end, the overall purpose of one's life. The virtues, according to Mattison, are those "qualities of persons" that "dispose toward action that is *constitutive of happiness*." In a virtue-based ethical theory, according to Mattison, the virtues give coherence to life. They are the qualities, habits, traits that ultimately make possible "a life well lived" (Mattison, email message to author, November 7, 2016.)

While the term "virtue ethics" is used to describe a plurality of moral theories, ancient and contemporary, the philosopher whose work serves as the principal source for virtue-based ethical theories, and who is regarded, Dorothea Frede observes, as "*the* protagonist of virtue ethics" (Frede 2015, 17), is Aristotle. And while his is neither the first nor the last word on virtue, it nonetheless seems fair to say that modern students of virtue typically depart from, build upon, and quarrel with Aristotle's work, even as they reject what Hursthouse described as "the lamentable, parochial details of Aristotle's moral philosophy," and in particular his "deplorable views on both slavery and women" (2). To understand virtue, and virtue ethics, then, we need to revisit Aristotelian moral theory.

ARISTOTELIAN VIRTUE ETHICS

For Aristotle, virtue was an element in a larger philosophical project concerning the purpose of human existence. Aristotle describes his ethics as an "inquiry" through which he might examine certain broad questions about how to live: What constitutes a good life? How does one become good? What is happiness, and how it is achieved? Aristotle does not treat these as abstract questions, nor is he interested in discovering universal moral laws or setting forth a program of "obligations, rules, duties, and principles" (Pakaluk 2005, 3). Indeed, Aristotle is clear that ethics cannot be reduced to categorical principles, and that in making judgments about moral issues we are arguing, as he writes in the *Nicomachean Ethics*, "for the most part" under the influence of custom and circumstance (Aristotle 2004, 1094b). In this sense, the *Nicomachean Ethics* is, according to Jonathan Barnes, "a work of practical science" (Barnes 2003, xvii), in which the aim is not to acquire knowledge about goodness but rather to become a good person. The *Ethics*, Barnes writes, "is expressly practical: its philosophy aims at changing the world, not at interpreting it" (xxx). Or as Aristotle expresses it in J. A. K. Thomson's translation, "because we are studying not to know what goodness is but how to become good . . . since otherwise it would be useless" (Aristotle 2004, 1103b28–29).

For Aristotle, the supreme good, the *summum bonum*, the end to which all other ends contribute, is what he calls *eudaimonia*, typically translated as "flourishing," "well being," or "happiness." *Eudaimonia* is not a transitory emotional happiness, the way we might be happy at learning we have won the lottery or landed a promotion, but rather represents what Hursthouse characterizes as "the sort of happiness worth having," by which she means the happiness that comes with a life of purpose (Hursthouse 1999, 10).[2] What constitutes "living well" in Aristotelian ethics is grounded in the idea of a "function," or purpose. All things, living and non-living, may be said to have a function distinctive to the thing: the purpose for which the thing exists, its final end, or *telos*. So, for example, the knife has the function to cut, the plant to grow, the horse to run.

Aristotle observes that things, animals, and people can perform their functions well or poorly. The knife that cuts cleanly may be said to have the virtues of cutting well: a sharp edge, a hard blade, a good handle. The plant that flourishes in sunlight can be considered to have the virtues of growing well: green leaves, a healthy stem, deep roots. The horse that runs fast may be said to have the virtues of racing well: a strong body, long legs, a bold spirit. Human beings, too, have a purpose, a telos, and the "distinctly human" activity in Aristotelian ethics, that which separates us from knives, plants, and horses, is rationality, the ability of humans to exercise practical reason. Human beings who perform their distinctively human function well, who are, in essence, good at being human beings are those who exercise the virtues of reasoning well (van Hooft 2006, 51),

To practice the "virtues of reasoning well" in Aristotelian ethics is to react appropriately to a given situation by finding the mean, the middle way, the path between extremes of excess and deficiency. The foolhardy person rushes heedlessly into danger, while the cowardly person flees from it. To practice the virtue of courage is to find the mean between these extremes. The wasteful person spends frivolously, while the stingy person cannot be persuaded to part with a dollar. The virtue of generosity is the mean between these ends of the continuum. And this provides Aristotle with his celebrated definition of virtue: "a state concerned with choice, lying in a mean relative to us, this being determined by reason and in the way in which the person of practical wisdom would determine it" (Aristotle 2004, 1106b35–1107a2).

What may sound like little more than "cautionary folk wisdom," Frede writes, is "one of the most original and central aspects of Aristotelian ethics" (Frede 2015, 20). Before Aristotle, virtues and vices were understood as pairs: courage and cowardice; justice and injustice; and so forth. Frede points out that Aristotle offered instead a "triadic schema of virtues and vices" (21), one that called for the exercise of judgment and practical wisdom to find a feasible and proper path: the Aristotelian mean. That path does not, however, necessarily advise moderation in all things. The right response to injustice, for example, is righteous indignation, not tempered forbearance (Pakaluk 2005, 108).

Aristotle provides a list of exemplary virtues, distinguishing between the "intellectual virtues," such as knowledge and wisdom, which, are acquired through formal learning and practical experience; and the "moral virtues," or virtues of character, such as kindness, self-control, and generosity, which are developed through practice and habituation. In instances where virtues appear to clash—Should I be honest and tell you I don't like the scarf you've given me as a present?—the good person will exercise the virtue of *phronesis*, or practical wisdom, which enables her to choose the right course of action in the specific circumstances.[3]

Van Zyl (2015) describes *phronesis* as "a kind of know-how, an ability to find the means to a given end" (190). The virtue of honesty, for example, calls for more than reflexive truth telling. "People who are in the habit of always telling the truth," Van Zyl writes, "end up in all sorts of trouble: hurting others' feelings for no good reason, breaching confidentiality when doing so is not warranted, and in general damaging relationships" (191–192). The person who has acquired the virtue of honesty, in contrast, understands and appreciates honesty's range of contexts and impacts. To be what Van Zyl calls "a truly honest person" is to tell the truth at the right time, in the right manner, for the right reasons.[4] And so, too, may we say of Aristotelian virtue that it calls for acting in the right way, at the right time, in the right manner, for the right reasons.

The conditions that enable human beings to practice virtue in the right ways are to be found in the context of the *polis*, the city-state established for the common good. Frede argues that Aristotle's selection of moral virtues—courage, self-control, magnanimity, and the like—are those virtues required for human beings to live communally. The city, or *polis*, becomes the scene for the development and practice of ethical communal living. "A *polis* is therefore much more," Frede writes, "than a community of law, economic, interest and mutual defense; it both educates its citizens and allows them to pursue their talents" (28). The role of the political leader and the purpose of politics more broadly, in this view, are thus to create and sustain communities in which it is possible for people to practice virtue and live happy, flourishing, and fulfilling lives. The political and the ethical, in other words, are inseparable, two aspects of a single discipline.

For writers, and teachers of writing, Aristotle's ethics provides a virtue-based framework for addressing ethical questions when assessing or composing texts. If the deontological writer searches for the right rules to follow, and if the consequentialist writer considers the possible outcomes of a given decision, the Aristotelian writer is guided by reflection upon those traits and habits characteristic of a good person—or in this case, the good writer. What would the good writer say in this argument about abortion? What words would she use? What sources of evidence, and which metaphors? When writing on topics about which she is passionate, how would the good writer characterize those who disagree with her? Is her language controlled, fair-minded, and tolerant when these virtues are appropriate; is it vehement, indignant, and intolerant when these qualities are required? To what degree has she developed the master virtue of Aristotelian ethics, *phronesis*, practical wisdom, knowing what needs to be said, when it must be said, and how to say it?

When June Jordan's students debated whether to write in Standard or Black English, they had no rules to guide their choices, nor were they ultimately swayed by the almost certain consequences of their decision. Rather, they acted, as Aristotle puts in in Book X of the *Nicomachean Ethics*, "in accordance with these virtues"—in this case, the virtues of solidarity, resolve, and righteous anger, all of which were called for in that rhetorical moment. The students in June Jordan's class, then, were writing in ways entirely consistent with Aristotelian moral theory, choosing the right words, at the right moment, in the right manner, for the right reasons.

Much of the Aristotelian edifice has been worn away by time, cultural changes, and emergent theories of virtue. Most contemporary virtue ethicists, for example, no longer propose foundational lists of virtues, as did Aristotle, but are more inclined to regard virtues as expressions of particular cultures, traditions, and narratives. MacIntyre, for example, makes the point that the heroic virtues of Homeric society differ from the catalog of virtues that might be extracted from the novels of Jane Austen or the writings of Benjamin Franklin. Others have discarded specific virtues idealized by Aristotle—few virtue ethicists today prize "liberality," or the getting and spending of money, as highly as did Aristotle—but have greatly expanded the list of what counts as virtues. The Virtues Project, for example, lists one hundred "Gifts of Character," including such decidedly non-Aristotelian virtues as "cleanliness," "gentleness," "mindfulness," and "wonder."[5]

If it is true, moreover, that Aristotle is "*the* protagonist of virtue ethics," neither is he the only character in the story. While neo-Aristotelianism is today the most prominent virtue-based ethical framework, inspiring the work of Hursthouse, MacIntyre, Annas, and others, the renewed interest in virtue-based ethics has resulted in greater attention to alternative accounts, contemporary and ancient. We shall briefly consider four such accounts, the Sentimentalist, the Feminist, the Non-Western, and the Applied, each of which has expanded our understanding of virtue and virtue ethics in ways that go beyond Aristotle in distinctive and original ways, and each of which contributes to a more robust understanding of rhetorical ethics and what it means to be a "good writer."

SENTIMENTALIST VIRTUE ETHICS

If the *eudaimonistic* virtue ethics of Aristotle accorded reason the central place in ethical life, what has become known as "sentimentalist virtue ethics" assigns that central place to emotion, variously called affect, passion, sympathy, or empathy. In the sentimentalist conception of ethics, the moral life is not a product of rational activity but rather of an innate "feel" for making moral judgments (Beauchamp 1998, 22). Forms of sentimentalist ethics can be found throughout the history of ethics, such as in Christian ethics, with its emphasis on love and mercy; in Buddhist ethics, which emphasizes compassion and kindness; and in the ancient Chinese ethics of Mencius, who regarded benevolence or sympathy (*ren*) as "essential to our humanity" (Frazer and Slote 2015, 197–198). However, the most considered philosophical movement toward a sentimentalist account of virtue is generally thought to begin in eighteenth century Britain, in the works of such figures as the Earl of Shaftesbury, Francis Hutcheson, Adam Smith, and David Hume.

In sentimentalist virtue ethics, we gain awareness of good and evil, right and wrong, by experiencing the pleasure that comes from approving of actions generally considered good, such as benevolence, and by disapproving of actions generally considered bad, such as selfishness. Why is benevolence good and selfishness bad? According to sentimentalist virtue ethics, because of our intuitive reactions to them. Hume, for example, held that emotions, or what he called the passions, were neither irrational nor confused, as others before him had maintained. Rather, writes Tom L. Beauchamp, Hume viewed the passions as "vital and worthy dimensions of human nature" that we should accept as an essential part of our humanity (14). Where Aristotle considered rational activity as the defining feature of human beings, Hume argued that reason was limited and uncertain. Reason can inform the passions, but reason alone cannot move us to action. And action, Alasdair MacIntyre, has argued, is "the whole point and purpose of the use of moral judgments" (MacIntyre 1996, 169).

Suppose, for example, that I am an undergraduate, and one night my best friend confides in me that he has cheated on a final exam. My college has an honor code, which I signed, that obligates me to report my friend's action. I like to think of myself as an ethical person, one who honors my commitments. However, I know that college policies will result in my friend's expulsion, and, besides, something inside me resists informing on a friend. I am torn as how to proceed. In such cases, Hume maintains, reason can help us consider choices, balance responsibilities, and weigh consequences. But after reason has had its say, "the approbation or blame, which then ensues, cannot be the work of judgment, but of the heart; . . . an active feeling or sentiment" (Hume 1998, App. 1.11., quoted in Taylor 2015, 160). Thus follows Hume's radical assertion in *A Treatise of Human Nature* on the role of emotions in moral judgments: "Reason is, and ought only to be the slave of the passions, and can never pretend to any other office than to serve and obey them" (Hume 1888, II., 3.3, 415).

Moral approval or disapproval, in other words, were rooted for Hume in "moral sentiments," and these are what move us to act in one manner rather than another. "Hume's idea was that the human world," argues J. B. Schneewind, "could be explained not in terms of the working or reason but in terms of the working of feeling" (Schneewind 1983, 5). And while our feelings are often self-interested, Hume believed, we also desire good for others. The virtues in Humean ethics are expressions of this desire. Hume defines virtues as "a quality of mind agreeable to or approved of by everyone, who considers or contemplates it" (Hume 1888, n.50, quoted in Beauchamp 1998, 28). Hume does not mean by this, Beauchamp cautions, that each one of us actually experiences feelings of approval or disapproval for a given action (28). Rather, Hume is appealing to what he calls "general opinion," or the shared moral response of impartial observers toward character traits and actions.

For example, when a story circulated on the Internet in 2013 about an El Paso, Texas, police officer buying a pair of shoes for an eighty-three-year-old homeless man during a winter storm (DailyMail.com 2013), many people experienced and expressed what Hume would call feelings of sympathy toward the homeless man and approval of the officer and his act. Let us imagine that those people approved of the kindness and compassion of the police officer's actions, and so they come to esteem, if they did not already, "kindness" and "compassion" as virtues.

Conversely, we instinctively regard as vices those traits or actions that cause us to feel pain or uneasiness. When the 2016 Republican presidential nominee Donald Trump attacked the family of the slain Muslim American soldier Humayan Khan, insinuating that Khan's mother, Ghazala Khan, was prevented from speaking for religious reasons, and declaring that Khan's father, Khizer Khan, had "no right" to criticize Mr. Trump, many people across the country were aghast, judging Mr. Trump's actions toward a Gold Star family to be ugly and intolerant (Burns et al. 2016). Our moral sentiments, using Hume's language, lead us to censure such actions as vices.

Hume's conception of virtues as qualities of mind produced by moral sentiment results in a catalog of virtues far more expansive and richer than anything to be found in Aristotle. In Hume's *An Enquiry Concerning the Principles of Morals* (EPM), there are "qualities," or virtues, useful to others, such as sociability, good-naturedness, gratitude, and beneficence (Hume 1888, EPM, Sec. II-V), and qualities useful to ourselves, such as discretion, good sense, discernment, and patience (EPM, Sec. VI). There are qualities agreeable to ourselves, such as cheerfulness, courage, tranquility, and poetic sensibility (EPM, Sec. VII), as well as qualities agreeable to others, including wit, ingenuity, eloquence, and decency (EPM, Sec. VIII). Hume further distinguished between what he called "natural virtues," such as benevolence, which are embedded in human nature, and "artificial virtues," such as justice, which are social constructions necessary for society to function effectively (Taylor 2015, 157–158).

While the Aristotelian rationality continues to dominate the landscape of contemporary virtue ethics, there has been a recent renewal of interest in sentimentalist virtue ethics. Perhaps the most prominent account of contemporary sentimentalist virtue ethics is that of Michael Slote (2010), who argues in *Moral Sentimentalism* that an action is morally right only if it does not demonstrate a lack of "empathic" concern for others (Frazer and Slote 2015, 203). The primary criterion for determining right actions, in this account, is empathy for others' ideas, concerns, and points of view. Frazer and Slote give the example of a historical case of hate speech. When neo-Nazis in 1977 announced that they planned to march through Skokie, Illinois, a predominantly Jewish community where many Holocaust survivors lived, the "typical Kantian liberal view," grounded in notions of rights and obligations, was that even hate speech should be legally protected (204). In the sentimentalist account of virtue ethics, however, the absence of empathy shown to the survivors, who would likely be traumatized by the march, rendered the event immoral and, by extension, impermissible.

This suggests that in cases where rights and values conflict, as in the Skokie example, the sentimentalist virtue ethicist does not look to abstract, rationalistic principles for resolution. Instead, the sentimentalist philosopher makes moral and perhaps legal judgments grounded in the "emotional attunement and attentiveness to the particular needs of others" (Stohr 2015, 274). Frazer and Slote argue that empathy makes it possible "to understand and fully respect those who differ from one on political and moral questions," and is therefore "absolutely necessary to the workability of modern-day pluralist societies" (Frazer and Slote 2015, 205). And this makes sentimentalist virtue ethics, the authors contend, superior to neo-Aristotelianism in the current cultural and historical moment.

For teachers of writing, the sentimentalist account suggests that ethical choices in the arguments, narratives, and other texts our students write are not defined principally by the rational principles of Aristotelian virtue ethics. Ethical choices are also grounded in the "working of feeling," in the judgments of the heart. Ethical discourse, in other words, is Aristotelian, which is to say rational, objective, open-minded, and even-tempered; it is the discourse of the academic journal, the philosophical dialogue, the op-ed page of *The Washingon Post*. However, ethical discourse is equally, or so the sentimentalist account suggests, passionate, empathic, censorious, and indignant; it is the language of the protest movement, the penitent's prayer, the lover's letter. It is the language of June Jordan's students decades ago, and of the Black Lives Matter movement today. These, too, are virtuous.

FEMINIST VIRTUE ETHICS

Perhaps the best way to begin a discussion of feminist virtue ethics is to acknowledge the apparent unlikeliness of the subject. The pairing of "feminist" and "virtue" has an oxymoronic feel, a coinage that juxtaposes two apparently contradictory perspectives, each suggesting separate if not opposing narratives, histories, and ideologies. Feminism, in the broadest sense, is committed to identifying and resisting all forms of oppression against women worldwide, while the concept of "virtue" has historically accommodated such oppression. Nonetheless, some feminist moral philosophers have continued to explore the possibilities of a feminist virtue ethic, explorations that might transform virtue ethics by linking it to critical and feminist politics, by revising the concept of "flourishing" to promote equality between men and women, and by expanding the catalog of virtues.

First, the difficulties. Feminist ethics begins with the recognition, Alison M. Jaggar writes, that much of the history of Western philosophy is "overtly misogynistic" and assumes "women should be subordinate to men because they are inferior to them in some way" (Jaggar 1991, 79). These were not the fringe views of marginal figures in moral philosophy, Jagger contends, but were expressed by some of the central figures in the Western canon, including Aristotle, Rousseau, Kant, and Hegel.

The concept of virtue was central to the subordination and control of women. Jaggar observes that the virtues ascribed to women in traditional ethical theory were regarded as inferior to those of men, and that the so-called "feminine virtues" tended to promote masculine dominance. Aristotle held, for example, that women's virtues consisted of "obedience, silence, and modesty," while Kant assigned women the virtues of "charm, docility, complaisance, beauty, and concern with a pleasing appearance" (1996, 101n3).

The British historian Lynne Abrams reminds us that the "ideal woman" in Victorian England was confined to the home and expected to enact the virtues of "piety, patience, frugality, and industry" (Abrams 2014, 2), while Jean Grimshaw writes that as middle-class women in industrialized nations of the eighteenth century became increasingly dependent on the institution of marriage for economic security, there emerged "a sentimental vision of the subordinate but virtuous and idealized wife and mother, whose specifically female virtues both defined and underpinned the 'private' sphere of domestic life" (Grimshaw 1993, 491).

While Victorian feminists fiercely resisted such representations—Mary Wollstonecraft's ([1793] 1989) nineteenth century manifesto, *Vindication of the Rights of Woman* was a powerful rebuke to the notion of gendered virtues—Victorian women were nonetheless assigned those virtues associated with motherhood and the domestic sphere. So if the project of feminist ethics, broadly speaking, is "the exploration of the ways in which cultural devaluation of women and the feminine may be reflected and rationalized in the central concepts and methods of moral philosophy" (Jaggar 1991, 348), an ethics of virtue would seem an unlikely means for contributing to that end.

Not surprisingly, many feminist moral philosophers remain skeptical of contemporary virtue ethics, particularly of its broad identification with neo-Aristotelianism. "Few feminists wholeheartedly endorse neo-Aristotelian theories such as communitarianism and virtue ethics," Jaggar writes (353), while Karen Stohr acknowledges that "Aristotle's notorious sexism might seem too deeply entrenched in his theory to make any form of Aristotelian virtue ethics compatible with feminism" (271). Okin is more definitive, asserting that "it is inconceivable to regard Aristotle as a feminist, and it seems doubtful that one would find much in his politics and moral philosophy that might be useful to those thinking through issues from a feminist point of view" (212).

Other feminists, however, are unwilling to abandon the potential of virtue-based ethical theories. While Sandrine Berges, for example, agrees that Aristotle "clearly considers women philosophically uninteresting" (Berges 2015, 4), she nonetheless suggests that a richer and more complex understanding of virtue can be realized "if we look outside of the central figures of the canon or, in the case of virtue ethics, outside Aristotle" (7). Berges's philosophical-historical project in her book *A Feminist Perspective on Virtue Ethics* is to recover the writing and histories or women working within a virtue ethics perspective, such as Heloise of Angenteuil, Christine de Pizan, Sophie de Grouchy, and Mary Wollstonecraft. A study of the writings of these women, argues Berges, reveals how they used constructs of virtue to address "issues in education, political participation, citizenship, sexuality and gender" (8). More, the study of such exemplars suggests that feminist virtue ethics has a long and rich tradition, one that has become obscured over time.[6]

Martha Nussbaum takes a different tack, offering a robust defense of Aristotle and arguing that Aristotelian moral theory is particularly well suited to account for the experiences of women. Nussbaum contends that Aristotle's attention to "the material conditions necessary for truly human functioning," such as food, shelter, and medical care, as well as education, employment, and citizenship—when so many women around the world are denied these basic goods—represents an important contribution to feminist moral theory (Nussbaum 1992, 1019). Nor does Nussbaum find Aristotelian theory irredeemably conservative. The "allegedly conservative method," Nussbaum contends, "actually prompts a sweeping and highly critical scrutiny of all existing regimes, and their schemes of distribution, as well as of the preferences that result from and support these distributions" (ibid.)

Still another feminist reading of virtue, in this case "the virtue of appropriate anger" in response to sexist oppression, is offered by Macalaster Bell in her essay, "Anger, Virtue, and Oppression" (Bell 2009). Those who would resist sexist oppression, Bell suggests, might consider "the aptness and value of developing a *character trait* of appropriate anger" (169). Such a character trait, or virtue, would be more than an episodic emotion in response to misogyny. More, it would be a settled disposition, enabling one who developed it to use practical reason, or *phronesis*, in determining when anger is called for, and when it is not. A person who developed this disposition, Bell writes, "would not only respond with anger to wrongs done to her but she would encourage others to do so as well; she would raise her children to recognize insults and teach them when anger would be an appropriate response to a specific injustice, and so on" (ibid.)

Two of the most significant feminist theorists of virtue are the psychologist Carol Gilligan and the philosopher Nel Noddings, both of whom are identified with the profoundly influential "ethics of care." In her 1982 book, *In a Different Voice: Psychological Theory and Women's Development*, Gilligan argued that women exhibit a psychology and manner of moral reasoning that is distinctive from but not, as was often assumed, inferior to that of men (Gilligan 1982). Rather, Gilligan argued, the standard measures of psychological and moral development are biased toward masculine ways of reasoning, which privilege the application of abstract principles to moral dilemmas and lack a language to capture the experiences and moral perspectives of women.

To illustrate, Gilligan revisited Harvard psychologist Lawrence Kohlberg's work on the moral development of children. Kohlberg posited a six-stage progression of moral development, in which the highest stage was based on principles of equality and reciprocity (Gilligan 1982, 27). Kohlberg's method for measuring moral development was to present children with a conflict between moral norms, and then discuss with the children the choices they made in resolving the dilemma. Jake and Amy, two eleven-year-old children in Kohlberg's study, were presented with the following scenario: Heinz's wife is sick, and Heinz cannot afford to pay for the life-saving drugs his wife requires. The druggist refuses to lower his prices. Should Heinz steal the drugs? Jake was emphatic that

Heinz should steal the drugs, his answer reflecting his understanding of rights and property: the right to life is greater than the right to property, justifying the decision to steal the drugs. Amy, however, understood the problem differently. Stealing the drugs might save his wife's life, but might also result in Heinz going to jail. Should his wife become sick again, Heinz would then be unable to help her. Amy suggested that Heinz try to borrow the money or talk with the druggist to see if a compromise might be reached.

Gilligan argues that Jake understands the problem, as Kohlberg did, mathematically, considering it as an equation with a rationally derived correct answer. Amy's understanding of the problem, in contrast, is grounded in relationships, narratives, and responsiveness to others. The proper response to the dilemma is not to steal from the druggist, but to try helping the druggist understand the responsibilities human beings have to care for one another. Since Kohlberg's understanding of morality was grounded in the deontological tradition of categorical rules and principles, his and other similarly gendered approaches to moral development invariably ranked women below men. However, Amy's understanding of Heinz's dilemma speaks to a world, Gilligan writes, "of relationships and psychological truths where an awareness of the connection between people gives rise to a recognition of the responsibility for one another, a perception of the need for a response" (30). In Amy's response, we hear the "different voice" that is the basis of an ethic of care.

Nel Noddings made similar arguments in *Caring: A Feminine Approach to Ethics and Moral Education* (Noddings 1978), in which she argued that care was a feminine ethic, if not a virtue.[7] Noddings argued that contemporary ethics was discussed largely in "the language of the father: in principles and propositions, in terms such as justification, fairness and justice" (1). She proposed instead to consider ethics in the language of the mother, which, she wrote, was "feminine in the deep classical sense— rooted in receptivity, relatedness, and responsiveness" (2). The ontological basis of ethics in this view was the caring relationship, comprised of the "one-caring" and the "cared-for," both having obligations toward the other. An ethics of care, as Noddings represented it, de-emphasizes the language of rules, principles, and demonstrations, which owe more to mathematics than moral reasoning, in favor of a more "intuitive or receptive" ethics, which could be "mysterious, internal, and nonsequential" (7). An ethics of care is particularly suited to women, Noddings argued, "who define themselves in terms of *caring* and work their way through moral problems from the position of the one-caring" (8).

Like Gilligan, Noddings understood caring as a feminine alternative to Kohlberg's six-stage model of moral development. Women do not reason, as Kohlberg understood the highest achievement of moral development, by considering ethical problems in the abstract and formulating deductive arguments. Rather, they "remain in the situation as sensitive, receptive, and responsible agents" (42). And while women have often been represented as being in an inferior state of moral development, Noddings countered that "a powerful and coherent ethic, and, indeed, a different sort of world may be built on the natural caring so familiar to women" (46).

Care ethics, then, has challenged male biases in psychological and philosophical literatures, and has offered an important alternative to deontological moral theories. Political scientist Susan J. Hekman has written of Gilligan's contributions, "It does not overstate the case to say that Gilligan's work has revolutionized discussions in moral theory, feminism, theories of the subject, and many related fields" (Hekman 2014, 1). That said, the care ethics of Gilligan and Noddings has also drawn its share of criticism, having been faulted as essentialist, as making unwarranted universal claims about women, as reinforcing stereotypes about feminine qualities, and as failing to take considerations of justice into account (McLaren 2001, 103).

John M. Broughton, for example, questions Gilligan's "dualistic psychology" and what he regards as her "tendency to essentialize gender, removing it from the context of relationships, discourse, culture, societal structure, and processes of historical formation" (Broughton 1993, 135). The anthropologist Carol B. Stack critiques Gilligan for conflating "gender" with a population of primarily white, middle-class women, even as feminist researchers have emphasized that "gender is a construct shaped by the experience of race, class, culture, caste, and consciousness" (Stack 1993, 110–111). Some feminist theorists, moreover, are wary of the stereotypes associated with the view that "morality is gendered," a notion that, Joan Tronto writes, "reinforces a number of existing moral boundaries and mitigates against change in our conceptions of politics, of morality, and of gender roles" (Tronto 1993, 61) Onora O'Neill similarly argues that "an appeal to 'women's experience', 'women's traditions', and 'women's discourse', does not escape but rather echoes ways in which women have been marginalized and oppressed" (O'Neill 1992, 55, quoted in Robinson 1999, 19). Sarah Hoagland is perhaps most emphatic, arguing that feminine virtues such as altruism and self-sacrifice maintain relationships of domination and subordination. The feminine virtues, Hoagland writes, are "virtues of subservience" (Hoagland 1988, 157, quoted in McLaren 2001, 107).

Margaret A. McLaren argues that such criticisms can be addressed by locating care ethics within a virtue-ethics framework. While virtue ethics and care ethics have certain commonalities—both challenge deontological moral theory, both locate moral choices in the context of particular situations, and both recognize the overlap between the ethical and the political—there is at least one significant difference: "care ethics is less attentive," McLaren writes, "to social and political context than virtue theory is" (McLaren 2001, 109). McLaren maintains that Aristotelian theories of virtue, for all their limitations, recognize "the importance of social institutions in promoting virtue" and represent virtues "as social goods to be fostered through social, political, and educational institutions" (110). To understand care as a virtue, McLaren suggests, is to place it in a moral framework in which gender is understood as a social construct, differences of race, ethnicity, and class are recognized, and distinctions between the public and the private life are no longer maintained.

However, McLaren also notes that virtue ethics lacks an explicit commitment to challenging male bias, and has historically perpetuated the feminine stereotypes that have subordinated and demeaned women. Before virtue ethics can offer a meaningful moral theory, McLaren suggests, it must engage feminist politics and provide "a conception of human flourishing that promotes equality" (112). To that end, McLaren advocates the development of a "feminist virtue theory," one that would emphasize the contextual character of moral situations, recognize the role of judgment and practical wisdom in moral decision-making, acknowledge the importance of character and friendship, and affirm the "inseparability of the ethical and the political" (112). In the work of ending the subordination of women, McLaren suggests, feminist virtue theorists might expand the catalog of "feminine virtues" to include such qualities as feistiness, self-respect, playfulness, self-awareness, and courage.

The ethical writer, the feminist account of virtue ethics suggests, is ultimately and necessarily a feminist: rejecting the misogynistic legacies of "virtue"; embracing alternative exemplars and histories; expanding the catalog of virtues; attending to the social, political, and economic conditions necessary for flourishing; affirming the inseparability of the personal and the political; and making choices when composing texts that encourage resistance to oppression. Such writing would seek to liberate both men and women from the burdens of a tradition that equated so-called "heroic" virtues, such as valor, with men and subordinate qualities, such as submissiveness and obedience, with women. In place of these, a feminist virtue ethics would provide an evolved moral framework and language for making choices in the writing class and would promote practices of gender equality across social and political contexts.

NON-WESTERN VIRTUE ETHICS

> *The Master said, That I have not cultivated virtue, that I*
> *have learned but not explained, that I have heard what is*
> *right but failed to align with it, that what is not good in me I*
> *have been unable to change—these are my worries.*
> —The Analects of Confucius, Book 7.3

In recent years, scholars have begun to explore what Lorraine Besser-Jones and Michael Slote characterize as "the seeds of virtue ethics" as these have been sown in non-Western traditions, especially Asian traditions (Besser-Jones and Slote 2015, xxi). These inquiries, which include considerations of virtue in Hindu, Buddhist, Confucian, and Islamic ethics, have informed theoretical understandings of virtue by placing them in a broader historical and geographical context. More, they have illustrated that virtue may be understood equally as transcultural, commonly embraced by many cultures throughout history, and as culturally specific, reflecting distinctive cultural values, narratives, practices, and aspirations.

Studies of virtue in non-Western contexts often address two issues. The first is whether the conception of virtue in a given culture can be considered "virtue ethics" as this has been developed in Western moral philosophy. So, for example, Roy W. Perrett and Glenn Pettigrove's essay, "Hindu Virtue Ethics," begins, "Is there a Hindu virtue ethics? Clearly, an answer to the question depends upon (1) what we mean by 'virtue ethics', and (2) how we restrict the scope of the term 'Hindu ethics'" (Perrett and Pettigrove 2015, 51). Perrett and Pettigrove go on to argue that one philosophical school within the Hindu tradition, Yoga Ethics, derived from a third century text, the *Yogasutra*, comes closest to the understanding of virtue ethics familiar to Western readers. Yoga ethics offers, the authors contend, a teleological theory of ethics that elevates "liberation" of the true self from ordinary human experience as the *summum bonum*, and provides an eight-stage process of mental and physical training, with each stage roughly akin to a Western virtue, through which to achieve such liberation.

Similarly, May Sim's essay, "Why Confucius' Ethics is a Virtue Ethics" (Sim 2015) addresses the arguments as to whether Confucianism is a form of virtue ethics. If virtue ethics is to be construed as a rival theory to deontology and consequentialism, then Confucian ethics cannot be considered, skeptics have argued, a form of virtue ethics. Confucius was unaware of other moral theories, did not distinguish between virtues and rituals, did not separate virtues from obligations, and was interested not in moral theory but in social practices—all of which would mitigate against classifying Confucianism as virtue ethics (63). However, Sim suggests, if virtue ethics "were more loosely defined" as an ethics focused on the dispositions, character, motivations, and general excellence of the moral agent, then it is possible to view Confucianism as a form of virtue ethics, which is Sim's position (ibid.).

There is a danger to these kinds of arguments, argue Stephen C. Angle and Michael Slote in their book, *Virtue Ethics and Confucianism* (Angle and Slote 2013). Angle and Slote contend that the Confucian tradition offers a rich and complex set of moral teachings, practical and spiritual. To reduce these teachings "into one sub-type of Western morality—and a relatively minor one (until recently) at that" is to sacrifice the richness and complexities of the tradition (3). Indeed, for many Chinese intellectuals, the Western concept of "philosophy" and its attendant categories of "ethics," "metaphysics," "epistemology," and so on, are not compatible with Confucianism and have little relevance to Chinese culture. To view Confucianism through the prism of virtue ethics, then, "can seem to privilege a historically contingent way of seeing the world" (ibid).

A second issue commonly addressed in studies of virtue ethics in non-Western cultures concerns the catalog of virtues recognized within a given tradition. In his essay on Buddhist ethical traditions, for example, Charles Goodman argues that the conceptual frameworks of Eightfold Path, the Ten Good Paths of Action, and the Ten Perfections can be understood as enumerating the virtues necessary for individuals to become "wise and compassionate beings, free from emotional confusion and misery" (Goodman 2015, 89). The Ten Perfections of the Mahayana tradition, Goodman writes, catalog the virtues (allowing for difficulties of translation) of generosity (*dana*), moral discipline (*sila*), patient endurance (*ksanti*), perseverance (*virya*), meditative stability (*dyana*), wisdom (*prajna*), skillful means (*upaya*), vow (*pranidhana*), power (*bala*), and pristine awareness (*jnana*) (ibid.). Goodman argues that while Buddhist ethics are diverse, comprising different schools and traditions, the conceptual frameworks of Buddhist ethics nonetheless "have important similarities with views about excellence of character found in Western virtue ethicists" (97).

Similarly, Majid Fakhry writes that early Islamic philosophers, drawing upon Socrates, Plato, and Aristotle, incorporated classical theories of virtue into Islamic ethical teachings (Fakhry 1998). The Islamic philosopher Al-Kindi (c. 866–73), whom Fakhry calls "the first genuine philosopher of Islam," drew upon Greek thought in his *Paving the Way to Virtue*, while al-Farabi (c. 870–950), "the first systematic writer on philosophical questions in Islam," followed Aristotle by classifying virtues as intellectual, including temperance, courage, liberality, and justice; and as moral, including practical reason, good judgment, and sound understanding. And Ibn Rushd (1126–98), regarded by many as the most important Islamic philosopher,[8] wrote a paraphrase and commentary on the *Nicomachean Ethics*, aligning Islamic and Aristotelian principles (Leaman 1998).

However, perhaps the most important philosopher of virtue in any culture, Western or non-Western, is Confucius (Kongzi) (571–479 BC), whose moral teachings are vastly more complex than we can address here. Even a cursory review of such central concepts as *dexing*, virtuous conduct or character, *junzi*, the exemplary person, and *xin*, truthfulness, illustrates the subtleties of the Confucian tradition and the difficulties of mapping Western virtue ethics onto Chinese moral thinking (Lai 2013; Sim 2015). For example, the concept of *dexing*, Chinese scholar Chen Lai explains, can be translated as both "virtuous conduct" and as "virtuous character," and that the "actual meaning" of the word can be ascertained only by examining both the context of the text *and* the historical period in which the term is used. "Generally speaking," Lai writes, "during the time of the Western Zhou Dynasty [1046–771 BC], within the texts of the Spring and Autumn period, *de* refers to virtuous conduct and behavior" (15). The use of *dexing* to refer to character came later, during the time of the Warring States [475–221 BC] "in the text of the Zhonyong" (Lai 2013, 16).

At times, Confucian moral teachings seem to suggest something close to Aristotle's concept of *phronesis*. Consider the application of *xin*, or truthfulness. Sim recounts the story of the villager who reported his father to the Governor of She for stealing a sheep. The governor praises the son as a "true person" (*zhi*) for reporting the father. Confucius disagrees, arguing that a son who covers for his father is a better example of a true person. Rather than reporting the father, Confucius says, the son might return the sheep and counsel the father how to avoid repeating his mistake in the future. This is preferable to having the father punished, which would only prevent him from truly understanding the nature of his crime. Moreover, by protecting the father from punishment, the son would be carrying out both his civic duties, returning the sheep, and his filial responsibilities, honoring his father. In this way would the son be observing the ritual proprieties (*li*) and acting as a true person.

"The Confucian tradition is preemptive," write the Confucian scholars Henry Rosemont Jr. and Roger T. Ames, "in trying to establish a social fabric that would reduce the possibility of crime, rather than adjudicating hard cases after the fact" (Rosemont and Ames 2008, 18, quoted in Sim 2015, 65). The narrative speaks to the contextual nature of *xin*, truthfulness, and the way the "true person" is embedded in a complex web of roles, relationships, and responsibilities. More, the story suggests a correspondence with Aristotelian *phronesis*, which enables one to make the right decision, in the right circumstances, for the right reasons.

However, there are clear differences in Confucian and Aristotelian ethics. Angle and Slote (2013), for example, emphasize the role of moral humility in Confucian ethics, a virtue absent from Aristotelian ethics (5). If someone harms you, Confucian texts advise, perhaps your first response should not be to retaliate. Instead, you might consider whether you have inadvertently harmed or insulted that person, and are thus the cause of the problem. Such humility is not to be found in Aristotle's catalog of virtues, which emphasize, Angle and Slote write, "proper pride as a virtue and leaves no room for the just-mentioned humility" (ibid.). Indeed, the absence of humility in Aristotle's virtuous person, Angle and Slote write, would seem to make that person ill-suited for life in complex, multi-cultural societies that call for tolerance, deference, and the ability to listen to others. And this suggests, conclude Angle and Slote, contemporary Aristotelian virtue ethics has something to learn from other traditions.

Non-Western virtue traditions tell us something of the dual nature of the virtues. We learn that virtue is transcultural and trans-historical, common to many world cultures and ages. Hindu, Buddhist, Confucian, Islamic, and other traditions contain their theories of virtue, and their distinctive catalogs of individual virtues. Virtue ethics is not, write Angle and Slote, "simply another name for the thought of Aristotle" (10). Nor it is the exclusive property of the ancient Greeks and their contemporary Western commentators, as the Asian, South Asian, and Middle Eastern traditions demonstrate.

However, non-Western virtue traditions also teach us about the culturally specific nature of virtue, and how virtues may be understood as the products of distinctive cultural values, narratives, practices, and traditions. For example, while the virtues of generosity and courage appear to be cross-cultural, recognized in both Asian and Greek traditions, other virtues are unique to particular cultures. Both the Aristotelian and Confucian traditions recognize "truthfulness" as a virtue, for example, but they depart, as we have seen, on the virtues of "pride" and "moral humility." Nor does the Aristotelian catalog include such virtues as "patient endurance," "meditative stability," and "pristine awareness," each of which may be found in the *Ten Perfections*.

And this dual nature of virtue is instructive, I submit, for our work as teachers of writing. One of the reservations of addressing virtue in the writing classroom, as we have seen, is Bizzell's concern that "any talk of teaching virtue will tend to introduce exclusions, as socially privileged groups in our diverse nation arrogate to themselves the right to define what virtue is taught" (1992b, 6). One response to such concerns is to note that socially privileged groups in any context often arrogate to themselves rights and entitlements they would deny others, whether legal, political, economic, cultural, or other forms of rights. There is nothing unique about virtues in this regard.

A more productive response to Bizzell's legitimate concerns, however, is to recall the transcultural character of the virtues, the fact that people of diverse cultures appear to share certain virtues. Are there many cultures in which the virtues of "knowledge," "truthfulness," "fairness," or "courage" are not valued, for example? Are there societies in which "justice" is not desirable? While these may have culturally specific expressions or take culturally inflected forms, they are recognizable throughout history and in diverse cultural contexts. So while there is always the possibility that one group will impose its moral framework upon another, there is also the possibility that the transcultural nature of the virtues will engender dialogue and the recognition of common values.

Yet is it equally true that in a multi-cultural, trans-global, digitally interconnected society such as our own, which is characterized by the mass movement of peoples across borders, whether immigrants, refugees, migrants, asylum seekers, or others, conceptions of virtue will inevitably differ, contradict, and conflict with one another. Perhaps nowhere will this be more evident than in our own classrooms, which are populated by writers of diverse nationalities, ethnicities, religions, languages, and rhetorical traditions. What counts as virtuous in such contexts cannot be assumed, but may need to be negotiated through arguments, testimonies, remembrances, dialogues, and other rhetorical actions.

Today's ethical writer, in other words, is not wholly Aristotelian, Confucian, Christian, Humean, or others, but is in all probability, given the moment in which we live, some fusion of these influences. And this means students and teachers of writing will be called upon to navigate— through extended and continuing classroom conversations, arguments, and sharing of student papers—the ethical complexities, uncertainties, and unknowns that may be present in our multicultural classrooms.

APPLIED VIRTUE ETHICS

In his seminal 1983 essay on environmental ethics, "Ideals of Human Excellence and Preserving Natural Environments," Thomas E. Hill Jr. tells the following story, recounted in Philip Cafaro's essay, "Environmental Virtue Ethics": a wealthy man buys a home surrounded by beautiful displays of grass, plants, and flowers, all of it shaded by a great avocado tree (Hill 1983, quoted in Cafaro 2015). But such natural surroundings demand attention: the grass must be cut, the flowers need care, and anyway the man wants more sun. So he cuts down the tree and paves over everything with asphalt. Hill wonders how to account for his sense that the man's actions are morally wrong. There is no argument of rights to be made; the man owns the property and has the legal right to pave it. Nor is Hill satisfied with arguments of consequence; his discomfort goes deeper than cost/benefit analyses. After some reflection, Hill decides the right question to ask is this: "What sort of person would do a thing like that?" And his answer is that such a person would be lacking certain traits or dispositions generally thought to be admirable, such as humility, the trait of accepting one's place in the natural order; and aesthetic sensitivity, the disposition to cherish what enriches one's life. A person's attitudes toward nature, Hill concludes, may ultimately be related to the possession or absence of certain qualities of character, or virtues.

One of the persistent criticisms of virtue ethics is that it fails to provide guidance as to how one should act in a given situation. While deontology offers categorical rules for making choices when confronted with moral dilemmas, and while consequentialism provides a kind of calculus based on the greatest good for the greatest number, virtue ethics locates goodness in human character and urges the cultivation of such traits as generosity, tolerance, and others said to be necessary for people to be good and live well. But how helpful is this really, the critic of virtue ethics asks, when confronted with specific moral problems associated with family, work, or friendship? And how will reflection on the lives of moral exemplars such as Nelson Mandela or Dorothy Day enable one to address ethical problems concerning, say, end-of-life decisions or a troubled marriage? Virtue ethics, in this perspective, would seem to have little practical use.

In recent years, however, philosophers and ethicists have begun to address this critique by developing a virtue-based perspective to ethical problems in such areas as education, business, law, political theory, and other topics. In the process, these scholars and researchers have broadened the range of virtue ethics, gradually transforming it from a normative ethical theory, concerned with principles of how one ought to live, to an applied theory, focused on specific questions and problems, often in specialized fields. Collectively, such work suggests that virtue ethics can provide what the moral philosophers call "action guidance," or direction as to the right way to act in a given situation (Hursthouse 1999, 26).

For example, Rebecca L. Walker and Philip J. Ivanhoe's edited collection *Working Virtue: Virtue Ethics and Contemporary Moral Problems*, contains thirteen essays on topics including medicine, psychiatry, animal rights, filial piety, famine, and others that illustrate, the editors write, "clear examples of virtue ethics actually *at work* in various practical fields" (Walker and Ivanhoe 2007b, 1; emphasis in original). Walker's contribution to the volume, "The Good Life for Non-Human Animals: What Virtue Requires of Humans" (Walker 2007), is representative.

Walker asks why we may feel troubled when we see non-human animals such as great apes or polar bears confined in a zoo. In seeking to explain our discomfort, we may say that captivity violates the rights of these animals, or that their confinement causes them to suffer. But what if we are uncertain, Walker asks, about the rights of apes and bears? And what if caretakers can persuade us that the animals are safer, better fed, and kept free from illness in the confines of a zoo? Walker contends that arguments made in the language of rights or suffering cannot fully account for our moral obligations to non-human animals. We need instead, she argues, a language that can speak to "the nature of the good life for particular types of animals." (174). Walker finds this language in virtue ethics, invoking Aristotle's concept of *eudaimonia* to develop an account of "animal flourishing" in which our ethical obligations to animals can be met by providing non-human animals with the necessary resources, whether habitat, privacy, or social relationships, to ensure "an animal's having a life that is a good one for its kind" (184). The question of whether great apes, bears, or any other animal belong in a zoo, in other words, can best be addressed by considering the virtue-ethical perspective of what constitutes a "good life" for that kind of animal, and whether the conditions of its existence allow it to flourish.[9]

Other moral theorists have turned to the language of virtue to explore moral questions related to environmental sustainability, the health care professions, and political theory. For example, Matthew Pianalto's "Humility and Environmental Ethics" (Pianalto 2013), advocates for humility as an environmental virtue. To walk along ocean shores, hike amid mountains, or stand beneath a forest canopy can often move us, Pianalto writes, to become aware of our place within the vast natural world. Should we develop the virtue of what Pianalto calls "ecological humility," we will become the kind of people who understand we are part of nature, who appreciate the intrinsic values of the natural world, and who are motivated to live in ways that preserve those intrinsic values and minimize our impact on the environment (143).

In a different domain, Edmund D. Pellegrino and David C. Thomasma argue that medicine is "at its heart a moral enterprise," that "the duties of doctors are the obligations voluntarily assumed by those . . . commit themselves to the ends of medicine," and that virtues are "those traits of character that dispose the agent—the doctor and the patient—to choices that will attain those ends" (Pellegrino and Thomasma 1993, 21). Virtues of "special importance in the medical relationship," write Pellegrino and Thomasma, include compassion, intellectual honesty, and benevolence (25–26).

For Lisa Tessman, Aristotelian virtue ethics can provide useful insights to those studying oppression and resistance. In her provocative book, *Burdened Virtues: Virtue Ethics for Liberatory Struggles* (Tessman 2005), Tessman argues that when targeted groups are subject to violence and abuse, denied adequate housing, food, and health care, exposed to environmental hazards, and unjustly imprisoned, members of those groups suffer "moral damage." When the "self under oppression" is "morally damaged," Tessman contends, the individual may be incapable of developing or exercising the virtues Aristotle regarded as necessary for flourishing (4). More, if the virtues that cannot be developed or exercised include those that enable resistance to oppression, the moral damage suffered by the members of targeted groups actually sustains their oppression.

Consider, as a troubling illustration, the case of Flint, Michigan, a low-income, primarily African American city that experienced a public health crisis in 2014 when city officials, as a cost-saving measure, switched its water supply from Detroit's system to the notoriously toxic Flint River (*New York Times* 2016). Despite numerous complaints from city residents that their water was discolored and that their children were suffering from mysterious rashes, state officials played down the problem, telling residents that the water was not "an imminent threat to public health" (ibid.). When scientists ran tests on local tap water, however, they discovered lead levels in the drinking water as high as 13,200 parts per billion (ppb) of lead. As a point of comparison, water contaminated with 5,000 ppb is considered "hazardous waste" by the US Environmental Protection Agency (*CNN Library* 2017.)

While exposure to lead is unhealthy for all human beings, decades of research have found that children are especially vulnerable because of their developing brains and nervous systems. Studies of lead exposure have found that even low levels of lead can affect children's growth, behavior, and intelligence, and that damage to a child's brain may be irreversible. "If you were going to put something in a population to keep them down for generations to come, it would be lead," said Dr. Hannah-Atisha, whose research, according to the *New York Times*, compelled Flint officials to address the crisis (Goodnough 2016). Will the children of Flint develop the virtues that enable them to flourish, and to contest the structural forces that have kept generations of African Americans in poverty, or will their exposure to lead poisoning—which the Michigan Attorney General charged was deliberately and criminally concealed from Flint residents (Livengood and Chambers 2016)—"keep them down for generations to come"?

A second consequence of moral damage, according to Tessman, is the development of virtues that are necessary for surviving oppressive social structures, but that do not contribute to the happiness or fulfillment of the moral agent. Tessman calls these "burdened virtues," or virtues "that have the unusual feature of being disjoined from one's own flourishing" (4). For example, political resistance to oppression may cause individuals to commit acts, such as lying, which in a normal society are considered antithetical to a virtuous life.

Resistance to oppression may also lead to the development of virtues that actually work to harm the individual. Sensitivity to the suffering of others, for example, is normally considered a virtue. In conditions of widespread suffering, however, the pervasiveness of injustice and its effects can overwhelm the moral agent rather than enabling her flourishing (96). Moral damage can equally lead to the development of virtues that are considered admirable in a just society, but cause the moral agent to feel regret, even anguish, if they are practiced in an unjust society. Imagine you live in a violently oppressive police state, and you learn that a family member is informing on your neighbors for small amounts of money. Integrity and loyalty to your community, virtues in a just society, would under ordinary circumstances compel you to reveal the identity of the informant to your neighbors. Nonetheless, the prospect of betraying your family member fills you with sorrow, undermining the presumed relationship of virtue to human flourishing.

In a world of such burdened virtues, Tessman asserts, the concept of Aristotelian *eudaimonism* must be revised to account for the contingent nature of the connection between virtue and flourishing. To that end, Tessman has proposed elsewhere the development of a "critical virtue ethics" that would both acknowledge the social, political, and economic systems preventing oppressed peoples from developing virtues conducive to flourishing, and that would identify the "radical virtues" that might be used in "communities of resistance" to bring about structural and liberatory transformations of the oppressive society (Tessman 2001).

So for example, the catalog of radical virtues in communities of resistance might include courage, but courage of a particular type: the courage to go to jail, to lose one's job, to be socially ostracized. The catalog of radical virtues might include, as well, the virtues of anger at injustice, of solidarity with the poor, of endurance in the face of loss, and of an aesthetic sense, Tessman writes, that regards "socially rejected bodies to be beautiful" (Tessman 2001, 95).

Applied virtue ethics removes virtue from the realm of contemplative rationality that Aristotle held to be the highest function of human beings, and locates it squarely in the midst of what Kenneth Burke described as "the Scramble, the Wrangle of the Market Place, the flurries and flare-ups of the Human Barnyard, the Give and Take, the wavering line of pressure and counterpressure, the Logomachy, the onus of ownership, the Wars of Nerves, the War" (Burke 1962, 23). Virtues in this sense are not only personal characteristics that mark one as a good person, living a good life. Beyond this, they are traits, dispositions, habits, that can serve to motivate practices of social action.

• • •

The primary aim of this chapter has been to answer two questions, "What do we mean by virtue?" and "What do we mean by virtue ethics?" I have also attempted to demonstrate that the vices of virtue, its identification with misogynist, exclusionary, and politically regressive discourse, are but one part of a rich, complex, and evolving story.

While the feminist critique of virtue, for example, is historically grounded and theoretically compelling, so too, we have seen, is the project of articulating feminist virtue theory, which emphasizes the contextual character of moral situations, recognizes the role of judgment and practical wisdom in moral decision-making, acknowledges the importance of character and friendship, and affirms, in McLaren's words, the "inseparability of the ethical and the political" (112).

Similarly, the identification of virtue with Christian doctrine becomes less apparent when we consider that traditions of virtue can be found in Hindu, Buddhist, Islamic, and other faiths, and that the origins of virtue can be traced back to the decidedly non-Christian ancient Greeks and to Confucian ethics long before that.

The politically regressive nature of virtue, finally, its identification with neo-conservative ideology, is countered by the project of developing a "critical virtue ethics," one in which a virtue ethics framework can be used by those "engaged in analyzing oppression and creating liberatory projects" (Tessman 2005, 79).

Such developments, in feminist, non-Western, and critical virtue ethics, suggest to us that the history of a term is not necessarily predictive of its future, and that the tensions between past and contemporary understandings of a word can be productive, causing us to see more clearly what the word has represented, what it represents currently, and what it might represent going forward, should we engage it. We need only look for an example to the word, "rhetoric," which accommodates diverse histories, conflicting narratives, and, for those of us who study and teach it, transformative possibilities.

The broad scope of applied virtue ethics recommends it to teachers and students of writing who may find in it a language for writing ethical arguments about economic inequality, environmental sustainability, human sexuality, and other equally urgent topics. However, what I have not done in this chapter is answer the question of how the virtues, or what I call "rhetorical virtues," are enacted in the everyday practices of the writing classroom, in the work of developing claims, presenting evidence, addressing counterarguments, and revising texts. Nor have I specified with any clarity which virtues are attached to these practices, and why they are attached. Let's do that now.

NOTES

1. The meanings of these terms, *arête* and *virtus*, are not precise. Philippa Foot (2002) notes that "When we talk about the virtues we are not taking as our subject everything Aristotle called *arête* an Aquinas *virtus* . . . . 'The virtues' are to us the moral virtues whereas *arête* and *virtus* refer also to the arts, and even to excellences of the speculative intellect whose domain is theory rather than practice" (2).
2. I am grateful to John Gallagher for pointing me toward this understanding of *eudaimonia*.
3. *Phronesis* is sometimes translated as "prudence." It was one of the four Cardinal Virtues, along with temperance, courage, and justice, recognized in classical antiquity.
4. In reflecting on how women philosophers construct moral theory, Annette Baier, in the essay, "What Do Women Want in a Moral Theory?" makes a similar point. "We

should not assume," Baier writes, "that promiscuous trustworthiness is any more a virtue than is undiscriminating distrust. It is appropriate trustworthiness, appropriate encouragement to trust which will be virtues, as will judicious untrustworthiness, selective refusal to trust, discriminating discouragement of trust" (Baier 2004, 181). Baier argues that women are "particularly well placed" to appreciate these virtues, since they have so often needed them.

5. https://www.virtuesproject.com/Pdf/100Virtueshandout.pdf.

6. In her essay "Feminist Virtue Ethics," Karen Stohr notes that many of the most important neo-Aristotelian moral philosophers—those who have been most responsible for the revival of Aristotelian virtue ethics—have been women: Elizabeth Anscombe, Philippa Foot, Rosalind Hursthouse, Martha Nussbaum, and Julia Annas, among others. The fact that a "higher-than-normal" percentage of women philosophers find Aristotelian moral theory compelling "hardly shows that it is compatible with feminism," Stohr acknowledges. "Still," she suggests, "it should give us reason to look more closely" (275).

7. Noddings does not identify the ethics of care with virtue ethics (McLaren 2001, 113, n.5), although she does acknowledge that care ethics and virtue ethics "share important moral understandings" (Noddings 2015, 401).

8. http://www.muslimphilosophy.com/ip/rep/H025.

9. Michael W. Austin's (2013) *Virtues in Action: New Essays in Applied Virtue Ethics* (2013) offers a similarly eclectic selection of essays on applied virtue ethics, including contributions on the place of virtue on such topics as education, business, sport, sexual relations, and psychology, which collectively undermine the claim, Austin asserts, that virtue ethics "fails to provide action guidance" (2). See also Axtell and Olson's (2012), "Recent Work in Applied Virtue Ethics" (2012).

4

RHETORICAL VIRTUES
Toward an Ethics of Practice

> *"What we can only do by practicing, we practice by doing."*
> —Aristotle, *Nicomachean Ethics* (1103 a31-b6)

Let us imagine a writing teacher, call her Professor A, teaching a lesson to her first-year writing class on what constitutes appropriate evidence in support of a claim. Professor A has distributed in advance of the class an op-ed essay from *The New York Times* and excerpts from several academic journal articles. The classroom conversation is lively as teacher and students work through each of these texts, discussing when writers need to incorporate evidence, where to locate evidence, the difference between primary and secondary sources, how to distinguish between weak and strong proofs, and related questions. One student asks about the use of personal experience as evidence, and this leads to a discussion of genre, and what kinds of proofs are appropriate in which rhetorical contexts. Professor A then projects onto the classroom whiteboard a series of websites—*The Washington Post, Scientific American, Breitbart, The Huffington Post,* The US Census Bureau, *ESPN*—inviting students to discuss which might be cited under what circumstances in an academic essay. The lesson concludes with Professor A asking students to list possible sources of evidence they might draw upon for a research essay they had begun earlier in the term.

Professor A, in the class I am imagining, is teaching skills familiar to teachers of rhetoric and writing. In teaching students to support their claims with evidence, select sources their readers will trust, and consider multiple perspectives, Professor A is teaching conventions of academic argument. More than this, however, Professor A is teaching a lesson in ethics, or more precisely in the rhetorical ethics of academic writing. When Professor A requires that students support their claims with proofs, she is insisting that they be accountable for their

DOI: 10.7330/9781607328278.c004

assertions. When she teaches them to choose sources their readers will find credible, she is teaching practices of rhetorical judgment. And when she exhorts them to examine multiple perspectives on a question, including perspectives that contradict their own, she is teaching her students to be open-minded, intellectually generous, and intellectually courageous. In the language of this book, Professor A is teaching writing practices that call upon students to develop and exercise rhetorical virtues.

In *After Virtue*, MacIntyre (2007) argues that in Homeric and Aristotelian accounts of virtue, the "exercise of a virtue" was tied to a particular type of social practice (187). In Homeric society, for example, to excel was to excel at the practice of war, as Achilles did, or at the practice of giving counsel, as Nestor did. Fighting in war and giving advice were regarded as social practices that enabled individuals to demonstrate their excellence, synonymous with virtuous behavior, in the social and cultural context of Homeric society. "Selected social practices," MacIntyre contends, may be understood to be "providing the arena in which the virtues are exhibited" (ibid.).

MacIntyre defines "practices" as "coherent and complex forms of socially cooperative human activity" through which degrees of excellence may be realized (ibid.). As examples of practices, MacIntyre offers the activities of chess, architecture, painting, and others. Practices enable individuals to realize the goods "internal" to the activity; for example, the practice of playing chess may lead, if the player is sufficiently devoted, to the pleasures of playing chess for its own sake, rather than for the sake of winning. To realize the internal goods of a practice, according to MacIntyre, one must subject and hold oneself to the rules and standards that govern that practice, such as learning the rules of chess. The standards of a practice are not "immune from criticism" (190), MacIntyre freely concedes. They are culturally specific, the product of particular histories, narratives, and traditions. But they are, at any given place and time, the standards outside of which excellence in a practice cannot be achieved.

Among other things, MacIntyre's concept of a practice provides an answer to the vexing question of whose virtues, in a diverse, multicultural society, we should teach: we should teach our own. As teachers of writing, we share a loosely defined set of practices that we recognize as essential to realizing to the internal goods of the activity of writing. Examples of our shared practices may be found in our common textbooks or in such documents as the *WPA Outcomes Statement (3.0)* and the Council of Writing Program Administrators' *Framework for Success in*

Postsecondary Writing, the latter of which lists the skills, experiences, and "habits of mind," such as curiosity, openness, engagement, and responsibility, said to be necessary for realizing the internal goods of becoming a successful college writer.

Nor are such shared practices, as MacIntyre noted, "immune from criticism." In a globalized, multi-cultural world of diverse ethnicities, languages, and more, the practices we teach in the writing class will continually be tested by other rhetorical traditions and other ethical commitments. If we cannot productively engage these other traditions and commitments, if we cannot adapt our shared practices in response, then we do indeed risk, as Bizzell cautioned, enforcing exclusions and privileges in the writing course.

To be clear, practices are not narratives. They do not, in and of themselves, tell a story of a people, a culture, or, for our purposes, an academic discipline. Rather, they serve as the basis, the raw materials, though which we may construct our collective narrative, the shared story of who we are, and what matters to us. And the story that matters to teachers of writing, I have suggested, is that the practices we teach are inherently ethical, that the teaching of writing is fundamentally the teaching of discursive ethics, and that this is suggestive for the future of public argument in the United States.

In this chapter, I examine four practices of argument commonly taught in the writing class: formulating claims, providing evidence, addressing counter-arguments, and revising texts. I argue that each of these practices, following MacIntyre, provides an "arena in which the virtues are exhibited." Each practice, that is, can be understood as a "coherent and complex form of socially cooperative human activity" through which degrees of excellence may be realized. In considering each practice, I will address two questions: what is the nature of the practice—what does it mean to make a claim, provide evidence, address counterarguments, revise texts—and what rhetorical virtues are exhibited when engaging in that practice?

In focusing on the practices named above, I do not mean to suggest they are the only practices we teach, that other practices are subordinate to them, or even that the teaching of writing is defined exclusively in terms of a "practice." Different writing programs respond to different needs, call upon different pedagogies, and teach different forms of rhetorical knowledge. I focus on these practices, however, because they are commonly taught in college writing programs, and because they illustrate well how the teaching of writing always and inevitably leads us, teachers and students, into ethical deliberations and decisions.

To characterize each practice—what we mean by a "claim," "evidence," "counterargument," and "revision"—I shall draw primarily upon several of the more well-known composition textbooks used in writing programs across the country. While not all teachers use or value textbooks, such texts, Laura Aull (2011) has argued, speak to the "core values and exemplary material" (2) of an academic field and provide "important materials which often serve as introductions for teachers and students new to a field" (Aull 2011, 142). Our textbooks, in this view, reflect at least something of our disciplinary commitments. We shall begin where so many college essays begin—with the writing of a claim.

VIRTUES OF CLAIMS

A claim, Richard Bullock, Maureen Daly Goggin, and Francine Weinberg state simply and clearly in *The Norton Field Guide to Writing*, is a "statement that asserts a belief or position" (Bullock et al. 2016, G/I–80). Claims do not exist in isolation but are inherently social practices: I make the claim to you and so begin our relationship of writer and reader. "'Claim' comes from the Latin *clamare*," writes James Crosswhite in his thoughtful treatment of the subject, "which means to call or cry out. There is something already social about a claim: someone makes a claim about something to *someone*; someone calls out to *someone else*" (Crosswhite 1996, 55; emphases in original).

I take Crosswhite to mean that when we make a claim of some kind, we are calling for a connection with another; we are crying out, in the Latin sense of the term, for dialogue and a measure of shared understanding, whether of concepts, beliefs, emotions, or some other human experience. The claim may assail accepted wisdom, seek common assent, address historical problems, call for radical change, or pursue other intentions entirely. Whatever the motive, the claim is an overture, an enticement, an invitation, as Crosswhite (1996) writes, "to share a particular way of making sense of something" (62). When we teach students to write claims, we are teaching them to share particular way of making sense of something with others, their readers.

For their relationship to flourish, in Aristotle's term, reader and writer must be confident in making certain assumptions about each another. The reader must be confident that claims are made without equivocation or deception, and the writer must be confident that readers will consider judiciously the ideas advanced in the claim. The reader may disagree with the claim, question its wisdom, or reject its underlying assumptions. You may instinctively disagree, for example, with claims

I make about gender relations or White Privilege in US society. Our disagreement, however, does not annul the invitation I have sent you through my claim. So long as you judge my claim to have been made in good faith, which Andre Comte-Sponville describes as the virtue corresponding to "love or respect for truth," (Comte-Sponville 1996, 195), there is at least the possibility of dialogue between us.

The writer, in turn, writes in the expectation that such dialogue can be achieved, which assumes that readers have the capacity and disposition to assess the writer's words cogently and reasonably. As I write this sentence, I do so in the of expectation you will give my ideas a fair hearing when you read them, and that your critiques will be informed, impartial, and equitable. For our relationship to flourish, then, we must place our trust in the other, assuming some degree of knowledge, intellectual honesty, and rationality. And this suggests that when teaching claims, we are teaching more than how to make or evaluate assertions. We are teaching practices of trust and trust-making. We are teaching students how to become trustworthy readers and writers.

To trust another person, the philosopher Adriaan T. Peperzak writes, involves "a kind of bonding" with another, the creation of a union between two or more people. "My trust in you involves me in one or more aspects of your life and activity" writes Peperzak; "it associates me with you and gives you a role in my dealing with the world." (Peperzak 2013, 10). And to be a morally trustworthy person, according to virtue theorist Nancy Nyquist Potter, evoking Aristotle, is to be *"one who can be counted on, as a matter of the sort of person he or she is, to take care of those things that others entrust to one and* (following the Doctrine of the Mean) *whose ways of caring are neither excessive nor deficient"* (Potter 2002, 16; emphases in original,).

Trust calls for judgment. Should the reader trust claims made about the economy on the editorial page of the *Wall Street Journal,* or claims made in the journal *Science* that the earth is warming? Potter argues that trust is conditioned by cultural, material, and ideological forces, and that the questions of trust and trustworthiness "can never be answered independently of questions of equality, nondomination, and justice" (19). The supervisor writing the performance review, the therapist writing the case file, the officer writing the police report—trust between readers and writers in such exchanges is mediated by conditions of institutional and individual power. Trust is risky. Trust makes us vulnerable to others, and it can be betrayed or exploited. To teach claims is to teach writers and readers how to make judgments about whether to trust, how and when to make themselves vulnerable to trust, how to be trustworthy themselves, and how to read the relations of institutional and individual power that condition the practices of trust.

Trust further calls for skepticism. Before we can trust another, we subject that person or that writer critical scrutiny, satisfying ourselves that the person or writer merits our trust. The philosopher Allan Hazlett describes the virtue of skepticism as excellence in the act of attributing ignorance to the person who does not know, suspending judgment of whether the person knows, and questioning whether the person knows (Hazlett 2015, 76). And being skeptical of our own claims, as Hazlett describes skepticism, is an act of intellectual humility: we attribute ignorance to ourselves, suspend judgment of whether we know, and question whether we know. I want to make the claim in my essay, say, that service-learning courses produce more active and politically engaged citizens. If I am appropriately skeptical of my own assertions, I will have addressed, before I write, the questions of what I know about this topic, whether I know enough, and how I have come by my knowledge.

To be skeptical of the claims of others, in turn, calls for questioning what such persons know about the claims that have made. Suppose I read an essay in a popular online health journal claiming that fluoridated water might actually be poisoning me. If I am properly skeptical, I ask myself such questions as what this writer knows about the topic, how the writer came by this knowledge, what sources inform the knowledge, whether the writer's motive for writing is forthright or ulterior, and so on. Trust without skepticism is mere credulity.

While trust between readers and writers calls for judgment and skepticism, one measure before all is necessary for establishing trust: the rhetorical virtue of truthfulness. The philosopher Sissela Bok defines truthfulness "as the disposition to tell the truth," and the truthful person "is someone who aims consistently to speak so as not to mislead others" (Bok 1998). For the philosopher Bernard Williams, "the virtues of truth," are those "qualities of people that are displayed in wanting to know the truth, in finding it out, and in telling it to other people" (Williams 2002, 7). Truthfulness is the virtue of opposites and avoidances. It is the opposite of mendacity, duplicity, and distortion. It is the avoidance of lies, dissembling, and equivocation. Truthfulness is what "we most obviously owe to others," MacIntyre writes, if we wish to form and sustain relationships with them (MacIntyre 1999, 150). Truthfulness is distinguished from what Bok calls "the larger cluster of traits called honesty" by its character as a discursive trait. In this sense, truthfulness is the rhetorical enactment of the virtue of honesty.

Truthfulness and truth are not identical. The former belongs, as Bok points out, to "the *moral* domain of intended truthfulness and deception," while the latter references "the *epistemological* domain of truth and falsity" (emphases in the original). Failing to distinguish between the two leads to what Bok calls "the conceptual muddle" when skepticism about the epistemological status of truth—is there such a thing as "truth," and could we know it if there were?—leads to doubting there are differences between the intention to speak truthfully and the intention to deceive. You and I may both have doubts about the foundational character of "truth," but if I remove $10 from your wallet and deny I having done so, then I have spoken, assuming I do not have a neurological condition that interferes with my ability to understand my actions, untruthfully.

Truthfulness is not a virtue of absolutes. We do not regard as lies things we may be told in error, or promises we cannot keep. If we mistakenly tell a friend that the concert is at three when it begins at four, we have not deliberately tried to mislead. If we promise an elderly parent we will never place her in a nursing home, but her health deteriorates to the point where we can no longer keep that promise, we have not lied. We may have shown poor judgment in making the promise in the first place, but we have not intentionally deceived her, assuming we intended to keep the promise. Nor do we regard as untruthful the plots of novels, the figurative language of poems and lyrics, or other instances of creative departure from the literally factual. An insightful metaphor can bring us closer to truth than a dull statement of fact.

Nor is truthfulness in communication always desirable. To be "honest to a fault" is a failing, asserts the moral philosopher Judith Andre, in its indifference to the social and individual goods that truthfulness is intended to achieve (Andre 2015). Andre gives the example of health care practitioners who commit the act of "truth-dumping," or telling patients more than they are emotionally prepared to handle. While the ostensible purpose of such disclosure is to help patients confront the challenges they face, "truth dumping," Andre writes, "instead overwhelms them. It also impairs the provider-patient relationship, making the provider a threat rather than a companion in a journey through pain" (103). Other instances in which the virtue of truthfulness may not result in a good involve children, the mentally ill, enemies in wartime, or, as we have considered in our review of Tessman's work on critical virtue ethics, oppressed peoples who need to deceive or withhold truth as a means to survive. People living under such conditions, Andre observes, "fall in different moral spaces" (ibid.). And we have noted previously Van Zyl's admonition that "people who are in the habit of always telling the truth end up in all sorts of trouble: hurting others' feelings for no good reason, breaching confidentiality when doing so is not warranted, and in general damaging relationships" (Van Zyl 2015, 191–192).

The practice of truthfulness, then, involves qualifications and judgments, as do most claims. And yet even allowing for these, some degree of truthfulness is central to most human relationships. Because "no society or human relationship could survive without at least a degree of truthfulness in communication," Bok contends, "all communities have stressed truthfulness as a trait to be fostered." When individuals and institutions deliberately reject truth and truthfulness, confidence in institutions wanes, objective information is discounted, and conspiracy theories flourish. The 2016 US presidential campaign, for example, provided so many examples of truth being twisted or simply disregarded that it eventually led to Oxford Dictionaries (2016) selecting "post-truth" as its 2016 Word of the Year. To the extent that writing teachers insist upon truthfulness in making of claims—insist, that is, on "the *moral* domain of intended truthfulness and deception" (Bok 1998)—the writing classroom effectively becomes a site of resistance to "post-truth" rhetoric and politics.

Review any number of writing textbooks or writing program websites and we find much good advice on the teaching and writing of claims: how to define a claim, the different kinds of claims, whether the claim is arguable, whether it is supported by evidence, whether it can acknowledge alternative points of view, whether it is relevant to its audience, and related concerns. These are useful guidelines for students and teachers of writing. Less often acknowledged in our pedagogical discussions of claiming, however, perhaps because it is simply assumed, is that successful claims presuppose some degree of trust between readers and writers, and that this trust is built of degrees of judgment, skepticism, and truthfulness. These are what readers and writers "most obviously owe" to one another if their relationships are to flourish. When we teach students how to formulate a claim, in this perspective, we are teaching an essential rhetorical skill; yet we are also teaching essential practices of ethical discourse. One is incomplete without the other.

VIRTUES OF EVIDENCE

Claims are not taught in isolation. Claims in an academic argument are but one part of a pairing, the first line in a couplet. Claims require, so our writing textbooks tell us, the accompaniment of evidence, variously called support, proofs, grounds, or good reasons. So, for example, we find the following admonitions in our writing textbooks:

> "A **claim** is an assertion of fact or belief that needs to be supported with **evidence**—the information that backs up a claim" (Greene and Lidinsky 2008, 47; emphases in original)

> "In an effective academic argument, the writer supports his or her claims with reasons, evidence, and explanations" (Wilhoit 2009, 9)

> "One of the best ways to make a claim more fully defensible, of course, is to support it with evidence" (Fletcher 2015, 161)

> "Writers of convincing arguments offer support for what they are asking their reader to believe or to do." (Roen, Glau, and Maid 2013, 247)

People in our field have thought carefully about evidence. We have studied what counts as proof, how it functions, and how to teach it. We teach our students, for example, about the different forms evidence can take, such as empirical facts, personal experience, or visual representations. We examine with students how beliefs and values shape the selection of evidence of evidence, and how these beliefs and values may be implicit in academic arguments. We help students understand how judgments about the sufficiency, accuracy, and relevance of evidence may be discipline-specific, determined at least partly by the conventions and epistemology of a given academic discipline. And we address, as well, the ethics of finding and using evidence, conversations typically if narrowly framed in terms of citing sources correctly and avoiding plagiarism.

When we call upon students to observe these norms—supporting their claims with proof, providing appropriate forms of proof, furnishing the citations that make it possible to check proofs, and so on—what, exactly, are we calling for? One obvious answer is that we are teaching skills that students will need to succeed as academic writers. We are teaching them how academic arguments work, how to write academic essays, and how to participate, more broadly, in academic conversations. We are providing them with the tools they will need to develop an ethos, conduct research, and persuade their readers to think, feel, or understand the world in particular ways.

Yet this is not all we are teaching when we teach students to find and supply evidence. We are teaching, as well, the ethical commitments inherent in providing evidence. When we teach students, for example, how to use library databases to support their claims about the effects of climate change, or how to use census data to back claims about child poverty, or when to use personal testimony in support of claims about gender discrimination, we are teaching, as Professor A was teaching, that writers have obligations to their readers, that they are responsible for the assertions they make. In teaching students to support their claims with evidence, in other words, we are teaching the rhetorical virtue of accountability.

"Accountability is a relation," the philosopher Margaret Urban Walker writes, in which I am accountable to you for the way I treat you relative to your legitimate expectations of me (Walker 2014, 41). Indeed, Walker describes accountability as "*the* relation at the core of morality as a living institution rather than a theory" and as "the motor of moral relations." Accountability connects us to others, Walker contends, "through the recognition of [our] responsibilities under shared norms of many kinds: we are accountable to each other under norms of law, morality, agreement, institutional roles, or common understanding" (ibid.) And when we hold one another accountable, when we insist on the recognition of those shared responsibilities, we are reinforcing the norms that regulate the mutual expectations existing between us. We are acknowledging the bonds that hold us together as readers and writers, and that unite us, however briefly and tenuously, as members of a community.

If I write that the practice of hydraulic fracturing, or "fracking," will not cause undue harm to the environment and will create jobs and feed families, you expect me to supply the evidence in support of that claim. If I provide that evidence to your satisfaction, whether you ultimately accept my claim or not, the relationship between us may proceed. You have held me accountable. But if I violate the shared norm of the academic essay by failing to provide evidence of the quality you legitimately expect to receive, then I have been unaccountable, and our relationship is no longer possible, or at the very least it is changed. "Accountability, in its core and basic sense," Walker writes, "means a presumption that someone can be called to answer, to stand before others for an examination of and judgment upon his or her behavior" (42).

When we insist that students provide evidence appropriate to their claims, we are teaching different things. We are teaching students to observe the norms that prevail in academic writing, the expectation that claims require proofs. We are teaching them to demonstrate their integrity, their commitment to providing the evidence by which their claims can be evaluated. Perhaps most of all, we are teaching students that when they make a claim they are called to answer, to stand before others to offer an account not just of their assertions, but of themselves.

VIRTUES OF COUNTERARGUMENTS

Perhaps the signature move in academic writing is the counterargument, alternately called the rebuttal, the refutation, the *refutatio*, the naysayer, or more simply, opposing views. The counterargument, we typically tell students, is that place in the text where the writer anticipates the possible objections of readers to the writer's arguments, and where the writer explains why those objections are misinformed, unwise, or in some other way misguided. Counterarguments compel the writer to deepen her knowledge of an issue by exploring it from multiple perspectives, and they strengthen the writer's ethos by demonstrating her willingness to consider views that differ from her own. In their collection, *Key Words for Academic Writers*, Rebecca Brittenham and Hildegard Hoeller write that the counterargument "is really fundamental to the academic writing process; we cannot arrive at an interesting and complex insight if we have not looked at all angles of an issue" (Brittenham and Hoeller 2004, 49). The counterargument demonstrates, Brittenham and Hoeller write, that "the writer is imaginative, argues rather than holds opinions, considers rather than asserts, and is strong enough to face uncertainty and complication" when writing about a topic (ibid.).

Certainly, there is a pragmatic dimension to counterarguments. They can create the appearance of thoughtful consideration even as they serve to discredit opposing views. My apparent concessions to your arguments on religious freedom, for example, while suggesting I am measured and unbiased, may be just a tactic for undermining your position. My acknowledgment of your views on transgender individuals, while suggesting my fair-mindedness, may be a pretext for advancing my own views. Just as *ethos* is the appearance though not necessarily the presence of practical wisdom, moral virtue, and goodwill, so too can the counterargument create perceptions of dialogue and accommodation where none exist. Our textbooks, many of them, recognize the pragmatic uses of counterarguments and offer advice on such practices as how to anticipate readers' critiques, where to position the counterargument, how to discredit opposing sources, and so on.

Yet if counterarguments are pragmatic and strategic, they are equally opportunities for student writers to rehearse practices of ethical discourse. Counterarguments call upon the writer to be open to other perspectives and, as Andrea Lunsford et al. write in *Everyone's an Author*, "to acknowledge them fairly and respectfully" (Lunsford et al. 2013, 405). To acknowledge other perspectives "fairly and respectfully" means engaging them on their own terms, representing those perspectives as their authors would represent them, and avoiding, as John D. Ramage,

John C. Bean, and June Johnson stipulate in *Writing Arguments: A Rhetoric with Readings*, "loaded, biased, or 'straw man' summaries that oversimplify or distort opposing arguments" (Ramage, Bean, and Johnson 2012, 102). The counterargument demands, as Greene and Lidinsky summarize, "That writers listen to different points of view, that they respect arguments that diverge from their own, and that they be willing to exchange ideas and revise their own points of view" (58). Collectively, these authors suggest that when we teach counterarguments, we are teaching, in the language of this book, the rhetorical virtues of open-mindedness, intellectual generosity, and intellectual courage.

Open-mindedness, the argumentation theorist Daniel Cohen has written, consists of "the ability to listen carefully, the willingness to take what others say seriously, and, if called for, the resolve to adopt [others' positions] as one's own" (Cohen 2009, 56). Open-mindedness involves a readiness to hear the other side, to suspend one's own beliefs, at least temporarily, and to refrain from making premature judgments. The open-minded person resists narrow-mindedness, prejudice, dogmatism, or other vices, demonstrating instead the qualities of receptivity, tolerance, perhaps empathy.

Open-mindedness need not involve intellectual disputes or disagreements, as the virtue theorist Jason Baehr has noted (Baehr 2011). Students exposed for the first time to Einstein's Special Theory of Relativity, for example, are challenged to think in new ways about space, time, velocity, and other concepts. They are called upon to "open their minds" to the unfamiliar and the exceptional. Open-mindedness in such instances is the capacity to think creatively, insightfully, even artistically.

Open-mindedness is finally "an attitude toward oneself as a believer," the philosopher Wayne Riggs argues, "rather than toward any particular belief. To be open-minded is to be aware of one's fallibility as a believer, and to be willing to acknowledge the possibility that anytime one believes something, *it is possible that one is wrong*" (Riggs 2010, 180; emphases in original).

When we teach students to write counterarguments, we are teaching them, following Riggs, to develop attitudes toward themselves as believers. We are asking them to acknowledge their inherent fallibility, their potential and actual blind spots. We are asking them to keep alive the possibility that in adopting a given position or attitude they may be, as the philosopher of education William Hare writes, "shutting out a conscious awareness of truths that are awkward or problematic" (Hare 2006). When we teach counterarguments, I am suggesting, we are asking students to become, as Socrates says of himself in Plato's *Gorgias*, one of those who would be just as glad "to be refuted as to refute" (Bizzell and Herzberg 2001, 94).[1]

To be open to the possibility of error, however, is not to grant the same credence to every challenge. Just as we teach students to be skeptical in assessing claims, and to be critical when evaluating source materials, the open-minded person must still make informed judgments about which intellectual challenges to consider seriously, and which to disregard. I can remain open-minded about the potential causes of lung cancer, for example, while declining to give serious attention to arguments made by the tobacco industry. You may be open-minded on the subject of fracking, but decide that arguments made by gas industry lobbyists do not merit extended consideration. The central criterion for deciding which challenges to accept and which to disregard, Baehr (2011) argues, is whether a particular challenge "may be helpful for reaching the truth" about a given question (210). And this calls for the exercise of discrimination and judgment as much as it calls for fairness and open mindedness. Perhaps this is why Baehr calls open-mindedness a "facilitating virtue," or one that encourages the enactment of others.

When we teach counterarguments, then, we are teaching students to judge the credibility of opposing views, to consider seriously those that deserve serious consideration, and to reflect upon how ideas that contradict our own may help us better understand the truth of a given issue. The counterargument challenges us to suspend, if only for a time, our own intellectual biases and commit ourselves to understanding those who think differently than we do. In its best sense, the counterargument calls upon us to read in a spirit of confidence and goodwill, regarding those who think differently than we do not as enemies to be destroyed but as potential colleagues and partners who can deepen our knowledge of an issue and, not incidentally, strengthen our arguments. And this suggests that when we teach the counterargument, we are teaching the rhetorical virtue of intellectual generosity.

Philosophers who write about generosity traditionally explain it in terms of giving, often material giving, and the principles that govern the act of such giving. So, for example, does Aristotle describe generosity as follows:

> Virtuous actions are fine, and done for a fine end; so the liberal man too will give with a fine end in view, and in the right way; because he will give to the right people, and the right amounts, at the right time, and will observe all other conditions that accompany right giving. And he will have pleasure, or at least no pain, in doing this; because a virtuous act is pleasant or painless, but certainly not painful. (Aristotle 1976, 143, quoted in Pybus 1991, 34)

Modern readings of generosity are more expansive, conceiving of generosity in terms of material but also non-material exchanges of goods. So, for example, does Andre argue, "many things worth giving—time, energy, attention, even some physical objects—have no monetary value. For something to count as a gift it need only be valued by the giver, and believed by her to be valued by the receiver" (Andre 2015, 80). The British philosopher Elizabeth Pybus expands the concept of generosity further, arguing that generosity is not "merely of a material kind" but encompasses as well "a generosity of spirit and understanding, crucially involving sympathy and imagination, without which people are not as good as they might be" (Pybus 1991, 29). Yi-Fu Tuan, who writes on the concept of "human geography," or the study of human relationships, attaches generosity to people and human goodness: "Generosity is not just the giving of things, time, and service. It is also how we think of another person, the merit of his or her work" (Tuan 2008, 50).[2]

Generosity is generally thought to benefit the giver as much as the receiver, though philosophers debate the moral worth of generosity because of the element of self-interest in the act of giving (Andre 2015, 80–83). And it is true that the practices of intellectual generosity that I claim are inherent in making counterarguments can lead to clear benefits for the giver—that is, the writer—while offering no immediately discernable benefits to the source of the opposing view.

Suppose, for example, the student writer arguing for the creation of a hate speech code at her university engages generously with the writing of the libertarian who opposes such codes as an infringement of free speech. The student writer may come away from that engagement with a more informed understanding of the issue, a greater sympathy for the principles of libertarianism, and a more nuanced argument in support of her views. We might argue that the source of the opposing view, the libertarian, receives no apparent benefit from the writer's practice of intellectual generosity, especially if the writer ultimately rejects libertarian views of free speech.

Such a conclusion, however, is predicated upon too narrow a conception of generosity, intellectual or otherwise. The benefits of generosity in an intellectual exchange are not limited to giver and receiver but extend to the community to which giver and receiver belong. Generosity benefits society, Andre writes, "through the relationships it fosters, which writ large are the networks of obligation, appreciation, and cooperation central to human activity" (92). Practices of intellectual generosity, in this reading, nurture activities of mind that go beyond whatever benefits may accrue to individual readers and writers.

I may disagree with the conclusions in your book about academic free-dom, but my willingness to take your ideas seriously, acknowledge your expertise, avoid characterizing you in mocking or abusive language, ultimately benefits us both if it promotes a society in which we are capable of addressing our differences without seeking to damage or humiliate one another. When we teach students how to write coun-terarguments, we are helping to develop such a society, essay by essay, argument by argument, word by word.

None of this is easy. To be open-minded and intellectually generous calls for a certain sort of resolve, a certain tenacity, one that involves the willingness to address ideas or beliefs that may be uncomfortable, offensive, or antithetical to our own values. When we engage with such ideas, we put some part of ourselves at risk. We run the risk of perceiving some truth in opposing ideas, and perhaps even of having our core values unsettled. We even risk that most radical of possibili-ties: the possibility we may come to change our minds. And that might threaten to destabilize some part of that ever-evolving medley of quali-ties, beliefs, quandaries, commitments, boundaries, and self-concepts that we understand to be our identities. And yet this is what we ask of students when we ask them to write counterarguments, is it not? When we teach the counterargument, in this perspective, we are asking stu-dents to take such risks and chance such unsettling possibilities. We are asking them, in other words, to cultivate the rhetorical virtue of intellectual courage.

In classical accounts, courage is typically discussed in terms of physi-cal valor, embodied by the soldier willing to die for his country in battle. *Dulce et decorum est pro patria mori*, wrote the Roman poet Horace: "It is sweet and glorious to die for one's country." Aristotle is predictably more prosaic: "So in the strict sense of the word the courageous man will be one who is fearless in the face of an honourable death, or of some sudden threat of death; and it is in war that such situations chiefly occur" (2004, III, vi., 1115b, 30–35). The association of courage with the warrior, what Richard White calls "the military model of courage," con-tinues to shape our understandings of courage and the words we use to describe it. "In any context involving courageous resolve," writes White, "we talk of standing firm in the face of difficulty, refusing to surrender our principles, and not laying down until we have finally prevailed" (White 2008, 23). This martial conception of courage, White maintains, "makes our moral life into a series of contexts or battles, with true virtue grasped as an absolute readiness to fight for whatever is right, and a refusal to compromise one's position" (ibid.)

The military model, however, does not account for the different contexts and meanings of courage. In their comprehensive handbook classifying character strengths and virtues, Christopher Peterson and Martin E. P. Seligman discuss distinctly different kinds of courage: physical, moral, and psychological (Peterson and Seligman 2004, 36). Physical courage, say the authors, is overcoming fear of injury or death to save another person; it is the courage, for example, of the first responder running into the World Trade Towers, or the soldier in the field in Afghanistan. Moral courage is maintaining ethical integrity at the risk of losing friends, employment, or prestige; it is the courage of the political leader who admits to a costly mistake, or the whistleblower reporting malfeasance when she knows it will cost her the job she loves. And psychological courage, according to Peterson and Seligman, is confronting the fears within ourselves; it is the courage of the patient facing up to a debilitating disease, or the drug addict who checks into a clinic to get clean. As Deidre McCloskey puts it, "'Courage' does not mean the same thing to a Roman knight as to a Christian knight, or to a samurai as to a cowboy, or to a free man in Athens of 431 BC as to an adult woman in the Paris of AD 1968" (364).

In the writing class, we encourage yet another kind of courage: intellectual courage, which calls upon students to engage conflicting views, read without bias or rancor, and acknowledge that they may, in fact, be wrong, or that the other side may have equally good or at least legitimate arguments.

Perhaps I can best illustrate with a personal narrative. Some years ago, teaching a first-year writing class at the University of Wisconsin, I had a student—I will call her Christine—whose family owned a fishing resort in the northern part of the state. This was during the period of the spearfishing controversy, sometimes called the Wisconsin Walleye War, in which white sports fishermen and resort owners clashed, sometimes violently, with members of the Native American Ojibwe tribe who claimed the legal right, based on treaty agreements with the US government dating back to the nineteenth century, to hunt and fish off-reservation, and to spearfish walleye during spawning season.[3] White protestors maintained that Ojibwe hunting practices were depleting the walleye stock and were therefore ruinous to the local economy, and that members of the tribe were unfairly accorded "special rights" to use spearfishing methods that were illegal for other fishermen. During the walleye spawning season, hundreds of protesters gathered at the lakes where the Ojibwe fished, shouting racial slurs, throwing rocks at Ojibwe fishermen, swamping their boats, and in some cases physically assaulting them. Riot police were eventually called in to maintain order.

Christine believed that her father and other resort owners were being discriminated against economically, and, worse, that they were being unfairly maligned as racists in local and national media. She decided she would write about the controversy to fulfill the final class assignment, which called for students to research and write about a question from multiple perspectives. As I remember her, Christine was one of the quieter students in class. She seldom contributed to class or small group discussions, and I rarely saw her outside of class. Moreover, the drafts she submitted were perfunctory, sketching the outlines of the conflict in a page or two. As the semester wore on, I was mostly in the dark about her progress.

One afternoon, she surprised me by appearing at my office to discuss her paper. She wanted to change her thesis. Was that alright? I said it was and asked about the new thesis. She would argue, she said, that the resort owners had legitimate grievances, as their livelihoods were threatened by the tribal fishing practices. But she had been reading, she told me. She now wanted to argue that the Ojibwe, too, had legitimate claims that had been negotiated in US courts, and their traditional hunting and fishing practices should be respected. Her new thesis would call for an accommodation of some kind.

I don't remember the paper Christine eventually wrote, or whether it achieved her purposes. I don't remember the grade I gave it. But I remember the admiration I felt for Christine that day she visited my office. I admired her commitment to the assignment, her work ethic, and her willingness to look at the controversy from multiple points of view, including one that potentially undermined her family's economic interests. Most of all, I admired what I now think of as Christine's intellectual courage.

In teaching counterarguments, we are teaching students to anticipate possible objections to their positions, to research such objections, and to respond to them appropriately. In learning these practices, we commonly tell students, they will become stronger writers. Yet we are equally teaching, when we teach the counterargument, the rhetorical virtues of open-mindedness, intellectual generosity, and intellectual courage.

VIRTUES OF REVISION

The word "revise," from the Latin, *revisere*, meaning "to look back on," or "to visit again"—from *re* ("again") and *videre* ("to see")—speaks to a fundamental charge in the teaching of writing. Certainly, we teach students to "look back on" and "see again" the writing they do in our classes, and we seek to impress upon them the importance of revision in virtually all other occasions for writing. Revision, we maintain, is central to the writing process and a habitual practice of accomplished writers. "To create the best possible writing," Doug Downs writes in his essay on revision, "writers work iteratively, composing in a number of versions, with time between each for reflection, reader feedback, and/or collaborator development" (Downs 2015, 66).

Revision as we teach it in the writing class is often, as Downs suggests, a collaborative undertaking, a point underscored in many of our textbooks. "Because it is hard to be objective about your own work," Timothy W. Crusius and Carolyn E. Channell counsel student writers, "getting a reading from a friend, classmate, teacher, or family member is a good way to see where revision would help" (Crusius and Channell 2003, 244). Greene and Lidinsky similarly advise, "Academic writing is a collaborative enterprise. By reading and commenting on your drafts, your peers can support your work as a writer" (227). So, too, do Roen, Glau, and Maid (2013) suggest, "Working with one or two classmates, read each other's paper and offer comments that will help each of you see your paper's strengths and weaknesses" (80). In our classrooms, we commonly make such collaborations possible in the form of peer tutoring groups, which provide students with opportunities to practice the skills of summarizing, paraphrasing, questioning, criticizing, and supporting the writing of others.

Revision involves us, then, teachers and students, in relationships with others. And it is in the context of relationships that we return to ethical questions and considerations. Let us assume for a moment the role of the student in the peer group. In such settings, we are expected to speak candidly and critically, offering a forthright appraisal of the writing of our fellow students. We are expected, in such settings, to exhibit the rhetorical virtues of honesty, self-confidence, and perhaps, again, intellectual courage, given that it is not always comfortable to critique the work of a peer. However, if our relationship with our fellow student is to proceed from its uncertain beginnings in the earliest days and weeks of the writing class, we must also practice, in most instances and with most peers, the moderating qualities of diplomacy and empathy. We must learn to listen as well as to speak, and when we speak we must do so—if our group is to achieve its purposes—in language that critiques the work but is free of personal criticism. Not so easy!

And when the comments of others are directed at our writing, when we receive unsparing and perhaps even biting criticism of our own work—the claims are unclear, the evidence is insufficient, the language is banal—we are called upon to demonstrate still other qualities and dispositions. We must, if we are willing to fully commit to improving as writers, have the fortitude not simply to listen to our critics, but to engage them in discussions of our deficiencies. How can I make my claims clearer and more specific? In what ways is my evidence inadequate? How can I write more compelling sentences? To open oneself to such discussions, to drive them forward by our questions and requests for clarification, calls for perseverance, humility, and perhaps even gratitude toward who are willing to take our work seriously. Is it any wonder that writing groups can be so challenging?

And after we have left the group, having relocated to the cafe or the library carrell to review the critiques of our work, we are called upon to make judgments that demonstrate something like the Aristotelian virtue of *phronesis*, or practical wisdom, "the ability," as Battaly (2015) writes, "to act rightly as a result of knowing what ought to be done" (47). What should be kept in our text, and what should be cut? What needs to be rewritten? Which comments made in the writing group can be safely ignored, and which must be addressed, even if they were delivered in language that stung us?

The act of revising, if we are to take it seriously, very often calls upon us to confront our inadequacies as writers. When we revise, we must come to terms with our muddled ideas, our failed metaphors, our unrealized ambitions. If we are to face these squarely, we will need to exercise still other virtues. We will require the honesty to admit our faults, the self-discipline to address them, and the resolve necessary to continue writing even as we understand how far we are from the writers we wish to become.

Nor are such commitments the work of a single sitting. Revision we tell students, in what has become a truism in our field, is a recursive process. Writers do not progress in linear, lockstep fashion through the stages of the writing process, from planning to drafting to revision to completion. Instead, we are continually circling back, beginning again, re-reading and re-writing. And this means that the virtues inherent in the work of revising must be learned and re-learned, practiced and practiced, until they are habitual, performed repeatedly and routinely throughout the writing process.

When we teach students the practices of revision, finally, we are teaching them to ask good questions about their claims, topics, evidence, counterarguments, and other rhetorical concerns. We are teaching them how to make changes in a text, when to cut and when to add words, when to rewrite and when to begin anew. Yet we are equally

teaching them, when we teach the habits of revision, to learn and practice a complex, interrelated, and often difficult set of rhetorical virtues.

CONCLUSION: VIRTUES OF ARGUMENT

When Professor A led her class so skillfully, as I imagined it, though her
lesson on providing evidence in support of claims, she and her students
made their classroom, after MacIntyre, into an "arena in which the virtues are exhibited." So it is, I would argue, with all writing classes. I have
focused in this chapter on practices of claims, evidence, counterarguments, and revisions, and the virtues inherent in these practices, including truthfulness, accountability, open-mindedness, and good judgment.
These are represented here as illustrative rather than comprehensive
accounts. We might equally have focused on the rhetorical virtues inherent in other writing practices.

We might have focused, for example, on how writing summaries calls
for exercising the qualities of diligence in reading carefully, detachment
in representing ideas impartially, and judgment in weighing prudently
what to include and exclude in the summary text. We might have discussed how writing personal narratives can encourage the habits of
attentiveness to detail, inventiveness in selecting words, and authenticity
in recounting experience. We might have considered as well how adapt-
ing to diverse rhetorical situations requires the traits of discernment
in assessing context, tactfulness in adjusting to circumstance, and wisdom in deciding what to say and how to say it. Alternatively, we might
have reflected on the rhetorical virtues inherent in our pedagogical
approaches to teaching writing. We might have considered, for instance,
how writing assignments in community-based classes may encourage
habits of cooperativeness, empathy, and civic responsibility, while assignments in critical literacy classes can inspire reflection on the virtue of
justice. In virtually all of the practices we teach, in all of our diverse
pedagogies, I am suggesting, we are teaching some account of rhetorical virtues.

Indeed, there is a sense in which argument itself—the whole that
is comprised of the parts of claims, proofs, counterarguments, and
the rest—can be said to serve as an "arena in which the virtues are
exhibited." Argument is frequently represented as an act of opposition,
an exercise of power, and an attempt to dominate others. No less an
argumentation scholar than David Zarefsky, for example, cautions that
argument can involve "an attempt to limit freedom of choice" by means
of "applying superior to inferior force" (Zarefsky 2005, 17). Deborah

Tannen captures this spirit, what she terms, the "adversarial frame of mind," in her popular book, *The Argument Culture*:

> The best way to discuss an idea is to set up a debate; the best way to cover news is to find spokespeople who express the most extreme, polarized views and present them as "both sides"; the best way to settle disputes is litigation that pits one party against the other; the best way to begin an essay is to attack someone; and the best way to show you're really thinking is to criticize. (Tannen 1998, 3)

Tannen is not endorsing such practices but is confirming how they are prevalent in an academic culture that prizes intellectual combat and the ability to "position our work in opposition to someone else's, which we prove wrong" (Tannen 2000).

Certainly, academics often represent argument in the language of conflict and war: We attack others' ideas. We gain and lose territory. We are victorious, or we are crushed, decisively. This is argument as intellectual domination. Such a model, Tannen writes, can have a baleful effect upon our students, who learn from us "that they must disprove others' arguments in order to be original, make a contribution, and demonstrate their intellectual ability" (Tannen 1998, 269). The need to prove others are wrong, moreover, can tempt students "to oversimplify at best, and at worst to distort or even misrepresent others' positions, the better to refute them" (ibid.). In this conception, argument serves as a means for dominating others, bending them to your will, and elevating yourself in the process.

I want to propose a different conception of argument, one that recalls the trope of argument as relationship. When we argue, in this view, we invite an exchange between others and ourselves. Argument in this understanding is not a monologue but a dialogue between two, or a conversation among many. More, argument from this perspective may be understood not as exercises in domination and control but rather as an act of radical humility.

Why "humility"? Because whenever we put pen to paper, or sit before the keyboard, or rise to speak for the purpose of making an argument, we subject ourselves to the evaluation of others. We put a proposition before our readers or listeners and invite them, as I am inviting you, the reader of this book, to make a judgment about our ideas, our values, even our character as individuals. Our readers or our listeners may agree with us, they may doubt us, they may reject and even revile us. But that is what we signed up for when we invited them to hear our argument. We have in essence said: these are my ideas, my proposals, my commitments. How should these be judged? We are not, of course, subservient. We don't accept any judgment. We resist certain conclusions. But the very act of making an argument, in this conception, calls upon us to stand before others to be judged.

And why call this "radical"? Because to conceive of argument this way is to make such a determined and thoroughgoing break with the customary conceptions of argument as war, power, and control as to constitute a radical departure. As an act of radical humility, argument functions not as a truncheon for dominating others but rather as an invitation to collaborate, to reason together and, perhaps, to find and inhabit common ground. Such a view calls for a different way of talking about and teaching argument. How we might do so is what we shall consider next.

NOTES

1.   To what extent this was actually true of Socrates is another question.
2.   What I am calling intellectual generosity might also be described—indeed, it has been described in the philosophical and theological literature—as charity, and in the exchange of ideas as the expression of intellectual charity. The word charity comes from the Greek, *agape*, or love, translated into Latin as *caritas*, or "mercy," "compassion," or "the giving of alms." The word steadily became associated with the Christian faith, as Catholic recognition of the theological virtues, faith, hope, and charity, or love—"and the strongest of these is love" (Corinthians 13:13). I have elected in this book to use the more every day and broadly understood term, generosity, to avoid unintended religious associations.
3.   The controversy was subject of the 1999 PBS documentary *Lighting the 7th Fire* (Osawa 1999).

5

TEACHING RHETORICAL VIRTUES

*"And I wish that you would, if possible, show me a little more clearly
that virtue can be taught. Will you be so good?"*

—Socrates, in Plato's *Protagorus*, 176

Just down the hall from Professor A, her colleague Professor Z is
also teaching a first-year writing course. The theme of the course is
"American Jurisprudence" and calls upon students to study and write
about significant legal decisions in the US justice system. On this day, the
class is discussing a case currently under review by a state supreme court.
The case concerns a student, we shall call her Hannah, who attended a
Catholic academy for high school and middle school students. Hannah
was enrolled in the middle school but denied admission to the academy
high school. Her family is suing the school under Persons with Disabilities
Civil Rights Act, claiming Hannah was wrongfully discriminated against
because she is learning disabled. Lawyers for the academy have moved
to dismiss the case, claiming that civil courts do not have jurisdiction to
review the administrative decisions of a religious institution.

At issue are two conflicting and seemingly incompatible rights granted
under US law. The school's position is based on the First Amendment
right to practice religion freely, which, the school's lawyers maintain,
prohibits the government from interfering in how a religious institution makes internal decisions. Hannah's position is that she was denied
admission to the academy neither on academic nor religious grounds,
but because she is disabled, which is a violation of her civil rights. The
court has been asked to rule on the question of whether civil courts have
jurisdiction in this case, whether the school does in fact have the right
to deny admission, and whether a previous precedent affirming the
school's position should be overturned.[1]

Professor Z's students offer different readings of the case. Some argue
the school is on solid ground claiming First Amendment protection, and
that government has no role in regulating the administrative policies of

DOI: 10.7330/9781607328278.c005

a faith-based institution. Should the courts be granted jurisdiction in this case, what else would they be empowered to regulate? Could they rule on hours of schooling, times for worship, or, most alarmingly, the academy's curriculum and educational materials? Other students see the case differently, asserting that anti-discrimination laws apply to all people and institutions, including religious institutions. If faith-based schools are exempt from anti-discrimination laws, the students argue, could they also choose to exclude LGBTQ students or students of color? Could they exclude, by the same logic, Mexican students, left-handed students, or students who wear braces on their teeth? Who is to say they cannot, if they are beyond the authority of the law?

Professor Z listens intently to each student's argument in the class discussion of the case, occasionally requesting clarifications of a given point or asking one student to respond to an argument made previously by another. From time to time, she offers carefully chosen vocabulary in response to student comments: So, would you say you are talking about *justice?* Is yours ultimately an argument about *fairness?* You seem to be making a case for *tolerance* and *practical wisdom?* Professor Z then writes these words—justice and fairness, tolerance and wisdom—on the white-board, asking students to discuss their understandings of each. She then asks students of differing views what they hold in common, and where they go their separate ways.

At the end of class, Professor Z distributes two readings for students to consider: Article 24 of the Convention on the Rights of Persons with Disabilities, which addresses the right of persons with disabilities to "inclusive education" directed toward "the full development of human potential and sense of dignity and self-worth" (United Nations 2006); and the Virginia Statute on Religious Freedom, authored by Thomas Jefferson in 1786, which prohibited both government interference with and support for religious activities, and which is thought to have inspired the First Amendment of the US Constitution (Virginia Historical Society 2017). The assignment, Professor Z tells the class, is to use one or both of these documents in writing an opinion on the lawsuit brought against the Catholic academy.

• • •

The teaching of writing, I have argued throughout, inevitably engages teachers and students in ethical deliberations and decision-making. And this is true, I have suggested, whether we are purposefully engaged in addressing ethical problems and topics in our classes, or whether we are indifferent to such questions. Regardless, we are necessarily teaching practices of ethical discourse. More, I have suggested that our students, our field, and indeed our communities can benefit from a deliberate engagement in our classes with the ethical dimensions of writing. But what would a "deliberate engagement" with rhetorical virtues mean in the context of our classes? How might discussions of the rhetorical virtues be framed in the writing class? What questions might be asked? What materials shared? If we are to make explicit what I have asserted is always implicit, how, exactly, are we supposed to do this? What strategies, approaches, or activities are available to us?

In attempting to address such questions in this chapter, I shall proceed cautiously. The teaching of rhetorical ethics in the writing class does not lend itself to off-the-rack syllabi or lesson plans that can be applied in all classes, for all students, at all times. Rather, such lessons are best worked out in the particulars of local contexts, accounting for the specific needs of students and communities, the distinctive goals of teachers and programs, and the resources available in different institutional settings. What is appropriate for one group of students may be inappropriate for others, and fruitful discussions of rhetorical ethics in one context may be unavailing in another. For writing programs "to be good," Bizzell has written, "they must be indigenous" (Bizzell 1992a, 15). Yet there are several broad strategies, I shall propose, that can inform the teaching of ethical rhetoric generally, and that can introduce students in diverse contexts to the language and practices of rhetorical virtue. For examples, let us return to the classroom of Professor Z.

To begin, Professor Z introduced students to a particular *situation*, one that called upon students to think about legal issues but also about such ethical qualities as justice, fairness, tolerance, and wisdom. Professor Z explicitly *named* these qualities, introducing them into students' deliberations, asking students to define their understandings of each term, and inviting students to locate points of agreement and disagreement in their application to the case at hand. More, by listening carefully to students, questioning them thoughtfully, requesting they clarify their arguments and respond to the arguments of others, Professor Z *modeled* the language practices of respectfulness and intellectual rigor. Following the discussion, Professor Z assigned readings to serve as *exemplars* that students might imitate or make use of in their own writings. And by welcoming all points of view and diverse student responses to the situation, Professor Z encouraged not consensus but rather its opposite, *dissensus*, or productive classroom disputations through which students might arrive at deeper understandings of the issue and the relationships of rhetoric, ethics, and writing. Finally, we may ask, in considering Professor Z's class, whether hers was the iso-lated effort of a single instructor in one classroom or reflected a wider *institutional culture* committed to the teaching of rhetorical ethics. I pro-pose that in these broad concepts, *situation, naming, modeling, exemplars, dissensus,* and *institutional culture,* we may find pathways for promoting ethical awareness and practice in the writing class. Let us consider each individually, beginning with situation.

SITUATION

In his under-appreciated essay, "In Pursuit of Rhetorical Virtue," John Gage argues that what makes for ethical argument, or argument that is "tolerant, judicious, and reasonable" (Gage 2005, 32) cannot be achieved through the formulation of abstract rules and precepts. Gage cites as an example the work of Jurgen Habermas, the philosopher of "communica-tive rationality," who has formulated a list of just such rules and precepts, including "No speaker may contradict himself" and "Everyone is allowed to question any assertion whatsoever" (32). In his essay, Gage presents his own more student-friendly version of Habermasian-style normative injunctions, including these:

1. Let us try to acknowledge that no matter what we might disagree about, we share a vastly larger number of agreements . . . There is always common ground somewhere to be found.

3. Let us try to acknowledge the necessity of disagreement, then, to the overall welfare of our culture . . . This principle I think I heard first from my mother, who would say, "If we agreed about everything, then one of us isn't necessary."

5. Let us then try to acknowledge the possibility that some claim or conclusion we wish to support might be wrong. Belief has a way of feeling permanent and inevitable, but all we have to do is recall when we have been wrong. Anyone here who hasn't been?

Gage offers 10 such rules in all, and they are, in my opinion, ter-rific guidelines for ethical discourse—wise and witty, sensible and civil, humane and just. And as normative rules of discourse, as Gage himself points out, they will likely never be observed. They will likely never be observed because in real life we do not argue on the basis of rules and precepts. We do not argue that way, Gage writes, because no one is bound to follow such rules, there are no consequences for discarding them, and there is an excellent chance, if we do follow them, that we will lose the argument. And we generally we do not argue to lose, as the cognitive scientists tell us. We argue to win.

122 TEACHING RHETORICAL VIRTUES

So where does that leave those of us who would represent the first-year writing class as a site for the teaching and practice of ethical discourse? As a scene for truthfulness, for vetting evidence, for the fair-minded consideration of multiple points of view? If ordinary argument is resistant to norms intended to promote rational communication, and if argument itself, as Mercier and the cognitive scientists have proposed, is a social adaptation evolved primarily for the purpose of winning, how do we help our students, if indeed we can help them, develop habits of ethical speech and writing?

Gage recommends we begin with virtue ethics. Gage recognizes in virtue ethics, as we do in this book, a conception of normative ethics based not on inflexible moral codes or the calculations of outcomes but rather on the qualities of character that guide moral decision-making. In the virtue-based approach, Gage advises, we make decisions about how to respond to ethical dilemmas by assessing the particulars of a situation, deliberating on possible choices, and finally choosing to act, speak, or write as a good person would in the absence of absolute knowledge.

But does this not lead us back to where we started? How do we promote such qualities of character in the student writer? How do we help students develop, for example, the rhetorical quality of *phronesis*, the wisdom of knowing which choices to make, and when, in which situations? When Professor Steven Salaita was fired in 2015 by the University of Illinois for his provocative Twitter comments about Israeli military actions in Gaza—Salaita wrote, among other things, "Zionists, take responsibility: if your dream of an ethnocratic Israel is worth the murder of children, just fucking own it already" (Salaita 2014)—were his remarks, as his critics argued, "loathsome" and "inexcusably violent" (Lubet 2014). Were they examples of "hate speech" (Leibovitz 2014)? Or were they, as his defenders had it, "an impassioned plea to end the violence taking place in the Middle East" (Illinois AAUP Committee 2014)? How do we help students assess such discourse? How do we help them develop the rhetorical virtues of judgment and practical wisdom they may use in deciding how to read Salaita's tweets or similarly provocative language?

For Gage, one answer to such questions can be found in the context of situations. Students can develop a greater ethical sensibility, in this view, if they have opportunities to write and speak in response to situations that call for ethical judgments. To that end, Gage recommends that we concern ourselves, we teachers of writing, less with teaching rhetorical strategies and more with creating situations that call for the exercise of those ethical qualities, traits, habits, and dispositions we most wish to promote. Gage writes:

What qualities do we look for in the situations we create for [students], that enable those situations to call for the exercise of practical wisdom? And how do we ask students to read in order to see how others have made such choices? Are there situations . . . in which pure self-interest must be set aside to arrive at assent? Are there situations in which knowledge must be discovered collectively rather than treated as a pre-determined commodity to be sold to someone else? The choices made in such situations can only be generated and evaluated by the application of what might be called virtue. This is a challenging re-orientation of a teacher's typical responsibility as promoter of rules. (Gage 2005, 36)

The role of the teacher, in this conception, shifts from promoter of rules to *creator of situations.* The teacher devises situations, whether concerning economic injustice, environmental destruction, gun violence or others, that require students to read about the issue, reflect on possible responses, advance a claim or series of claims, listen to the claims of classmates, reflect again in light of what may have been learned, and finally make a judgment as to how a good person would speak or write in response to the situation. Taking the example of Salaita's case, students might read more about the context in which the tweets were written, deliberate on whether or not they were an appropriate response, and discuss which rhetorical virtues were or were not enacted in Salaita's tweets. The goal of the discussion would not be to reach consensus on the issue, which would be unlikely in any case, but rather to engage students in reflection on what a good writer might say in that situation, how she might say it, and why it should be said in precisely that way. In such discussions might students engage in the kind of reasoned discourse that will help them develop the quality of *phronesis,* or the practical wisdom that will aid them in making such judgments.

But here we confront a difficulty. Many of the rhetorical situations our students will encounter will be characterized not by reasoned exchanges of differing views, as we know, but instead by practices of bias, bigotry, dishonesty, and other manifestations of toxic discourse. In a rhetorical culture increasingly defined by "post-truth" and "alternative facts," what is the place of the ethical writer and speaker? And how should our students respond to situations characterized not by idealized conditions of fact-based, reasoned argument but instead by injustice, violence, and other forms of oppression? What constitutes the good writer in such contexts?

Gage provides one answer to such questions by arguing that normative ethics of speech and writing must be augmented by what he calls "ab-normative ethics," by which he means those examples of speech and writing that "openly defy prevailing discourse norms and rules . . .

because there is a need to speak outside those norms" (35). Speech and writing "outside those norms" may be angry, confrontational, and unreceptive to compromise. And yet may be no less ethical, no less virtuous, for that. Rhetorical virtue, as we have noted previously, does not presuppose civility, and ethical discourse is not defined by adherence to norms that function to preserve social or economic inequities. In situations where reasoned argument is not productive or even possible, the relevant questions become: "How does a good writer resist such conditions?" or "How might my words and actions promote the virtue of justice in this situation?"

To address such questions, teachers might, in their role as creators of situations, provide scenarios, real or fictional, in which individuals or groups are confronted with injustices, and to which students would respond in discussion and in writing. Together, students and teacher would consider all the available means of a virtuous response, whether verbal, written, or "ab-normative." In such conversations, the teacher could pose questions related to ethical discourse practices: How would an ethical writer respond to this situation? What would she say or write? What rhetorical virtues would be expressed or enacted in her response? Why those virtues and not others? The purpose of such discussions would be to afford students opportunities to exercise judgment and practical wisdom, and the practice the rhetorical virtues they have identified as relevant to the situation.

NAMING

Perhaps the most straightforward way of introducing rhetorical virtues to students is to name them explicitly. In discussing a rhetorical situation, a course reading, or a student essay, teachers might name the virtues enacted in the particular text or context, discuss its range of meanings with students, and consider when and in which rhetorical contexts it applies. As education researcher Ron Ritchhart argues, "before one can effectively engage in a way of thinking, perspective taking, for example, it is helpful to know just what perspective taking is, why it is important, what it looks like in different situations, and when it is likely to be useful" (Ritchhart 2002, 48). So it is, too, in our discussions of truthfulness, courage, indignation, and the like.

Our students do not, of course, come to us *tabula rasa*, innocent of such concepts. They arrive, rather, as complex moral beings with their own conceptions of what it means to be truthful, courageous, and righteously indignant. Perhaps fewer of our students, however, come to our classes having learned to associate such ethical qualities with acts of speaking and writing. Fewer of our students, that is, arrive with the understanding that their rhetorical practices, their claims, proofs, and counterarguments, speak as much to their character as to their messages. In this sense, the explicit naming of rhetorical virtues can make unfamiliar what was previously familiar, and so suggest to students new and potentially generative ways to think about the activities of speaking and writing.

How might we do this? In my classes, I have introduced, as Professor Z introduced, the language of rhetorical virtues in the context of classroom discussions, asking, for example: Is this text, paragraph, analogy, or word illustrative of *empathy*? What do we mean by empathy? Is empathy warranted in this case? Does it conflict with other ethical imperatives?[2] Alternatively, teachers might consider designing a syllabus, as did Professor Angel Matos when he taught at the University of Notre Dame in 2013, grounded in the explicit teaching of the rhetorical virtues: assigning and discussing readings grounded in honesty, courage, generosity, and so on.[3] Teachers, too, can ask students to bring to class their own examples of rhetorical virtues, raising the possibility that virtues commonly privileged in the college writing class, such as honesty, accountability, open-mindedness, may be challenged or at the very least supplemented by virtues that speak directly to students' experiences, traditions, histories, and narratives.

What is common to each of the approaches suggested above is the explicit naming of virtues in the context of classroom discussion. "Although dispositions aren't formed," Ritchhart writes, "through such direct instruction, the presence of explicit instruction within a supportive cultural context over time supports their development" (Ritchhart 2002, 48) Our classrooms can serve, if we choose, as that supportive cultural context.

MODELING

Critiquing their own classroom teaching practices, Stephen D. Brookfield and Stephen Preskill, authors of *Discussion as a Way of Teaching: Tools and Techniques for Democratic Classrooms* (Brookfield and Preskill 1999), report that one of the mistakes they have often made is to announce on the first day of class that they believe in class discussion, tell students why such discussion is good for them, and then place students into small groups to begin discussing. "The trouble with this scenario," the authors write, "is that it omits a crucial element: we have neglected to model for students how to engage in the activity we are urging on them . . . As teachers, we have to earn the right to ask students to engage seriously in discussion by first modeling our own serious commitment to it" (41). If we are committed to teaching students to speak and write truthfully, generously, and courageously, Brookfield and Preskill's critical self-evaluation suggests, we must model these behaviors ourselves—in our classroom dialogues with our students certainly, but also in our interactions with colleagues and in our own scholarly and public writing.

When Professor Z listened carefully in her class to student responses to the problem she had placed before them, when she did not interrupt, contradict, or belittle their ideas, she was modeling for her students the rhetorical qualities of respect, open-mindedness, and restraint, holding back her own views until students had the opportunity to express theirs. Professor Z was in a sense practicing the virtue of humility by refusing, at that moment and in that situation, to make herself the center of the class and treating her students as empty vessels to be filled with the teacher's knowledge.

In the daily give-and-take of the classroom, we teachers of writing are offered innumerable opportunities to model ethical discourse practices for our students. When students ask questions, or make comments on classroom readings, we can demonstrate attentiveness by listening carefully and thoughtfully. When students offer opinions that differ markedly from our own, we can model tolerance by withholding judgment and hearing them out. When conflicts between students become heated, we can model diplomacy by addressing differences calmly, tactfully, and honestly.

None of this implies that we should paper-over conflicts to achieve a false semblance of agreement. An ethical speaker in classroom dialogue is committed, to use Parker Palmer's language, to making "the painful things possible, things without which no learning can occur—things like exposing ignorance, testing tentative hypotheses, challenging false or partial information, and mutual criticism of thought" (Palmer 1993, 74, quoted in Brookfield and Preskill 1999, 9). Yet we can model for students how to express the "painful things" in a language of fair-mindedness, generosity, and goodwill. In doing so, we can help to create conditions of trust in our classrooms—trust between teachers and students, trust among students in one another, and, perhaps most critically, trust in the project of becoming an ethical speaker and writer.

We can also model ethical discourse in interactions with colleagues. Brookfield and Preskill recommend inviting colleagues into our classrooms to engage in unrehearsed conversations about a contentious issue. As students look on, Brookfield and Preskill advise faculty to "listen attentively to each other's comments, reframe and rephrase what you've heard, and check with colleagues to make sure you've caught their meaning accurately" (52). Such conversations offer opportunities to demonstrate how ideas may be clarified and new perspectives gained through respectful disagreement. However, note Brookfield and Preskill, such conversations can also demonstrate that consensus on complex political or moral questions is not always possible. "But also allow yourself," Brookfield and Preskill write, "to reject [ideas] and to show that you don't feel obliged to change your views because of colleagues' comments. You want to show students that it is quite permissible to be the only one holding a dissenting view in a discussion and that groups should avoid trying to convert holdouts to the majority opinion" (ibid.). Arguments cannot always be resolved and differences may defy reasonable attempts at compromise. This, too, we can model.

We might equally model ethical discourse in our own writing, which provides, recalling MacIntyre, yet another "arena in which the virtues are exhibited." We may demonstrate in our own publications, in other words, those dispositions of truthfulness, accountability, open-mindedness, and intellectual confidence that we would have our students learn.

MacIntyre provides an example from his own work. In the Preface to the Second Edition of his book, *A Short History of Ethics*, MacIntyre responds to what he calls "the most pertinent criticisms" leveled at the first edition (MacIntyre 1996). Of his treatment of Christian ethics, for instance, MacIntyre characterizes as a striking "defect" his "overnumerous intentions," which resulted in his attempting to address "the distinctive moral outlook of the Christian religion *and* to bridge the gap of 1,300 years between Marcus Aurelius and Machiavelli *and* to give some account of the importance of medieval moral philosophy"—all in ten "sandwiched" pages. "What an absurdity!" he writes of his efforts (ix). Of his discussion of Christian conceptions of law and virtue, and how these stood in relationship to conceptions of virtue and human good in the ancient world, he states, "Because I had not understood [the issue] adequately, I was unable to pose the right questions about that relationship" (x). Of his neglect of Islamic ethics, he avers, "It was as great a mistake to have made no mention of such Islamic philosophers as ibn Sina (Avicenna), al-Ghazali, and above all ibn Rushd (Averroes)" (xi). And to the charge made by one Peter Winch that *A Short History of Ethics* is not merely relativistic but "incoherent," a charge that MacIntyre characterizes as having been made "justly" and "rightly," MacIntyre responds, "What I had certainly been unable to do was reconcile two positions [concerning how to make judgments about rival moral standpoints], to each of which I was committed" (xvi). MacIntyre concludes the Preface by writing, "Every philosopher is indebted to her or his critics, and I perhaps more than most. Let me conclude therefore by emphasizing how very grateful I am to all the critics of the *Short History*, whether named or unnamed" (xix).

To be clear, ethical discourse does not call upon us to accede to every charge made against us, or to be grateful for every criticism fired our way. Some criticisms will be wrong, and others unfair. Neither does it mean we decline to defend our ideas as vigorously and pointedly as we are able. Ethical writing is not without its edges and sharp elbows. What it does require, however, is that our communicative practices be guided by those dispositions and habits that will allow us to grow as ethical speakers and writers, and thus to serve as better models for our students. And while it may well be true that many of our students are unlikely to read much of what we write, whether we are publishing in our professional journals, in *Mother Jones* or *Commentary*, it is worth remembering Aristotle's view that "we become just by doing things that are just, temperate by doing things that are temperate, and courageous by doing things that are courageous" (2004, 1103b). By choosing to model virtuous writing, in other words, we become virtuous writers. Perhaps, in the end, the language practices of our students will not be the only ones transformed by the classroom engagement with rhetorical virtues.

EXEMPLARS

The practice of promoting virtuous behavior through exposure to moral exemplars can be traced as far back, as we have seen in chapter 3, to the teachings of Confucius and the concept of the *junzi*, or "the exemplary person" (Sim 2015, 64–65). The *junzi* is a combination, Hunter McEwan writes, of a teacher and a guide, one whose purpose, as stated in the *Xueji*, the text describing the pedagogical practices of the Imperial Academy during the Han period, is "to enlighten: to lead students forward through reasoning and inspiration rather than drag them . . . to open their minds rather than provide them with fixed answers" (McEwan 2016, 69). Aristotle, too, held that what he classified as moral virtues were developed through a combination of formal instruction, imitation of exemplars, and practice.

The virtue theorist Linda Zagzebski describes the exemplar as "a paradigmatically good person," a person whose actions or life fills us with feelings of admiration, and whom we are moved to imitate (Zagzebski

2010). "Moral learning, like most other forms of learning," contends Zagzebski, "is principally done by imitation. Exemplars are those persons who are most imitable, and they are most imitable because they are most admirable" (52). Just who should be regarded as an exemplar, as imitable and admirable, speaks to a complex blend of ideological, cultural, religious, and other commitments, but commonly cited as exemplary figures are spiritual leaders, such as Buddha, Jesus, and the Dalai Lama; historical actors, such as Gandhi, Dorothy Day, and Nelson Mandela; and fictional characters, such as Scout Finch, Hermione Granger, and Lisbeth Salander.

When the heavyweight boxing champion Muhammad Ali refused to be inducted into the US Army during the Vietnam War, stating flatly, "I ain't got no quarrel with them Vietcong," (Hauser 1991, 144–145), he was thrust into the center of a national debate, making him both a national hero and a reviled public figure. The philosopher Bertrand Russell wrote to congratulate Ali—"I am sure you know that you spoke for your people and for oppressed people everywhere in the courageous defiance of American power"—while others called to express their hatred and hope that he would die (Remnick 1998, 287–288). Sportswriters rebuked Ali as an unworthy champion, and US senators and congressmen denounced him as a traitor. "The heavyweight champion of the world," said Rep. Frank Clark of Pennsylvania, "turns my stomach" (Hauser 1991, 147).

The personal costs to Ali for his decision were considerable. He was stripped of his title, his boxing license was revoked, and he was placed under FBI surveillance. He would later be convicted of draft evasion, fined $10,000 and sentenced to five years imprisonment—a conviction overturned on appeal (Remnick 1998, 290–291; Tischler 2016, 114). Nonetheless, Ali continued to speak out, identifying resistance to the war with the civil rights struggle of African Americans. After a meeting with Martin Luther King Jr. in Louisville, in which Ali spoke in support of the struggle for fair housing practices in the city, he made the following statement to reporters:

> Why should they ask me to put on a uniform and go 10,000 miles from home and drop bombs and bullets on Brown people in Vietnam while so-called Negro people in Louisville are treated like dogs and denied simple human rights? No I'm not going 10,000 miles from home to help murder and burn another poor nation simply to continue the domination of white slave masters of the darker people the world over. This is the day when such evils must come to an end. I have been warned that to take such a stand would cost me millions of dollars. But I have said it once and I will

say it again. The real enemy of my people is here. I will not disgrace my religion, my people or myself by becoming a tool to enslave those who are fighting for their own justice, freedom and equality. If I thought the war was going to bring freedom and equality to 22 million of my people they wouldn't have to draft me, I'd join tomorrow. I have nothing to lose by standing up for my beliefs. So I'll go to jail, so what? We've been in jail for 400 years. (Hauser 1991, 167).

Teachers could ask students whether Ali should be considered an exemplar, whether his words and actions were admirable, and whether his statement to the press offered examples of rhetorical virtues that should be imitated. If not, why not? If yes, why? Students might discuss which virtues were enacted in Ali's speech, and where in the text these are expressed. Teachers might ask students to locate other texts that exemplify the virtues expressed in Ali's speech and share these with the class. If students objected to the speech, they might find and share texts that exemplified those virtues said to be lacking in Ali's statement. Finally, teachers and students might discuss whether the rhetorical virtues of Ali's speech might be practiced in students' writings, and what rhetorical situations students might call for such virtues.

A different kind of rhetorical exemplar can be found in the 2013 exchange of emails between blogger Kari Wagner-Peck, the mother of a child with Down Syndrome, and Chuck Klosterman, then the "Ethicist" columnist at *The New York Times*. After reading some of Klosterman's writing, Wagner-Peck (2013b) published the following "open letter" to Klosterman on her blog *a typical son*:

Dear Mr. Klosterman,

Words like "that's so *gay*" or "homo" were used regularly and with impunity in our society. Often to elicit a cheap laugh. Those words came to denote something or someone that is stupid, peculiar or undesirable. As gay rights flourished the majority of society realized they were not just using words—they were using words that hurt people. Words that devastated people.

Today people with cognitive disabilities and their allies are asking members of society to refrain from using the word "retarded" (along with all mutations of the word) for the same exact reasons. My question to you:

Is it ethical to contribute to the denigration of the vulnerable?

I am particularly interested because you, Chuck Klosterman, are The Ethicist for the New York Times and the author of the following:

"Well, okay . . . not everyone. Not boring people and not the profoundly retarded. But whenever I meet dynamic, non-retarded Americans I notice they all seem to share a single unifying characteristics [sic] *. . ."* (Chuck Klosterman on Film and TV: A Collection of Previously Published Essays, 2010)

"You used to be able to tell the difference between hipsters and homeless people. Now, it's between hipsters and retards. I mean, either that guy in the corner in orange safety pants holding a protest sign and wearing a top hat is mentally disabled or he is the coolest fucking guy you will ever know." (New York Magazine 2008)

"I don't want to come across as insensitive, but show me a person whose intelligence equates to that of a dolphin and I will show you a fucking retard." (Fargo Rock City: An Odyssey in Rural North Dakota, 2002)

Mr. Klosterman, you appear to be an unrepentant hater of people with cognitive disabilities. You are not using the word in an "I don't mean it like that way . . ." sort of ignorance which I think would be much easier to redress. You are using the word in a "Those people are exactly who I am talking about" way.

Please enlighten me: What are the ethics of using the R-word?

I am the mother of a seven-year-old son who has Down syndrome. I believe your response to my question could make all the difference in the world.

Sincerely,
Kari Wagner-Peck

Klosterman's reply to Wagner-Peck was published on her blog five days later (Wagner-Peck 2013a). He responded as follows:

Dear Ms. Wagner-Peck:

I have spent the last two days trying to figure out a way to properly address the issue you have raised on your web site. I've slowly concluded the best way is to just be as straightforward as possible: I was wrong. You are right.

I should not have used "retard" pejoratively. It was immature, hurtful, and thoughtless. I have no justification for my actions. I realize the books that contain those sentiments were published over 10 years ago, but that is no excuse; I was an adult when I wrote them and I knew what I was doing. I feel terrible about this and deeply embarrassed. I take full responsibility for my actions and understand why this matters so much to you. I'm truly sorry.

Feel free to re-post this message on your web site. I deserve the criticism I am receiving, and I want other people to know that I realize I was wrong. I would also like to donate $25,000 to whatever charity you feel is most critical in improving the lives of people with cognitive disabilities— . . . , . . . , * or any other organization you recommend. I have done something bad, so help me do something good.

Again, I apologize—and not just to you and your son, but to anyone else who was hurt by this.

—Chuck Klosterman [emphasis in original]

As with Ali's speech, students can discuss the rhetorical virtues expressed in each of the letters. They might address, for instance, the candor and justified anger of Wagner-Peck's letter. They might remark upon the devotion and love for her son that motivated her to write. They might reflect on the letter's insistence that people with intellectual disabilities be treated with respect and justice. They might note, despite everything, the temperance in Wagner-Peck's letter, which does not demand that Klosterman be fired or that his newspaper be boycotted. Students and teachers might then take up, among other issues, the questions of how to balance rhetorical anger and restraint, and under what circumstances each is appropriate.

Students and teachers could then turn to Klosterman's reply. Is his response "profoundly and beautifully simple," as Wagner-Peck wrote after reading it? (Wagner-Peck 2014). Is it an expression of the rhetorical virtues of humility and compassionate understanding as the author accepts full responsibility for the pain his language has caused? Do students find in Klosterman's letter an exemplar of the virtuous public apology? In what ways does it contrast with the many self-serving public apologies that begin, "If anyone was offended . . ." Or is the letter, as a student once suggested to me, a cynical ploy by the author? Is his gesture of donating money to charity little more than an attempt to buy off those who might rebuke him? The teacher might ask students how they would reply to Klosterman and what rhetorical virtues that would motivate their responses.

There are many examples of rhetorically exemplary texts from which we might choose. Some we know well, such as Dr. Martin Luther King Jr.'s "Letter from a Birmingham Jail" (King 1963) or Ronald Reagan's eloquent address to the nation after the Shuttle Challenger disaster

(Reagan 1986). Others are perhaps less known to our students, such as Carrie Chapman Catt's 1916 speech, "The Crisis," on women's suffrage, or Missouri Highway Patrol Captain Ron Johnson's (2014) address to the congregation at the Greater Grace Church in Ferguson, Missouri, after the shooting of Michael Brown in 2014, a speech that a *Newsweek* report described as "riveting" (Mejia 2014). We might study such speeches and writings to see how they embody rhetorical virtues, and how these same virtues might animate the writings of our students. Finally, we might, as before, ask students to supply their own exemplars, their own examples of the *junzi*, by bringing to class rhetorical texts that reflect the manifold traditions, languages, narratives, and histories that have enriched contemporary writing classroom.

Dissensus

Dissensus as I mean it here refers to the teacher's practice of encouraging students to offer diverse perspectives on a given issue, of making space for debate among those perspectives, and of allowing that reconciliation of incommensurable points of view in such discussions, as Brookfield and Preskill noted, may not be possible or even productive. When Professor Z put before her class a case of two legally guaranteed rights in conflict with one another, the purpose was not to achieve consensus on the right outcome. Rather, the classroom discussion required that students read the case closely, weigh the available evidence, develop their arguments, listen to the arguments of others, and finally offer their best judgments of the case.

In such discussions, consensus might be unachievable, and insisting upon it, upon a resolution of some kind, risks imposing a false sense of unanimity upon students, who may hold fundamentally incommensurable views on certain issues. More, it risks silencing minority perspectives, as adherents to those perspectives may feel pressured to go along with the views of the majority. Dissensus, in contrast, acknowledges that conflicting positions may frustrate compromise and elude the search for common ground. And while consensus implies closure—the group having agreed to a position is now free to move on—dissensus speaks to continuing conversation, ongoing negotiation, and, perhaps, evolving points of view over time. Finally, dissensus makes clear that ethical discourse can thrive in conditions of agreement and disagreement, harmony and dissonance, unity and division. The virtuous writer operates in all such contexts.

Institutional Culture

A critical question for those who would support Professor Z's efforts to promote ethical speech and writing in her classroom is whether hers is the work of an isolated instructor forging her own path, or whether her efforts are supported by a robust institutional or programmatic culture, one in which the commitment to ethical discourse is embedded in the mission of the writing program. If the latter, then decisions about curriculum, materials development, teacher evaluation, and more will reflect the program's commitment to teaching rhetorical ethics. More, the program will represent itself to the wider college or university community as a site for teaching ethical discourse, and will articulate this on its webpage, in its annual reports, and in other representations of its work.

What might this mean, an institutional culture committed to the teaching of rhetorical ethics? Let us speculate by returning, one last time, to the classroom of Professor Z for a brief thought experiment. Let us suppose Professor Z works at a small private college in a small Midwestern state. Each semester, she teaches three sections of first-year writing in classes capped at twenty students per section. Let us further suppose that the writing program in which Professor Z teaches offers thirty-five sections in the fall and spring semesters, none in summer. That means each year, assuming Professor Z works in a writing program with a strong institutional culture committed to the teaching of rhetorical virtues, some 1,400 students—let's say 1,300, adjusting for attrition—will graduate from Professor Z's college having had one course, at least, in which students received explicit instruction in ethical practices of writing and speech. (If there is no such institutional commitment, the number is closer to 120, or the number of students who have taken Professor Z's class.)

Looking ahead we can estimate, assuming course and cap numbers remain relatively stable and the institutional commitment to teaching ethical discourse remains strong, that in five years some 6,500 students will have graduated having taken a writing course that introduces relationships of rhetoric, writing, and ethics. In ten years, the number rises to about 13,000 students. In fifteen years, the number is just under 20,000 students, many of whom by then will be launched in their careers and established in their communities, where they will have opportunities, and perhaps responsibilities, to speak and write about the political, economic, educational, and other issues affecting their lives and the welfare of their communities.

Let's think further. Professor Z, we have said, works at a small private college. However, Big State University, some two hundred miles to the

south, has a much larger writing program, offering one hundred sections of first-year writing each semester, capped at twenty students per
section. If the writing program at Big State has a similar institutional
culture to that at Professor Z's college, if it too is committed to teaching
practices of ethical discourse, then the numbers we are envisioning grow
substantially. Every year, we may estimate that some 3,500 students, again
allowing for attrition, will graduate from Big State having taken at least
one class in which they received instruction in practices of rhetorical
ethics. In five years, the number is 17,500; in ten years, 35,000; in fifteen
years, more than 52,000 students would have left the university having
had opportunities to examine the place of truthfulness, accountability,
open-mindedness, and intellectual courage in their communications
with others.

Now let us add to this those numbers all the students who will graduate from the state university's numerous branch campuses, each of
which has its own writing program; now add the graduates of the state's
community colleges, technical schools, and religious colleges. Now let
us add all the other private, liberal arts institutions in the state. What if
the graduates of each of those institutions had also taken at least one
writing course in which rhetorical ethics was an explicit topic of discussion? What if they learned to think of arguments as ethical activities?
How might this influence the practice of public discourse in that state?
How might it influence public arguments in surrounding states?

Let's go further still. We said Professor Z is employed at a college in
a small Midwestern state. Now let us imagine that same commitment
to ethical rhetoric has been made in writing programs in institutions
in other states across the country. What if we add to our numbers all
the students who will graduate having studied ethical rhetoric in colleges, universities, community colleges, and technical schools in Ohio,
Kentucky, Illinois, and Michigan? In Florida, Georgia, Alabama, and
Texas? In Pennsylvania, New York, Maryland, and Virginia? What if we
look west and add to our numbers all the students who will graduate
having studied practices of ethical rhetoric in colleges and other postsecondary institutions in Arizona, California, Oregon, and Washington?
How might public discourse be transformed if millions of students
each year graduated from universities and colleges having studied
writing in programs committed to the teaching of rhetorical ethics, to
promoting the discursive enactments of truthfulness, accountability,
fair-mindedness, intellectual generosity, and intellectual courage? How
might that alter the character of our public arguments? What might it
mean for our democracy?

What we do in the classroom matters. The institutional cultures we establish in our writing programs may matter even more.

• • •

I have offered in this chapter five strategies, *situation, naming, modeling, exemplars,* and *dissensus,* instructors might call upon for teaching for teaching rhetorical virtues in the writing class. To these, I have added a discussion of *institutional culture,* considering how writing programs supported by a strong institutional commitment to the teaching of ethical rhetoric might inspire, gradually and over time, constructive changes in the character of our public argument.

These strategies do not attach to any particular pedagogy but are equally applicable in the expressivist classroom and the critical pedagogy course, the community-based learning course, and the writing about writing classroom. More, the strategies I recommend can be employed in the basic writing course and the advanced writing section, in writing across curriculum courses and in second language writing classes. They can be practiced, moreover, in disciplinary courses—history, philosophy, literature, political science, and others, where writing is a focus. Understood from this perspective, the entire university becomes, recalling MacIntyre, an "arena in which the virtues are exhibited."

What I have not considered in this chapter, however, is whether the teaching of rhetorical virtues will finally result, as the old Roman teacher Quintilian dreamed it would, in the formation of good people, speaking well, and in the consequent improvement of our public arguments. That is what I consider next, in the conclusion to this book.

NOTES

1. This scenario is based on a case that went before the Michigan Supreme Court (see *Detroit Free Press* 2017).
2. My thinking on empathy has been influenced by Eric Leake's (2016) excellent treatment of the subject in his *Composition Forum* essay, "Writing Pedagogies of Empathy: As Rhetoric and Disposition." http://compositionforum.com/issue/34/empathy.php.
3. To review Professor Matos's (2013) syllabus, go here: https://www.academia.edu/16746792/Course_Syllabus_Popular_Culture_and_Rhetorical_Ethics.

CONCLUSION
Revisiting the Q Question

"They ask, 'Was not then Demosthenes a great orator? Yet we have heard that he was not a good man. Was not Cicero a great orator? Yet many have thrown censure upon his character.' How shall I answer such questions?"

—Quintilian, XII.1.14 (414)

The morning the letter from the rock star Iggy Pop arrived, recalled Laurence, then twenty-one years old and living in Paris, her family was being evicted from their home by the bailiff (Letters of Note 2010). Nine months earlier, Laurence had written Iggy Pop a twenty-page letter in which she described, in her words, "my description of being the child of an acrimonious divorce with the string of social workers, lawyers, greedy estate agents and bailiffs at the door, the fear, the anger, the frustration, the love." Not only had Iggy Pop read "the whole 'fucking' 20 pages, including the bit about my Adidas dress (a semi-innocent allusion on my part)"—he had sent Laurence a handwritten reply that, she said, left her in tears. He wrote:

> Dear laurence,
>
> thankyou for your gorgeous and charming letter, you brighten up my dim life. i read the whole fucking thing, dear. of course, i'd love to see you in your black dress and your white socks too. but most of all i want to see you take a deep breath and do whatever you must to survive and find something to be that you can love. you're obviously a bright fucking chick, w/ a big heart too and i want to wish you a (belated) HAPPY HAPPY HAPPY 21st b'day and happy spirit. i was very miserable and fighting hard on my 21st b'day, too. people booed me on the stage, and i was staying in someone else's house and i was scared. it's been a long road since then, but pressure never ends in this life. 'perforation problems' by the way means to me also the holes that will always exist in any

DOI: 10.7330/9781607328278.c006

story we try to make of our lives. so hang on, my love, and grow
big and strong and take your hits and keep going.
all my love to a really beautiful girl. that's you laurence.

iggy pop (Letters of Note, 2010)

• • •

Will teaching rhetorical virtues in our classrooms help our students write
as compassionately as Iggy Pop? Will they write as empathetically and
as wisely? Can we claim with any confidence, resting on any evidence,
that the rhetorical practices we teach, the claims, proofs, counter-claims
and the rest, will inspire in our students' writings such qualities as truthfulness, accountability, and open-mindedness, or those of generosity,
courage, and goodwill? Will a deliberate engagement in our classes with
rhetorical virtues help our students know when to demonstrate tolerance and when to display anger, and how to direct these to the right
person, in the right amount, at the right time, for the right end, and in
the right way? Implicit in these are other, arguably more fundamental
questions: Does the teaching of ethical rhetoric lead to the development
of ethical people? Does the good writer become, necessarily, the good
person? And will the virtues of the good writer, assuming we explicitly
teach them, ultimately make for a better, healthier, more constructive
public discourse? "How shall I answer such questions?" asked Quintilian.

"Such questions" relocate to our classrooms the historical problem that
Richard Lanham called, in his essay of the same name, "The Q Question,"
so titled in honor of "its most famous nonanswerer," Quintilian. *Vir bonus
dicendi peritus*, proclaimed Quintilian: let us define the orator as the
good [person], skilled in speaking. The Q Question addresses, Lanham
writes, the issue of whether "the perfect orator," whom Quintilian sought
so assiduously to form throughout the twelve volumes of his *Institutio
Oratoria*, is by definition a good person, a person of high moral character,
by which Quintilian means a person who has obtained "a thorough knowledge of all that is just and honorable" (Lanham 1993, 418).

At the heart of the Q question, writes Lanham, is the entire project of
Western humanism, which assumes that education in the curriculum the
ancient Greeks called the *paidea*, and which today we call the liberal arts,
will result in persons more enlightened than ignorant, more just than
unjust, more virtuous than vicious. And nestled within that assumption
is yet another, larger, more socially directed premise: that the just and
good person, so formed through instruction in moral discourse, will
contribute through her speech and writing to the formation of a just,
enlightened, democratic society.

Should we doubt the staying power of this ancient conception we need only to sample the mission statements of US colleges and universities that offer a liberal arts education, such as that of Yale College, which promises to develop students' "intellectual, moral, civic, and creative capacities to the fullest" (Yale University 2017); or that of the University of Virginia, which commits itself to developing a community "bound together by distinctive foundational values of honor, integrity, trust, and respect" (University of Virginia 2014); or that of Denison University, which aspires that its students become "discerning moral agents and active citizens of a democratic society" (Denison University n.d); or that of the University of San Diego, which seeks to prepare "leaders who are dedicated to ethical conduct and compassionate service" (University of San Diego 2004). The language may not be as pithy as *vir bonus dicendi peritus*, but the message is comparable. The good person—moral, honorable, discerning, and compassionate—is one who has undertaken the study of the liberal arts curriculum, and who will, as a result of that study, promote those values we associate with democracy, justice, and freedom.

Is it so? Does the study of rhetoric, and by extension the humanistic curriculum, indeed make us, as Quintilian would have it, good people, skilled in speaking? Quintilian himself, Lanham notes, fails to answer the very question that he raised, or at least he evades the issue. If the orator is not by definition a good person, Quintilian asks, raising a bright red herring, then what has been the purpose of my life? What have I spent my life doing? And what would it say of nature, Quintilian protests tangentially, were proven that it designed speech to be "the promoter of crime, the oppressor of innocence, and the enemy of truth" (413)? This would not do at all. And so "with that genial resolution which illustrates his sweet nature throughout the *Institutio*," writes Lanham, Quintilian simply assumes the answer he desires and moves on (155).

Lanham is more skeptical. Much as humanists may have assumed the benefits of a liberal arts education for students and society, "no one has ever been able to prove," contends Lanham, "that it does conduce to virtue more than to vice" (ibid.). Nor has Quintilian's conception of the orator, Lanham notes, attracted much in the way of spirited defenders. The sixteenth century French philosopher Peter Ramus called Quintilian's definition of the orator as a good person "useless and stupid," pointing out, not unreasonably, that while students of rhetoric may become subtle of mind, they can nevertheless be persons "of the utmost depravity" (Ramus 1986, 83–84, 87, quoted in Lanham 1993, 157). Erasmus endorsed the relationship of "piety . . . and the systematic works on humanistic eloquence" (Grafton and Jardine 1986, 139, quoted in

Lanham 1993, 163), but offered little in the way of evidence beyond
iteration, or simply repeating what cannot be proven. In our own time,
Gerald Graff's *Professing Literature: An Institutional History* challenges
what Graff calls "the humanist myth," which holds that humanistic
study leads inexorably to the development of public and personal virtue
(Graff 1987, quoted in Lanham 1993, 173). Graff's history, Lanham
avers, makes clear that literary study and humanism more broadly have
failed "to supply any convincing self-justification, any real answer to the
Q question" (ibid.).

Could we do any better, those of us who teach writing? Could we
provide a more convincing answer to the Q Question? Probably not.
Certainly not if we were tasked with proving that such teaching "does
conduce to virtue more than to vice." Arguments of causation, we have
seen, rarely provide absolute proofs. Rather, they more often assert,
speculate, imply, providing probabilistic rather than positive conclusions about the relationships of cause and effects. While epidemiologists
may be able to demonstrate a causal relationship between, say, smoking
and lung cancer, such certainties are largely unavailable to teachers of
rhetoric and writing. And so the necessary connection between textual
practices and the ethical life is unavailable to us, just as it was unavailable
to Quintilian. We have joined the ranks of the non-answerers, genial
or otherwise.

Perhaps, however, we are asking the wrong question. If we cannot
affirmatively answer the question of whether the orator is by definition
is a good person, and by extension whether the teaching of oratory, or
in our case writing and rhetoric, will lead to practices of better public
argument, perhaps we might ask a more modest question. Perhaps we
might revisit and reframe the Q Question, asking not what the teaching
of ethical discourse proves, but what it makes *possible*. Let us call our new,
less intrepid interrogatory, The P Question, formulated as follows: What
possibilities does the teaching of rhetorical virtue make available? What
does it make possible for our students, our discipline, our practices of
public argument?

For our students, I propose, the teaching of rhetorical virtues makes
available a language that can speak to students' pasts, present, and possible futures. Let us begin with the past. When students arrive in our
classes, we have noted, they do not come as ethical blank slates attentively awaiting the wise counsel of our instruction. They arrive, rather
with well-developed ethical commitments shaped, as Annas has argued
(21), in the overlapping contexts of home, school, church, work, neigh-
borhoods, and the Internet. Some will come to our classes possessed

of a singular and defining conception of what constitutes a moral life, such as that prescribed by religious faith, while others may arrive struggling with the diverse and contending forms of moral understanding they have encountered throughout their lives. And some will come with ethical commitments that diverge from our own, inviting us to become learners exposed to new understandings of morality and ethical practice.

What the language of rhetorical virtues offers our students, then, is not an introduction to the traits, habits, and dispositions commonly counted as virtues. They already have formed ideas of these. Rather, we offer, when we teach in the language of rhetorical virtues, instruction in how to enact such language and virtues in students' speech and writing. What does it mean to speak and write truthfully and courageously? When should one's writing display attitudes of tolerance, and when should it express justified anger? In such conversations, we are proposing new and potentially generative ways for students to connect experiences of past learning with their present writing practices.

If the language of rhetorical virtues might speak to students' past experiences, so, too, does it hold out the possibility of speaking to the present moment. Students arrive in our classrooms, as we have discussed, at a moment in which civic arguments, whether on questions of war and peace, wealth and poverty, sickness and health, are contested in language that is irrational, vituperative, and sometimes violent. More, they arrive the context of a contemporary public struggle in which the concepts of truth, facts, evidence, and knowledge have been set against "post-truth," "alternative facts," "truthful hyperbole," and other such constructs used to propagate falsehoods in the pursuit of power. And while none of this is new, it is intensified by our extraordinary technological capacities, which enable individuals and institutions to disseminate their messages faster, further, and more ceaselessly to greater numbers of people than at any time previously in human history.

The language of rhetorical virtues provides an alternative to this discourse. In place of irrationality, we teach a language grounded, for the most part, in reason and evidence. In place of intolerance and vituperation, we propose a discourse of open-mindedness and intellectual generosity. And when students confront the dishonesty of "post-truth," "alternative facts," and "truthful hyperbole," we teach that the relationship of reader and writer thrives in the exchange of truthful claims and credible evidence.

So when discussions in the writing class turn, as they often do, to controversial topics such as abortion, guns, immigration, and the like, topics on which students' views may be fixed, if not calcified—as might well be true of our own views, if we are being honest—arguments informed by rhetorical virtues begin not with the recitation of the same exhausted and uncompromising assertions, but with the questions and qualities characteristic of a good person, arguing well. Have I examined my assumptions? Have I listened to the other side? What can I learn from their arguments? On which principles am I unwilling to compromise? How would a good person argue these questions?[1] In the course of such arguments, students will undoubtedly disagree, as we likely would, on exactly what constitutes honesty, tolerance, justifiable anger and the like. Simply to name a virtue is not to live it, and what counts as fairness or justice will always be disputed. Yet if such exchanges do not lead to common ground, acknowledging that accommodation is neither always possible nor desirable, they may nonetheless engender among persons of different and even incompatible values a shared commitment to practices of ethical argument. And this in turn may lead students to reject the discourses of irrationality, venom, violence, and post-truth. This, at least, is a possibility.

And this speaks to a possible future for our students, one they may have a hand in making. By the time students enroll in our classes, as noted, many are already perceptive consumers and critics of contemporary public discourse. They have learned the arts of contesting, interrogating, and debunking. They can speak and write, many of them, in the languages of skepticism, irony, and detachment. And these are necessary skills in a world of toxic discourse.

But are our students also learning, in our classes or elsewhere, how to write in languages that allow for receptivity and goodwill? Are they learning how and when to trust, how to demonstrate fair-mindedness, how to speak and write, when the situation calls for it, with humility and compassion? Are students learning to argue in ways that allow for the possibility that, regardless of how deeply held their convictions, they might be wrong? "We need never deny the presence of strife, enmity, factions, as a characteristic motive of rhetorical expression," Kenneth Burke has written. "We need not close our eyes to their almost tyrannous ubiquity in human relations" (Burke 1962, 20). Yet neither do we need to regard strife, enmity, and factions as the only motives and languages available to our students. We have other motives and an alternative language to offer students, motives and language grounded in practices of ethical discourse.

To provide this language to students, to speak it deliberately with them in our classes, is to suggest to students a possible future in which they might come to conceive of themselves, long after they have left our classrooms, not only as consumers and critics of contemporary discourse, but equally as makers and shapers of an ethical public rhetoric. This, again, is a possibility.

And for us? If the teaching of rhetorical virtues can indeed speak to students' past, present, and possible futures, what might it offer to teachers and scholars of writing? How might it influence the way we understand our diverse, divergent, and sometimes fractious discipline of Writing Studies? How might it shape the ways we explain ourselves?

To address such questions, let us begin by acknowledging our formidable scholarly and pedagogical accomplishments. The breadth and depth of our inquiries has allowed us to explore questions related to language, literacy, and rhetoric from multiple perspectives, practiced by diverse populations, in distinctive settings. And this, in turn, has informed the variety of innovative pedagogical approaches we have brought to our classrooms. Today, we arguably know more about writing—what it is, what it does, how it is learned, and how to teach it—than at any time in the history of the discipline.

Yet the diversity that is the source of our strength, as I suggested earlier, may equally undermine us. As we range far and wide, we risk becoming isolated within increasingly specialized discourses, theoretical and methodological silos that have little to say to one another, and that recognize, as Smit argued, few communal assumptions about the nature and value of writing. We appear to be reaching a disciplinary moment in which we have many languages, but no common language; many stories, but no shared narrative about the significance of the work we have undertaken.

More, our fragmentation into increasingly specialized discourses is taking place in a political climate in which institutions of higher education face increasing pressure from interests that seek to regulate what we study and teach (Purdy 2015), to dictate the material conditions under which we work (Flaherty 2017a), and to mandate who can and cannot gain access to our classes (Redman, 2017). In a cultural moment when trust in higher education is eroding among large sections of the general public (Flaherty 2017b), we are challenged to tell a coherent and convincing story of who we are, what we do, and why the teaching of academic literacy skills is essential to the civic and economic health of the nation.

In the discourse of rhetorical virtues, we are offered a language for telling that story.

In the virtue-based narrative, we are teaching writing to prepare students for academic success in courses they will take after leaving our classrooms, but we do not teach only for that purpose. We are teaching writing to equip students with an essential skill for the workplace, but we do not teach for that purpose alone. We are teaching writing so that students might become more effective communicators, but neither do we teach solely for that end. And we are teaching writing so that our students might come to savor the intellectual, aesthetic, and indeed the sensual pleasures of the written word, but not even these fully capture our purpose, our *telos*, as teachers of writing. We have yet a further purpose, one that speaks to the health of our communities and our society. In his wonderfully eloquent essay, "A Thousand Writers Writing," Robert Yagelski writes:

> If the overriding purpose of formal education is to enable us to imagine and create just and sustainable communities that contribute to our individual and collective well-being. . . . then teaching writing cannot be defined exclusively by the widely accepted but limited goals of producing effective communicators and academically successful learners for the existing consumer-oriented culture and for workplaces defined by economic globalization. . . . Rather, writing instruction, like schooling in general, should ultimately be about creating a better world. (2009, 8)

If we might connect the ancient and the contemporary, Quintilian and Yagelski, we teach writing so that our students might become good people, skilled in speaking on behalf of that better world. We teach writing, to say it another way, so that our students will speak and write as ethical human beings, committed to the discursive practices of truthfulness, tolerance, justice, discernment, and others. That, at any rate, is the language and the story the rhetorical virtues makes available to our discipline. It is a story, I submit, worth telling.

Finally, we end by returning to where we started. The profoundly toxic condition of our public arguments serves, if not as a rebuke, then at least as a reminder that for all we have accomplished—for all the research on writing and rhetoric we have conducted, for the programmatic structures we have created, and for the millions of students we have taught—our collective efforts appear to have had scant effect in the public worlds beyond our classrooms. To be sure, we are not responsible for the noxious and bitter brew that is contemporary public argument. We did not stir this drink. But neither have we effectively produced an antidote.

Perhaps it is expecting too much to think we might. Perhaps it is an exercise in magical thinking to believe that the first-year writing class, so long considered the dank and musty basement offices of academe, might contain the seeds of transformative social change. Perhaps such thoughts are no more than moments of disciplinary self-delusion.

Yet should we abandon such extravagant aspirations and retire to the everyday work of the classroom, to what would we return? We would return to the ordinary work of teaching students to frame their claims truthfully, demonstrate accountability in supporting those claims with evidence, and consider opposing arguments thoughtfully, fairly, and fearlessly. We would return to teaching students to exercise judgment in revising their papers, and to interact respectfully and generously while critiquing the work of peers in the writing group. We would return, in other words, to teaching what we have always taught and are already teaching: the ethical activities that are inherent in the everyday work of composing and evaluating texts. Whether we approach this dimension of our work explicitly or implicitly, whether we regard it as central or marginal, we are teaching, most of us, on most days, to most students, one way or the other, practices of ethical discourse. Shall we acknowledge as much?

From our contemporary vantage, Quintilian overplayed his hand in making a necessary connection between rhetoric and the good person. *Vir bonus dicendi peritus* is ill suited to our anxious and ironic times. So we may set aside for now, appreciative of his sweet nature and genial resolution, Quintilian and the question associated with his name. For us, the better question is what a deliberate engagement with the rhetorical virtues in our classrooms might make possible, our P Question, for our students, our discipline, and for practices of public argument. What becomes possible if we acknowledge the ethical dimensions of our work? What might be possible if some portion of the millions of students who leave our classrooms and graduate from our institutions do so having learned that writing is an ethical activity, and that their arguments speak as much to their character as to their topics? How might practices of public argument be repaired and reinvigorated if we were to commit ourselves, in our classrooms, our conferences, and our scholarship, to addressing the question of just what it means in the twenty-first century to be a good writer? What knowledge, transformations, and provocations might follow?

We cannot say for certain. Yet such questions, I have tried to suggest in this book, are worth asking, and their answers worth seeking.

NOTE

1.   I am grateful to my colleague Lois Agnew for helping me see this.

REFERENCES

Aberdein, Andrew. 2007. "Virtue Argumentation." In *Proceedings of the Sixth Conference of the International Society for the Study of Argumentatation*, ed. Frans H. van Eemeren, J. Anthony Blair, Charles A. Willard, and Bart Garssen, 15–19. Amsterdam: Sic Sat.

Abrams, Lynn. 2014. "Ideals of Womanhood in Victorian Britain." *History Trails, Victorian Britain*: 1–9. September 18, 2014. http://www.bbc.co.uk/.

Alexander, Larry. 2000. "Deontology at the Threshold." *San Diego Law Review* 37:893–912.

Allen, Danielle S. 2004. *Talking to Strangers: Anxieties of Citizenship Since Brown v. Board of Education*. Chicago: University of Chicago Press. https://doi.org/10.7208/chicago/9780226014685.001.0001.

Anderson, Ashley A., Dominique Brossard, Dietram A. Scheufele, Michael A. Xenos, and Peter Ladwig. 2014. "The 'Nasty Effect:' Online Incivility and Risk Perceptions of Emerging Technologies." *Journal of Computer-Mediated Communication* 19 (3): 373–387. https://doi.org/10.1111/jcc4.12009.

Andre, Judith. 2015. *Worldly Virtue: Moral Ideals and Contemporary Life*. Lanham, MD: Lexington Books.

Angle, Stephen C., and Michael Slote. 2013. *Virtue Ethics and Confucianism*. New York: Routledge.

Annas, Julia. 2011. *Intelligent Virtue*. Oxford: Oxford University Press. https://doi.org/10.1093/acprof:oso/9780199228782.001.0001.

Anscombe, G. E. M. 1958. "Modern Moral Philosophy." *Philosophy (London, England)* 33 (124): 1–19. https://doi.org/10.1017/S0031819100037943.

Aquinas, Thomas. [1911] 1981. *Summa Theologica. Published in English in 1911. Translated by Fathers of the English Dominican Province*. Vol. 2. Westminster, MD: Christian Classics.

Aristotle. (1953/1976) 2004. *The Nicomachean Ethics*. Trans. J. A. K. Thomson, and revised with notes and appendices by Rev. Hugh Tredennick (1976). London: Penguin Books.

Aull, Laura Louise. 2011. "Forgotten Genres: The Editorial Apparatus of American Anthologies and Composition Textbooks." PhD diss., University of Michigan, Ann Arbor.

Austin, Michael W., ed. 2013. *Virtues in Action: New Essays in Applied Virtue Ethics*. Basingstoke, UK: Palgrave MacMillan. https://doi.org/10.1057/9781137280299.

Axtell, Guy, and Philip Olson. 2012. "Recent Work in Applied Virtue Ethics." *American Philosophical Quarterly* 49 (3): 183–204.

Baehr, Jason. 2011. "The Structure of Open-Mindedness." *Canadian Journal of Philosophy* 41 (2): 191–213. https://doi.org/10.1353/cjp.2011.0010.

Baier, Annette. 2004. "What Do Women Want in a Moral Theory?" In *Virtue Ethics*, ed. Stephen Darwall, 168–183. Malden, MA: Wiley-Blackwell.

Barnes, Jonathan. 2003. "Introduction." In *Aristotle: The Nicomachean Ethics*, trans. J. A. K. Thomson, and revised with notes and appendices by Rev. Hugh Tredennick (1976), ix–lxi. London: Penguin Books.

Bartholomae, David. 1980. "The Study of Error." *College Composition and Communication* 31 (3): 253–269. https://doi.org/10.2307/356486.

Barton, Ellen. 2008. "Further Contributions from the Ethical Turn in Rhetoric/Composition: Analyzing Ethics in Interaction." *College Composition and Communication* 59 (4): 596–632.

Battaly, Heather. 2015. *Virtue*. Cambridge, UK: Polity Press.

DOI: 10.7330/9781607328278.c007

Bauman, Zygmunt. 1993. *Postmodern Ethics*. Malden, MA: Blackwell Publishing.

Beauchamp, Tom L. 1998. "Editor's Introduction." In *An Enquiry concerning the Principals of Morals*, ed. Tom L. Beauchamp, 7–53. Oxford: Oxford University Press.

Bell, Macalaster. 2009. "Anger, Virtue, and Oppression." In *Feminist Ethics and Social and Political Philosophy: Theorizing the Non-Ideal*, ed. Lisa Tessman, 165–183. New York: Springer. https://doi.org/10.1007/978-1-4020-6841-6_10.

Bender, Thomas. 2003. "The Thinning of American Political Culture." In *Public Discourse in America*, ed. Judith Rodin and Stephen P. Steinberg, 27–34. Philadelphia: University of Pennsylvania Press.

Berges, Sandrine. 2015. *A Feminist Perspective on Virtue Ethics*. New York: Palgrave Macmillan. https://doi.org/10.1057/9781137026644.

Berlin, James A. 1984. *Writing Instruction in Nineteenth-Century American Colleges*. Carbondale: Southern Illinois University Press.

Berlin, James A. 1990. "Postmodernism, Politics, and Histories of Rhetoric." *Pre/Text* 11 (3–4): 170–187.

Berry, Jeffrey M., and Sarah Sobieraj. 2014. *The Outrage Industry: Political Opinion Media and the New Incivility*. Oxford: Oxford University Press.

Berry, Patrick W., Gail E. Hawisher, and Cynthia L. Selfe. 2012. *Transnational Literate Lives in Digital Times*. Logan: Computers and Composition Digital Press/Utah State University Press.

Besser-Jones, Lorraine, and Michael Slote, eds. 2015. *The Routledge Companion to Virtue Ethics*. New York: Routledge.

Bizzell, Patricia. 1992a. *Academic Discourse and Critical Consciousness*. Pittsburgh: University of Pittsburgh Press. https://doi.org/10.2307/j.ctt7zwb7k.

Bizzell, Patricia. 1992b. "The Politics of Teaching Virtue." *ADE Bulletin* 103:4–7. https://doi.org/10.1632/ade.103.4.

Bizzell Patricia, and Bruce Herzberg. 2001. *Gorgias. In The Rhetorical Tradition: Readings from Classical Times to the Present*, 2nd ed. Boston: Bedford/St. Martin's.

Black, Edwin. 1970. "The Second Persona." In *Readings in Rhetorical Criticism*, ed. Carl R. Burghardt. 68-77. State College, PA: Strata Publishing.

Blackburn, Simon. 2015. "Deontology and Human Rights with Simon Blackburn." New College of the Humanities. YouTube, May 27, 2015. https://www.youtube.com/watch?v=s4ve3n3uIL4.

Blue, Miranda. 2015. "David Horowitz: 'Traitor' Obama Letting Terrorists Bring Nukes Over Southern Border." *Right Wing Watch*, April 21, 2015. http://www.rightwingwatch.org/post/david-horowitz-traitor-obama-letting-terrorists-bring-nukes-over-southern-border/.

Bok, Sissela. 1998. "Truthfulness." In *Routledge Encyclopedia of Philosophy*. Milton Park, UK: Taylor and Francis; https://www.rep.routledge.com/articles/thematic/truthfulness/v-1.

Brainard, Lori A. 2004. *Television: The Limits of Deregulation*. Boulder, CO: Lynne Reinner.

Brittenham, Rebecca, and Hildegard Hoeller. 2004. *Keywords for Academic Writers*. New York: Pearson/Longman.

Bromwich, Jonah Engel. 2017. "CNN Fires Kathy Griffin from New Year's Eve Broadcast Over Trump Photo." *New York Times*, May 31, 2017. https://www.nytimes.com/2017/05/31/arts/trump-kathy-griffin.html?_r=0.

Brookfield, Stephen D., and Stephen Preskill. 1999. *Discussion as a Way of Teaching: Tools and Techniques for Democratic Classrooms*. San Francisco: Jossey-Bass.

Brooks, Deborah Jordan, and John G. Geer. 2007. "Beyond Negativity: The Effects of Incivility on the Electorate." *American Journal of Political Science* 51 (1): 1–6. https://doi.org/10.1111/j.1540-5907.2007.00233.x.

Broughton, John M. 1993. "Women's Rationality and Men's Virtues: A Critique of Gender Dualism in Gilligan's Theory of Moral Development." In *An Ethic of Care: Feminist and Interdisciplinary Perspectives*, ed. Mary Jane Larrabee, 112–139. New York: Routledge.

Bullock, Richard, Maureen Daly Goggin, and Francine Weinberg. 2016. *The Norton Field Guide to Writing with Readings and Handbook*. New York: W. W. Norton and Company.

Burke, Kenneth. 1962. *A Rhetoric of Motives*. Berkeley: University of California Press.

Burns, Alexander, Maggie Haberman, and Ashley Parker. 2016. "Donald Trump's Confrontation with Muslim Soldier's Parents Emerges as Unexpected Flash Point." *New York Times*, July 31, 2016. https://www.nytimes.com/2016/08/01/us/politics/khizr-khan-ghazala-donald-trump-muslim-soldier.html?_r=0.

Cafaro, Philip. 2015. "Environmental Virtue Ethics." In *The Routledge Companion to Virtue Ethics*, ed. Lorraine Besser-Jones and Michael Slote, 427–444. New York: Routledge.

Calhoun, Cheshire. 2000. "The Virtue of Civility." *Philosophy & Public Affairs* 29 (3): 251–275. https://doi.org/10.1111/j.1088-4963.2000.00251.x.

Cappella, Joseph, and Kathleen Hall Jamieson. 1997. *Spiral of Cynicism: The Press and the Public Good*. New York: Oxford University Press.

Carr, David. 1991. *Educating the Virtues: An Essay on the Philosophical Psychology of Moral Development and Education*. London: Routledge.

Carroll, Lauren. 2015. "Fact-Checking Trump's Claim That Thousands in New Jersey Cheered When World Trade Center Tumbled." *Politifact*, November 22, 2015. http://www.politifact.com/truth-o-meter/statements/2015/nov/22/donald-trump/fact-checking-trumps-claim-thousands-new-jersey-ch/.

Carter, Stephen L. 1998. *Civility: Manners, Morals, and the Etiquette of Democracy*. New York: Harper Perennial.

Catt, Carrie Chapman. 1916. "The Crisis." *American Rhetoric Top 100 Speeches*. September 7, 1916. Updated October 26, 2017. http://www.americanrhetoric.com/speeches/carrie chapmancattthecrisis.htm.

Chapman, John Jay. 1912. "The Coatesville Address." In *American Issues: A Sourcebook for Speech Topics*, eds. Edwin Black and Harry P. Kerr, 1961, 111-114. New York: Harcourt, Btace, and World.

Chokshi, Niraj. 2015. "Nevada Lawmaker Says 'Shoot 'Em in the Head' Remark Applied to Terrorists, Not Refugees." *Washington Post*, December 8, 2015. https://www.washingtonpost.com/news/the-fix/wp/2015/12/08/nevada-lawmaker-says-shoot-em-in-the-head-remark-applied-to-terrorists-not-refugees/?utm_term=.3ab0edd468b4&nore direct=on.

Cohen, Daniel H. 2009. "Keeping an Open Mind and Having a Sense of Proportion as Virtues in Argumentation (Manteniendo una mente abierta y teniendo un sentido de proporción como virtudes en la argumentación)." *Cogency* 1 (2): 49–64.

Cohen, Patricia. 2011. "Reason Seen More as Weapon Than Path to Truth." *New York Times*, June 14, 2011. https://www.nytimes.com/2011/06/15/arts/people-argue-just-to-win scholars-assert.html.

Comte-Sponville, Andre. 1996. *A Short Treatise on the Great Virtues*. London: Heinemann.

Connors, Robert J. 1997. *Composition-Rhetoric: Backgrounds, Theory, and Pedagogy*. Pittsburgh: University of Pittsburgh Press. https://doi.org/10.2307/j.ctt5hjt92.

Council of Writing Program Administrators. 2014. *WPA Outcomes Statement for First-Year Composition (3.0)*. Approved July 17, 2014. http://wpacouncil.org/positions/outcomes .html.

Council of Writing Program Administrators, National Council of Teachers of English, National Writing Program. 2011. *Framework for Success in Postsecondary Writing*. http://wpacouncil.org/files/framework-for-success-postsecondary-writing.pdf.

Council on American-Islamic Relations (CAIR). 2015. "Syndicated Radio Host Compares Muslims to 'Cockroaches.'" March 11, 2015. http://www.cair.com/press-center/cair-in-the-news/9798-syndicated-radio-host-compares-muslims-to-cockroaches.html.

Crosswhite, James. 1996. *The Rhetoric of Reason: Writing and the Attractions of Argument*. Madison: The University of Wisconsin Press.

Crowley, Sharon. 1998. "Composition in the University." In *Composition in the University: Historical and Polemical Essays*, by Sharon Crowley, 1–18. Pittsburgh: University of Pittsburgh Press. https://doi.org/10.2307/j.ctt5hjpc7.5.

Crowley, Sharon. 2009. "The Evolution of Invention in Current-Traditional Rhetoric: 1850–1970." In *The Norton Book of Composition Studies*, ed. Susan Miller, 333–346. New York: W. W. Norton & Company.

Crusius, Timothy W., and Carolyn E. Channell. 2003. *The Aims of Argument: A Text and Reader*. 4th ed. Boston: McGraw Hill.

Cummins, Joseph. 2015. 2007. *Anything for a Vote: Dirty Tricks, Cheap Shots, and October Surprises in U.S. Presidential Campaigns*. Revised Edition. Philadelphia: Quirk Books.

DailyMail.com. 2013. "Heartwarming Moment Police Officer Buys Winter Boots for Homeless Man Who Stumbled into Lowe's in Search of Warmth." January 29, 2013. http://www.dailymail.co.uk/news/article-2269924/Heartwarming-moment-police-officer-buys-winter-boots-homeless-man-tattered-shoes.html.

Daniel, Marcus. 2009. *Scandal and Civility: Journalism and the Birth of American Democracy*. Oxford: Oxford University Press.

Davis, Nancy. (Ann). 1993. "Contemporary Deontology." In *A Companion to Ethics*, ed. Peter Singer, 205–218. Malden, MA: Blackwell Publishing.

Denison University. n.d. *Vision and Values*. Accessed November 7, 2017. https://denison.edu/campus/about/vision-values.

DeStigter, Todd. 2015. "On the Ascendance of Argument: A Critique of the Assumptions of Academe's Dominant Form." *Research in the Teaching of English* 50 (1): 11–34.

Detroit Free Press. 2017. "Michigan Supreme Court Looks at Decisions at Catholic School." April 9, 2017. https://www.freep.com/story/news/local/michigan/2017/04/09/michigan-supreme-court-catholic-school/100255906/.

Donaldson, Thomas. 1992. "Kant's Global Rationalism." In *Traditions of International Ethics*, ed. Terry Nardin and David R. Mapel, 136–157. Cambridge: Cambridge University Press. https://doi.org/10.1017/CBO9780511521768.008.

Donnelly, Tim. Twitter post, March 4, 2014, 7:29 a.m. https://twitter.com/PatriotNotPol/status/440871558920568832.

Downs, Doug. 2015. "Revision Is Central to Developing Writing." In *Naming What We Know: Threshold Concepts in Writing Studies*, 66–67. Boulder: University of Colorado Press.

Dunlap, Riley E., and Aaron M. McCright. 2011. "Organized Climate Change Denial." In *The Oxford Handbook of Climate Change and Society*, ed. John S. Dryzek, Richard B. Norgaard, and David Schlosberg, 144–160. Oxford: Oxford University Press.

Eagan, Kevin, Ellen Bara Stolzenberg, Hillary B. Zimmerman, Melisa C. Aragon, Hannah Whang Sayson, and Cecilia Rios-Aguilar. 2017. *The American Freshman: National Norms Fall 2016*. Higher Education Research Institute, Prepublication Version, April 19, 2017. https://www.insidehighered.com/sites/default/server_files/files/TheAmericanFreshman2016PREPUB.pdf.

Ellis, Anthony. 1992. "Utilitarianism and International Ethics." In *Traditions of International Ethics*, ed. Terry Nardin and David R. Mapel, 158–179. Cambridge: Cambridge University Press. https://doi.org/10.1017/CBO9780511521768.009.

Erickson, Eric. 2009. "At What Point Do People Revolt?" *RedState*, March 31, 2009. https://www.redstate.com/diary/erick/2009/03/31/at-what-point-do-people-revolt/.

Faigley, Lester. 1992. *Fragments of Rationality: Postmodernity and the Subject of Composition*. Pittsburgh: University of Pittsburgh Press.

Fairclough, Norman. 1992. *Discourse and Social Change*. Cambridge: Polity Press.

Fakhry, Majid. 1998. *Ethics in Islamic Philosophy*. October 26, 2017. http://www.muslimphilosophy.com/ip/rep/H018.

Fehrenbacher, Don E. 1982. "The Anti-Lincoln Tradition." *Journal of the Abraham Lincoln Association* 4 (1): 6–28. https://quod.lib.umich.edu/j/jala/2629860.0004.103/-anti-lincoln-tradition?rgn=main;view=fulltext.

Fisher, Mary. 1992. "Republican National Convention Address." *American Rhetoric Top 100 Speeches*, August 19, 1992. http://www.americanrhetoric.com/speeches/maryfisher19 92rnc.html.

Flaherty, Colleen. 2017a. "Killing Tenure." *Inside Higher Ed*, January 13, 2017. https://www .insidehighered.com/news/2017/01/13/legislation-two-states-seeks-eliminate-tenure -public-higher-education.

Flaherty, Colleen. 2017b. "'Regaining Public Trust.'" *Inside Higher Ed*, January 27, 2017. https://www.insidehighered.com/news/2017/01/27/academics-consider-how-rebuild -public-trust-higher-education.

Fletcher, Jennifer. 2015. *Teaching Arguments: Rhetorical Comprehension, Critique, and Response*. Portland, ME: Stenhouse Publishers.

Fontaine, Sheryl I., and Susan M. Hunter. 1998. "Ethical Awareness: A Process of Inquiry." In *Foregrounding Ethical Awareness in Composition and English Studies*, ed. Sheryl I. Fontaine and Susan M. Hunter, 1–11. Portsmouth, NH: Heinemann.

Foot, Philippa. 2002. *Virtues and Vices*. Oxford: Oxford University Press. https://doi.org /10.1093/0199252866.001.0001.

Forni, P. M. 2008. *The Civility Solution: What to Do When People Are Rude*. New York: St. Martin's Press.

Fox News. 2012. "Maxine Waters Calls Republican Leaders 'Demons.'" February 15, 2012, http://www.foxnews.com/politics/2012/02/15/maxine-waters-calls-republican -leaders-demons.html.

Fowler, H. W. [1926] 1965. *A Dictionary of Modern English Usage*. Revised, Sir Ernest Gowers. Oxford: Oxford University Press.

Frazer, Michael L., and Michael Slote. 2015. "Sentimentalist Virtue Ethics." In *The Routledge Companion to Virtue Ethics*, ed. Lorraine Besser-Jones and Michael Slote, 197–208. New York: Routledge.

Frede, Dorothea. 2015. "Aristotle's Virtue Ethics." In *The Routledge Companion to Virtue Ethics*, ed. Lorraine Besser-Jones and Michael Slote, 17–29. New York: Routledge.

Frey, R. G. 2000. "Act-Consequentialism." In *The Blackwell Guide to Ethical Theory*, ed. Hugh LaFollette, 165–182. Malden, MA: Blackwell Publishing.

Friend, Christy. 1994. "Ethics in the Writing Classroom: A Nondistributive Approach." *College English* 56 (5): 548–567. https://doi.org/10.2307/378606.

Fritz, Janie M. Harden. 2013. *Professional Civility: Communicative Virtue at Work*. New York: Peter Lang. https://doi.org/10.3726/978-1-4539-0947-8.

Fulkerson, Richard. 1996. *Teaching the Argument in Writing*. Urbana, IL: National Council of Teachers of English.

Gage, John. 2005. "In Pursuit of Rhetorical Virtue." *Lore*: 29–37.

Gardiner, Stephen M. 2005. "Introduction: Virtue Ethics, Here and Now." In *Virtue Ethics, Old and New*, ed. Stephen M. Gardiner, 1–7. Ithaca: Cornell University Press.

Garofoli, Joe. 2017. "The pro-Russia, pro-Weed, pro-Assange GOP congressman Who Will Be Tough to Beat." *San Francisco Chronicle*, September 14, 2017. https://www.sfchronicle .com/politics/article/The-pro-Russia-pro-weed-pro-Assange-GOP-12195944.php.

Gilligan, Carol. 1982. *In a Different Voice: Psychological Theory and Women's Development*. Cambridge, MA: Harvard University Press.

Goodman, Charles. 2015. "Virtue in Buddhist Ethical Traditions." In *The Routledge Companion to Virtue Ethics*, ed. Lorraine Besser-Jones and Michael Slote, 89–98. New York: Routledge.

Goodnough, Abby. 2016. "Flint Weighs Scope of Harm to Children Caused by Lead in Water." *New York Times*, January 29, 2016. https://www.nytimes.com/2016/01/30/us/flint-weighs -scope-of-harm-to-children-caused-by-lead-in-water.html.

Goodstein, Laurie. 2011. "Founder of Civility Project Calls It Quits." *The New York Times*, January 12, 2011.

Gould, Jon B. 2005. *Speak No Evil: The Triumph of Hate Speech Regulation*. Chicago: University of Chicago Press. https://doi.org/10.7208/chicago/9780226305134.001.0001.

Gowers, Ernest. 1965. "Preface to the Revised Edition." In *A Dictionary of Modern English Usage*, H. W. Fowler, Revised, Sir Ernest Gowers, iii-x. Oxford: Oxford University Press.

Graff, Gerald. 1987. *Professing Literature: An Institutional History*. Chicago: University of Chicago Press.

Graff, Harvey J., and John Duffy. 2016. "Literacy Myths." In *Literacies and Language Education, Encyclopedia of Language and Education*, 3rd ed., ed. Brian V. Street and Stephen May, 31–42. New York: Springer.

Grafton, Anthony, and Lisa Jardine. 1986. *From Humanism to the Humanities: Education and the Liberal Arts in Fifteenth- and Sixteenth-Century Europe*. London: Duckworth.

Greene, Stuart, and April Lidinsky. 2008. *From Inquiry to Academic Writing: A Text and Reader*. Boston. Bedford: St. Martin's.

Grimshaw, Jean. 1993. "The Idea of a Female Ethic." In *A Companion to Ethics*, ed. Peter Singer, 491–99. Malden, MA: Blackwell Publishing.

Grobman, Laurie. 2002. "'Just Multiculturalism': Teaching Writing as Critical and Ethical Practice." *JAC* 22 (4): 813–845.

Hall, John A. 2013. *The Importance of Being Civil: The Struggle for Political Decency*. Princeton, NJ: Princeton University Press. https://doi.org/10.1515/9781400847495.

Halloran, S. Michael. 1990. "From Rhetoric to Composition: The Teaching of Writing in America to 1900." In *A Short History of Writing Instruction from Ancient Greece to Twentieth-Century America*, ed. James J. Murphy, 151–182. Davis, CA: Hermagoras Press.

Hansen, Kristine. 2011. "Are We There Yet? The Making of a Discipline in Composition." In *The Changing of Knowledge in Composition*, ed. Lance Massey and Richard C. Gebhardt, 236–263. Logan: Utah State University Press.

Hanson, Victor Davis. 2010. "Obama and the New Civility." *National Review Online*, April 21, 2010. http://victorhanson.com/wordpress/obama-and-the-new-civility/.

Hare, William. 2006. "Why Open-Mindedness Matters." *Think (London, England)* 5 (13): 7–16. https://doi.org/10.1017/S1477175600001482.

Hauser, Thomas. 1991. *Muhammed Ali: His Life and Times*. New York: Simon and Schuster.

Hazlett, Allan. 2015. "Intellectual Humility and Intellectual Criticism." In *Intellectual Virtues and Education: Essays in Applied Epistemology*, ed. Jason Baehr, 71–93. London: Routledge.

Heigl, Jana. 2017. "A Timeline of Donald Trump's False Wiretapping Charge." *Politifact*, March 21, 2017. http://www.politifact.com/truth-o-meter/article/2017/mar/21/time line-donald-trumps-false-wiretapping-charge/.

Hekman, Susan J. 2014. *The Feminine Subject*. Cambridge: Polity Press.

Herbst, Susan. 2010. *Rude Democracy: Civility and Incivility in American Politics*. Philadelphia: Temple University Press.

Hill, Thomas. 1983. "Ideals of Human Excellence and Preserving Natural Environments." *Environmental Ethics* 5 (3): 211–224. https://doi.org/10.5840/enviroethics19835327.

Hill, Thomas E. Jr. 2000. "Kantianism." In *The Blackwell Guide to Ethical Theory*, ed. Hugh LaFollette, 227–246. Malden, MA: Blackwell Publishing.

Hoagland, Sarah Lucia. 1988. *Lesbian Ethics: Toward New Value*. Palo Alto, CA: Institute of Lesbian Studies.

Holdstein, Deborah. 2005. "From the Editor: CCC in 2005." *College Composition and Communication* 56 (3): 405–409.

Hooker, Brad. 2000. "Rule-Consequentialism." In *The Blackwell Guide to Ethical Theory*, ed. Hugh LaFollette, 183–204. Malden, MA: Blackwell Publishing.

Hudson, David L. Jr. 2003. "Fighting Words." First Amendment Center, November 5, 2003. http://www.firstamendmentcenter.org/fighting-words/. https://doi.org/10.1080/030 64220308537290.

Hume, David. 1888. *A Treatise of Human Nature, Reprinted from the Original and Edition in Three Volumes*. Ed. L. A. Selby-Bigge. Oxford: Clarendon Press.

Hume, David. 1998. *An Enquiry Concerning the Principles of Morals*. Ed. Tom L. Beauchamp. Oxford: Oxford University Press.

Hursthouse, Rosalind. 1999. *On Virtue Ethics.* Oxford: Oxford University Press.

Illinois AAUP Committee. 2014. "Illinois AAUP Committee: A Statement on Steven Salaita and UIUC." *Academe Blog*, August 6, 2014. https://academeblog.org/2014/08/06 /illinoisaaup-committee-a-statement-on-steven-salaita-and-uiuc/.

Information Clearing House. n.d. *Language: A Key Mechanism of Control, Newt Gingrich's 1996 GOPAC Memo.* http://www.informationclearinghouse.info/article4443.htm.

Jacobi, Martin. 1996. "Professional Communication, Cultural Studies, and Ethics." *South Atlantic Review* 61 (2): 107–129. https://doi.org/10.2307/3201412.

Jacobson, Louis. 2016. "Donald Trump's Pants on Fire Claim That Millions of Illegal Votes Cost Him Popular Vote Victory." *Politifact*, November 28, 2016. http://www.politifact .com/truth-o-meter/statements/2016/nov/28/donald-trump/donald-trumps-pants -fire-claim-millions-illegal-vo/.

Jacobson, Louis, and Linda Qiu. 2016. "Donald Trump's Pants on Fire Claim Linking Ted Cruz's Father and JFK Assassination." *Politifact*, May 3, 2017. http://www.politifact.com /truth-o-meter/statements/2016/may/03/donald-trump/donald-trumps-ridiculous -claim-linking-ted-cruzs-f/.

Jaggar, Alison M. 1991. "Feminist Ethics: Projects, Problems, Prospects." In *Feminist Ethics*, ed. Claudia Card, 78–104. Lawrence: University of Kansas Press.

Johnson, Ron. 2014. "Speech." Archived in *Fox 2 Now, St. Louis* ("Watch Capt. Ron Johnson's amazing Michael Brown Speech"), August 17, 2014. http://fox2now.com /2014/08/17/watch-capt-ron-johnsons-amazing-michael-brown-speech/.

Jordan, June. 1988. "Nobody Mean More to Me than You and the Future Life of Willie Jordan." *Harvard Educational Review* 58 (3): 363–375. https://doi.org/10.17763/haer .58.3.d171833kp7v732j1.

Kahn, Seth, and JongHwa Lee, eds. 2010. *Activism and Rhetoric: Theories and Contexts for Political Engagement.* New York: Routledge.

Kant, Immanuel. 1996. "On a Supposed Right to Lie from Philanthropy." In *Practical Philosophy*, ed. and trans. Mary J. Gregor, 611–615. Cambridge: Cambridge University Press.

Kessler, Glenn, and Salvador Rizzo, and Meg Kelly. 2018. "President Trump Has Made 6,420 False or Misleading Claims Over 649 Days." *Washington Post*, November 2, 2018.

Kessler, Glenn, and Michelle Ye Hee Lee, and Meg Kelly. 2017. "President Trump's List of False and Misleading Claims Tops 1,000." *Washington Post*, August 20, 2017.

https://www.washingtonpost.com/politics/2018/11/02/president-trump-has-made-false -or-misleading-claims-over-days/?utm_term=.e6dc7dc45fd5

King, Martin Luther Jr. 1963. "Letter from a Birmingham Jail." African Studies Center, University of Pennsylvania. April 15, 1963. https://www.africa.upenn.edu/Articles _Gen/Letter_Birmingham.html.

King, Martin Luther Jr. 1967. "Beyond Vietnam." *King Encyclopedia*, April 4, 1967. https://kingencyclopedia.stanford.edu/encyclopedia/documentsentry/doc_beyond _vietnam/.

Kinneavy, James L. 1999. "Ethics and Rhetoric: Forging a Moral language for the English Classroom." In *Ethical Issues in College Writing*, ed. Fredric G. Gale, Phillip Sipiora, and James L. Kinneavy, 1–20. New York: Peter Lang.

Kopan, Tal. 2015. "10 Groups Donald Trump Offended Since Launching His Campaign." *CNN Politics*, November 29, 2015. https://www.cnn.com/2015/11/27/politics/donald -trump-insults-groups-list/index.html.

Kraemer, Don J. 2017. "The Good, The Right, and the Decent: Ethical Dispositions, the Moral Viewpoint, and Just Pedagogy." *College Composition and Communication* 68 (4): 603–628.

LaBarre, Suzanne. 2013. "Why We're Shutting Off Our Comments." *Popular Science*, September 24, 2013. https://www.popsci.com/science/article/2013-09/why-were-shutting-our -comments.

Lai, Chen. 2013. "Virtue Ethics and Confucian Ethics." In *Virtue Ethics and Confucianism*, ed. Stephen C. Angle and Michael Slote, 15–27. New York: Routledge.

Lanham, Richard A. 1993. "The Q Question." In *The Electronic Word: Democracy, Technology, and the Arts*, by Richard A. Lanham, 154–194. Chicago: University of Chicago Press. https://doi.org/10.7208/chicago/9780226469126.001.0001.

Lapsley, Daniel K., and Darcia Narvaez. 2006. "Character Education." In *Psychology in Practice*, vol. 4. ed. William Damon, Richard M. Lerner, and Irving I. Sigel, 248–296. Handbook of Child Psychology. Hoboken, NJ: John Wiley and Sons, Inc.

Latour, Bruno. 2004. "Why Has Critique Run Out of Steam? From Matters of Fact to Matters of Concern." *Critical Inquiry* 30 (2): 225–248. https://doi.org/10.1086/421123.

Leake, Eric. 2016. "Writing Pedagogies of Empathy: As Rhetoric and Disposition." *Composition Forum* 34. http://compositionforum.com/issue/34/empathy.php.

Leaman, Oliver. 1998. *Ibn Rushd, Abu'l Walid Muhammed (1126–98)*. October 26, 2017. http://www.muslimphilosophy.com/ip/rep/H025.

Leibovitz, Liel. 2014. "Steven Salaita's Academic Work Is Just as Hateful as Tweets." *Tablet (Brooklyn, N.Y.)*, September 5, 2014. http://www.tabletmag.com/jewish-news-and-politics/183813/steven-salaita-academic-work.

Letters of Note. 2010. "Hang on, My Love, and Grow Big and Strong." January 15, 2010. http://www.lettersofnote.com/2010/01/hang-on-my-love-and-grow-big-and-strong.html.

Levinas, Emmanuel. 1969. *Totality and Infinity*. Duquesne, PA: Duquesne University Press.

Library, C. N. N. 2017. "Flint Water Crisis Fast Facts." Updated October 23, 2017. https://www.cnn.com/2016/03/04/us/flint-water-crisis-fast-facts/.

Livengood, Chad, and Jennifer Chambers. 2016. "Schuette: Workers Hid Discovery of Lead in Blood." *The Detroit News*, July 29, 2016. https://www.detroitnews.com/story/news/michigan/flint-water-crisis/2016/07/29/flint-water-charges/87699876/.

Lozano-Reich, Nina M., and Dana L. Cloud. 2009. "The Uncivil Tongue: Invitational Rhetoric and the Problem of Inequality." *Western Journal of Communication* 73 (2): 220–226. https://doi.org/10.1080/10570310902856105.

Lubet, Steven. 2014. "Professor's Tweets about Israel Crossed the Line." *Chicago Tribune*, August 14, 2014. http://www.chicagotribune.com/news/opinion/commentary/ct-speech-steven-lubet-salaita-university-illinois-20140814-story.html.

Lucaites, John Louis, and Celeste Michelle Condit. 1999. "Introduction." In *Contemporary Rhetorical Theory: A Reader*, ed. John Louis Lucaites, Celeste Michelle Condit, and Sally Caudill, 1–18. New York: The Guilford Pres.

Lucas, Scott. 2015. "Michelle Fiore Says She Wants to Shoot Syrian Refugees." *Las Vegas Sun*, December 7, 2015. https://lasvegassun.com/news/2015/dec/07/michele-fiore-says-she-wants-to-shoot-syrian-refug/.

Lunsford, Andrea, Lisa Ede, Beverly J. Moss, Carole Clark Papper, and Keith Walters. 2013. *Everyone's an Author*. New York: W. W. Norton and Company.

MacIntyre, Alasdair. 1990. "The Privatization of Good: An Inaugural Lecture." *Review of Politics* 52 (3): 344–377. https://doi.org/10.1017/S0034670500016922.

MacIntyre, Alasdair. 1996. *A Short History of Ethics*. 2nd ed. Notre Dame, IN: University of Notre Dame Press.

MacIntyre, Alasdair. 1999. *Dependent Rational Animals: Why Human Beings Need the Virtues*. Chicago, IL: Open Court.

MacIntyre, Alasdair. 2007. *After Virtue*. 3rd ed. Notre Dame, IN: University of Notre Dame Press.

Mack, Peter. 2004. "Utilitarian Ethics in Health Care." *International Journal of the Computer, the Internet and Management* 12 (3): 63–72.

Makau, Josua M., and Debian L. Marty. 2013. *Dialogue and Deliberation*. Long Grove, IL: Waveland Press.

Massey, Lance. 2011. "The (Dis)Order of Composition: Insights from the Rhetoric and Reception of *The Making of Knowledge in Composition*." In *The Changing of Knowledge in*

Composition, ed. Lance Massey and Richard C. Gebhardt, 305–322. Logan: Utah State University Press.

Mathieu, Paula. 2005. *Tactics of Hope: The Public Turn in English Composition*. Portsmouth, NH: Boynton/Cook.

Matos, Angel. 2013. "Popular Culture and Rhetorical Ethics." (Syllabus, University of Notre Dame, Notre Dame, IN.) *Academia.edu.* https://www.academia.edu/16746792/Course _Syllabus_Popular_Culture_and_Rhetorical_Ethics.

Matsuda, Mari, Charles R. Lawrence, III, Richard Delgado, and Kimberle Williams Crenshaw. 1993. *Words That Wound: Critical Race Theory, Assaultive Speech, and the First Amendment.* Boulder, CO: Westview Press.

Matsuda, Paul Kei. 2012. "Teaching Composition in the Multilingual World: Second Language Writing in Composition Studies." In *Exploring Composition Studies: Sites, Issues, Perspectives*, ed. Kelly Ritter and Paul Kei Matsuda, 36–51. Logan: Utah State University Press. https://doi.org/10.2307/j.ctt4cgjsj.6.

McCloskey, Deirdre N. 2006. *The Bourgeois Virtues: Ethics for an Age of Commerce*. Chicago: Chicago University Press. https://doi.org/10.7208/chicago/9780226556673.001 .0001.

McDonald, Soraya Nadia. 2014. "Gaming Vlogger Anita Sarkeesian Is Forced from Home after Receiving Harrowing Death Threats." *Washington Post*, August 29, 2014. https:// www.washingtonpost.com/news/morning-mix/wp/2014/08/29/gaming-vlogger-anita -sarkeesian-is-forced-from-home-after-receiving-harrowing-death-threats/?tid=a_inl& utm_term=.43cec23b01ef.

McEwan, Hunter. 2016. "Conduct, Method, and Care of the Soul." In *Chinese Philosophy on Teaching and Learning: Xueji in the Twenty-First Century*, ed. Xu Di and Hunter McEwan, 61–75. Albany, NY: SUNY Press.

McLaren, Margaret A. 2001. "Feminist Ethics: Care as a Virtue." In *Feminists Doing Ethics*, ed. Peggy DesAutels and Joanne Waugh, 101–117. Lanham, MD: Rowman & Littlefield Publishers.

Mejia, Paula. 2014. "Sharpton, Captain Johnson Give Moving Speeches at Ferguson Memorial for Michael Brown." *Newsweek*, August 17, 2014. http://www.newsweek.com /community-members-rally-ferguson-church-memorial-michael-brown-265148.

Mercier, Hugo. 2011a. "Researcher Responds to Arguments Over His Theory of Arguing." *New York Times*, June 15, 2011. https://artsbeat.blogs.nytimes.com/2011/06/15/researcher -responds-to-arguments-over-his-theory-of-arguing/.

Mercier, Hugo. 2011b. "What Good is Moral Reasoning?" *Mind & Society*. https://papers .ssrn.com/sol3/papers.cfm?abstract_id=1781319. https://doi.org/10.1007/s11299 -011-0085-6.

Mercier, Hugo. n.d. "The Argumentative Theory of Reasoning." Accessed November 4, 2017. https://sites.google.com/site/hugomercier/theargumentativetheoryofreasoning.

Mercier, Hugo, and Dan Sperber. 2011. "Why Do Humans Reason? Arguments for an Argumentative Theory." *Behavioral and Brain Sciences* 34 (2): 57–74. https://doi.org/10 .1017/S0140525X10000968.

Mercier, Hugo, and Helene Landemore. 2012. "Reasoning Is for Arguing: Understanding the Successes and Failures of Deliberation." *Political Psychology* 33 (2): 243–258. https://doi.org/10.1111/j.1467-9221.2012.00873.x.

Moore, Michael. 2003. *Bowling for Columbine*. United States: MGM Home Entertainment.

Mutz, Diana, and Byron Reeves. 2005. "The New Videomalaise: Effects of Televised Incivility on Political Trust." *American Political Science Review* 99 (1): 1–15. https://doi .org/10.1017/S0003055405051452.

NASA. 2017. "Scientific Consensus: Earth's Climate Is Warming." *Global Climate Change: Vital Signs of the Planet.* Last updated, November 7, 2017. https://climate.nasa.gov/.

National Center of Education Statistics. 2016. *Digest of Education Statistics 2015.* June 2016. https://nces.ed.gov/programs/digest/d15/.

Neiwert, David. 2009. *The Eliminationist: How Hate Talk Radicalized the American Right.* Sausalito, CA: PoliPointPress.

New York Times. 2016. "Events That Led to Flint's Water Crisis." January 21, 2016. https:// www.nytimes.com/interactive/2016/01/21/us/flint-lead-water-timeline.html.

Nocera, Joe. 2011. "The Ugliness Started with Bork." *The New York Times,* October 21, 2011. https://www.nytimes.com/2011/10/22/opinion/nocera-the-ugliness-all-started -with-bork.html.

Noddings, Nel. 1978. *Caring: A Feminine Approach to Ethics and Moral Education.* Berkeley: University of California Press.

Noddings, Nel. 2015. "Care Ethics and Virtue Ethics." In *The Routledge Companion to Virtue Ethics,* ed. Lorraine Besser-Jones and Michael Slote, 401–414. New York: Routledge.

Norman, Jim. 2016. "Americans' Confidence in Institutions Stays Low." *Gallup News,* June 13, 2016. http://news.gallup.com/poll/192581/americans-confidence-institutions -stays-low.aspx.

Nussbaum, Martha C. 1992. "Aristotle, Feminism, and Needs for Functioning." *Texas Law Review* 70:1019–1028.

Nyhan, Brendan, and Jason Reifler. 30 March, 2010. "When Corrections Fail: The Persistence of Political Misperceptions." *Political Behavior* 32 (2): 303–330. https://doi .org/10.1007/s11109-010-9112-2 https://www.unc.edu/~fbaum/teaching/articles/ PolBehavior-2010-Nyhan.pdf.

Okin. Susan Moller. 1996. "Feminism, Moral Development, and the Virtues." In *How Should One Live? Essays on the Virtues,* ed. Roger Crisp, 211–229. Oxford: Oxford University Press.

Olson, Gary A. 1999. "Encountering the Other: Postcolonial Theory and Composition Scholarship." In *Ethical Issues in College Writing,* ed. Fredric G. Gale, Phillip Sipiora, and James L. Kinneavy, 91–105. New York: Peter Lang.

O'Neill, Onora. 1992. "Justice, Gender, and International Boundaries." In *International Justice and the Third World,* ed. Robin Attfield and Barry Wilkins, 47–72. London: Routledge. https://doi.org/10.4324/9780203421772_chapter_3.

O'Neill, Onora. 1993. "Kantian Ethics." In *A Companion to Ethics,* ed. Peter Singer, 175–185. Malden, MA: Blackwell Publishing.

Oreskes, Michael. 1991. "Lee Atwater, Master of Tactics for Bush an G.O.P., Dies at 40." *The New York Times,* March 30, 1991. https://www.nytimes.com/1991/03/30/obituaries /leeatwater-master-of-tactics-for-bush-and-gop-dies-at-40.html?pagewanted=all.

Oreskes, Naomi, and Erik M. Conway. 2010. *Merchants of Doubt: How a Handful of Scientists Obscured the Truth on Issues from Tobacco Smoke to Global Warming.* New York: Bloomsbury.

Osawa, Sandy Sunrising. 1999. *Lighting the 7th Fire.* Seattle, WA: Upstream Productions.

Oxford Dictionaries. 2016. "Oxford Dictionaries Word of the Year 2016 is . . . Post-Truth." November 16, 2016. https://www.oxforddictionaries.com/press/news/2016/12/11 /WOTY-16.

Pakaluk, Michael. 2005. *Aristotle's Nicomachean Ethics: An Introduction.* Cambridge: Cambridge University Press. https://doi.org/10.1017/CBO9780511802041.

Palmer, Parker P. 1993. *To Know as We Are Known.* San Francisco: Harper San Francisco.

Pandey, Iswari P. 2007. "Researching (with) the Postnational 'Other': Ethics, Methodologies, and Qualitative Studies of Digital Literacy." In *Digital Writing Research: Technologies, Methodologies, and Ethical Issues,* ed. Heidi A. McKee and Dánielle Nicole DeVoss, 107– 125. Cresskill, NJ: Hampton Press.

Pellegrino, Edmund D., and David C. Thomasma. 1993. *The Virtues in Medical Practice.* New York: Oxford University Press.

Pence, Greg. 1993. "Virtue Theory." In *A Companion to Ethics,* ed. Peter Singer, 249–288. Malden, MA: Blackwell Publishing.

Peperzak, Adriaan T. 2013. *Trust: Who or What Might Support Us?* New York: Fordham University Press. https://doi.org/10.5422/fordham/9780823244881.001.0001.

Perlstein, Rick. 2012. "Exclusive: Lee Atwater's Infamous 1981 Interview on the Southern Strategy." *Nation (New York, N.Y.)*, November 13, 2012. https://www.thenation.com /article/exclusive-lee-atwaters-infamous-1981-interview-southern-strategy/.

Perrett, Roy W., and Glen Pettigrove. 2015. "Hindu Virtue Ethics." In *The Routledge Companion to Virtue Ethics*, edited Lorraine Besser-Jones and Michael Slote, 51–62. New York: Routledge.

Peterson, Christopher, and Martin E. P. Seligman. 2004. *Character Strengths and Virtues: A Handbook and Classification.* Oxford: Oxford University Press.

Pew Research Center. 2015. "Beyond Distrust: How Americans View Their Government." November 23, 2015. http://www.people-press.org/2015/11/23/beyond-distrust-how -americans-view-their-government/.

Pew Research Center. 2017. "The Partisan Divide on Political Values Grows Even Wider." Last modified October 5, 2017. http://www.people-press.org/2017/10/05/the -partisan-divide-on-political-values-grows-even-wider/.

Pianalto, Matthew. 2013. "Humility and Environmental Ethics." In *Virtues in Action: New Essays in Applied Virtue Ethics*, ed. Michael W. Austin, 132–149. Basingstoke, UK: Palgrave MacMillan. https://doi.org/10.1057/9781137280299_10.

Plato. 2001. *Gorgias. In The Rhetorical Tradition: Readings from Classical Times to the Present*, 2nd ed., ed. Patricia Bizzell and Bruce Herzberg: 87–138. Trans. W. R. M. Lamb, 1925. Boston: Bedford/St. Martin's.

Plato. 2001. *Five Dialogues: Euthyphro, Apology, Crito, Meno, Phaedo.* Translated by G.M.A. Grube, and revised by John M. Cooper. Indianapolis, IN: Hackett Publishing Company.

Porter, James E. 1993. "Developing a Postmodern Ethics of Rhetoric and Composition." In *Defining the New Rhetorics*, ed. Theresa Enos and Stuart C. Brown, 207–223. Newbury Park, CA: Sage Publications.

Porter, James E. 1998. *Rhetorical Ethics and Internetworked Writing.* Greenwich, CT: Ablex.

Potter, Nancy Nyquist. 2002. *How Can I be Trusted?: A Virtue Theory of Trustworthiness.* Lanham: Rowman & Littlefield.

Powell, Katrina M., and Pamela Takayoshi. 2003. "Accepting Roles Created for Us: The Ethics of Reciprocity." *College Composition and Communication* 54 (3): 394–422. https:// doi.org/10.2307/3594171.

Public Broadcasting Service (PBS). n.d. *The American Experience: Running for President.* http://www.pbs.org/wgbh/americanexperience/features/presidents/.

Purdy, Jedediah. 2015. "Ann Rand Comes to U.N.C." *The New Yorker.* March 19, 2015. https:// www.newyorker.com/news/news-desk/new-politics-at-the-university-of-north-carolina.

Pybus, Elizabeth. 1991. *Human Goodness: Generosity and Courage.* Hertfordshire, UK: Harvester Wheatsheaf.

Quintilian. 2001. *Institutes of Oratory.* In *The Rhetorical Tradition: Readings from Classical Times to the Present*, 2nd ed., ed. Patricia Bizzell and Bruce Herzberg, 359–428. Trans. Rev. John Selby Watson, 2 vols., 1856. Boston: Bedford/St. Martin's.

Ramage, John D., John C. Bean, and June Johnson. 2012. *Writing Arguments: A Rhetoric with Readings.* Boston: Pearson.

Ramus, Peter. 1986. *Rhetoricae Distinctiones in Quintilianum (1549).* Trans. Carole Newlands. DeKalb: Northern Illinois University Press.

Reagan, Ronald W. 1986. "Explosion of the Space Shuttle Challenger Address to the Nation, January 26, 1968." National Aeronautics and Space Administration, NASA History Office. Updated June 7, 2004. https://history.nasa.gov/reagan12886.html.

Redman, Jeremy. 2017. "Georgia Lawmakers Readying Raft of Tough Bills on Immigrant, Refugees." *Politically Georgia*, January 4, 2017. https://www.myajc.com/news/state -regional-govt-politics/georgia-lawmakers-readying-raft-tough-bills-immigrants-refugees /JOTJhhuKFhnY2npRkdt4iN/.

Rehm, Diane. 2017. "How Journalists Are Rethinking Their Role Under a Trump Presidency." *The Diane Rehm Show*, November 30, 2017. https://dianerehm.org/shows/2016-11-30/how-journalists-are-rethinking-their-role-under-a-trump-presidency.

Reid, Ronald F. 1959. "The Boylston Professorship of Rhetoric and Oratory, 1806–1904: A Case Study in Changing Concepts of Rhetoric and Pedagogy." *Quarterly Journal of Speech* 45 (3): 239–257. https://doi.org/10.1080/00335635909382357.

Remnick, David. 1998. *King of the World: Muhammad Ali and the Rise of an American Hero.* New York: Random House.

Riggs, Wayne. 2010. "Open-Mindedness." *Metaphilosophy* 41 (1–2): 172–188. https://doi.org/10.1111/j.1467-9973.2009.01625.x.

Ritchhart, Ron. 2002. *Intellectual Character: What It Is, Why It Matters, and How to Get It.* San Francisco: Jossey-Bass.

Robinson, Fiona. 1999. *Globalizing Care: Ethics, Feminist Theory, and International Relations.* Boulder, CO: Westview Press.

Rodin, Judith, and Stephen P. Steinberg. 2003. "Introduction: Incivility and Public Discourse." In *Public Discourse in America*, ed. Judith Rodin and Stephen P. Steinberg, 1–23. Philadelphia: University of Pennsylvania Press.

Roen, Duane, Gregory G. Glau, and Barry M. Maid. 2013. *The McGraw-Hill Guide: Writing for College, Writing for Life.* 3rd ed. New York: McGraw-Hill.

Rood, Craig. 2013. "Rhetorics of Civility: Theory, Pedagogy, and Practice in Speaking and Writing Textbooks." *Rhetoric Review* 32 (3): 331–348. https://doi.org/10.1080/07350198.2013.797879.

Rose, Mike. 1989. *Lives on the Boundary.* New York: Penguin Books.

Rosemont, Henry Jr. and Roger T. Ames. 2008. "Family Reverence (xiao 孝) as the Source of Consummatory Conduct (ren 仁)." *Dao* 7:9–19. https://doi.org/10.1007/s11712-008-9035-3.

Rountree, Clarke. 2013a. "Afterword: Reconstituting the Commonweal and Civil Society." In *Venomous Speech: Problems with American Political Discourse on the Right and Left*, ed. Clarke Rountree, vol. 2., 431–442. Santa Barbara, CA: Praeger.

Rountree, Clarke, ed. 2013b. *Venomous Speech: Problems with American Political Discourse on the Right and Left.* Vol. 1–2. Santa Barbara, CA: Praeger.

Russell, Daniel C. 2013. "Virtue Ethics, Happiness, and The Good Life." In *The Cambridge Companion to Virtue Ethics*, ed. Daniel C. Russell, 7–28. Cambridge: Cambridge University Press. https://doi.org/10.1017/CCO9780511734786.002.

Salaita, Stephen. Twitter post, July 19, 2014, 9:37 AM. https://twitter.com/stevesalaita/status/490535944169484288.

Sanchez, Yvonne Wingett, and Mary Jo Pitzl. 2017. "Democratic Lawmaker on Voucher-Bill Sponsor: 'I Wanted to Punch Her in the Throat'" *Azcentral*, April 13, 2017. https://www.azcentral.com/story/news/politics/politicalinsider/2017/04/13/democratic-jesus-rubalcava-voucher-bill-sponsor-wanted-punch-her-throat/100389028/.

Sanchez, Yvonne Wingett, Rob O'Dell, and Alia Beard Rau. 2017. "Gov. Doug Ducey Signs Expansion of Arizona's School-Voucher Program." *Azcentral*, April 7, 2017. https://www.azcentral.com/story/news/politics/arizona-education/2017/04/07/arizona-gov-doug-ducey-signs-school-voucher-expansion/100159192/.

Santhanam, Laura. 2017. "New Poll: 70% of Americans Think Civility Has Gotten Worse since Trump Took Office." *PBS*, July 3, 2017. https://www.pbs.org/newshour/politics/new-poll-70-americans-think-civility-gotten-worse-since-trump-took-office.

Sarkeesian, Anita. 2015. "One Week of Harassment on Twitter." *Feminist Frequency, Tumblr*, January 20, 2015. https://femfreq.tumblr.com/post/109319269825/one-week-of-harassment-on-twitter.

Schneewind, J. B. 1983. "Introduction." In *David Hume, An Enquiry Concerning the Principles of Morals*, ed. J. B. Schneewind, 1–10. Indianapolis: Hackett Publishing Company.

Schneewind, J. B. 2003. "Seventeenth- and Eighteenth-Century Ethics." In *A History of Western Ethics*, 2nd ed., ed. Lawrence C. Becker and Charlotte B. Becker, 79–94. New York: Routledge.

Selby, Gardner W. 2015. "Jason Villalba said Bernie Sanders is a Democratic Socialist and 'Nazis were Democratic Socialists.'" *Politifact Texas*, October 16, 2015. http:// www.politifact.com/texas/statements/2015/oct/16/jason-villalba/jason-villalba-said -bernie-sanders-democratic-soci/.

Selfe, Cynthia, and Richard Selfe Jr. 1994. "The Politics of Interface: Power and Its Exercise in Electronic Contact Zones." *College Composition and Communication* 45 (4): 480–504. https://doi.org/10.2307/358761.

Shafer-Landau, Russ. 2007. "Introduction to Part VIII" and "Introduction to Part IX." In *Ethical Theory: An Anthology*, ed. Russ Shafer-Landau, 521–524. Malden, MA: Blackwell Publishing.

Sharockman, Aaron. 2017. "Infowars' Alex Jones falsely says George Soros, Hillary Clinton instigated Charlottesville violence." *Politifact*, August 14, 2017. http://www.politifact .com/punditfact/statements/2017/aug/14/alex-jones/infowars-alex-jones-falsely-says -george-soros-hill/.

Shaughnessy. Mina. 1977. *Errors and Expectations: A Guide for the Teacher of Basic Writing*. New York: Oxford University Press.

Shaw, William. 2007. "The Consequentialist Perspective." In *Ethical Theory: An Anthology*, ed. Russ Shafer-Landau, 463–474. Malden, MA: Blackwell Publishing.

Sher, George. 1992. "Knowing About Virtue." In *Nomos XXXIV: Virtue*, ed. J. W. Chapman and W. A. Galston, 91–116. New York: New York University Press.

Siegel, Barry. 1993. "Fighting Words: It Seemed Like a Noble Idea—Regulating Hateful Language. But When the University of Wisconsin Tried, Its Good Intentions Collided with the First Amendment." *Los Angeles Times*, March 28, 1993. http://articles.latimes .com/1993-03-28/magazine/tm-15949_1_fighting-word/4.

Sigelman, Lee, and Mark Kugler. 2003. "Why Is Research on the Effects of Negative Campaigning So Inconclusive? Understanding Citizens' Perceptions of Negativity." *Journal of Politics* 65 (1): 142–160. https://doi.org/10.1111/1468-2508.t01-1-00007.

Sim, May. 2015. "Why Confucius' Ethics is a Virtue Ethics." In *The Routledge Companion to Virtue Ethics*, edited Lorraine Besser-Jones and Michael Slote, 63–76. New York: Routledge.

Sirota, David. 2010. "Mudslinger Who Created Willie Horton Politics Decries Lack of Civility In Politics." *Huffington Post*, May 25, 2011. https://www.huffingtonpost.com/david -sirota/mudslinger-who-created-wi_b_328475.html.

Slote, Michael. 2010. *Moral Sentimentalism*. New York: Oxford University Press.

Smit, David W. 2004. *The End of Composition Studies*. Carbondale: Southern Illinois University Press.

Smit, David W. 2011. "Stephen North's *The Making of Knowledge in Composition Studies* and The Future of Composition Studies 'Without Paradigm Hope.'" In *The Changing of Knowledge in Composition: Contemporary Perspectives*, ed. Lance Massey and Richard C. Gebhardt, 213–235. Logan: Utah State University Press.

Stack, Carol B. 1993. "The Culture of Gender: Women and Men of Color." In *An Ethic of Care: Feminist and Interdisciplinary Perspectives*, ed. Mary Jane Larrabee, 108–111. New York: Routledge.

Steutel, Jan, and David Carr. 1999. "Virtue Ethics and the Virtue Approach to Moral Education." In *Virtue Ethics and Moral Education*, ed. David Carr and Jan Steutel, 3–18. London: Routledge.

Stohr, Karen. 2015. "Feminist Virtue Ethics." In *The Routledge Companion to Virtue Ethics*, ed. Lorraine Besser-Jones and Michael Slote, 271–282. New York: Routledge.

Stolberg, Sheryl Gay. 2012. "Gingrich Stuck to Caustic Path in Ethics Battles." *The New York Times*, January 26, 2012. https://www.nytimes.com/2012/01/27/us/politics/the-long -rungingrich-stuck-to-caustic-path-in-ethics-battles.html.

Stotsky, Sandra. 1992. "Conceptualizing Writing as Moral and Civic Thinking." *College English* 54 (7): 794–809. https://doi.org/10.2307/378259.

Strunk, William, and E. B. White. 1999. *The Elements of Style*. 4th ed., Longman.

Swanton, Christine. 2003. *Virtue Ethics: A Pluralistic View*. Oxford: Oxford University Press. https://doi.org/10.1093/0199253889.001.0001.

Talbott, William J. 2013. "Consequentialism and Human Rights." *Philosophy Compass* 8 (11): 1030–1040. https://doi.org/10.1111/phc3.12084.

Tannen, Deborah. 1998. *The Argument Culture*. New York: Ballantine Books.

Tannen, Deborah. 2000. "Agonism in the Academy: Surviving Higher Learning's Argument Culture." *Chronicle of Higher Education*, March 31, 2000. http://www.chronicle.com /article/Surviving-Higher-Learnings/18745.

Taylor, Jacqueline. 2015. "Hume." In *The Routledge Companion to Virtue Ethics*, ed. Lorraine Besser-Jones and Michael Slote, 155–164. New York: Routledge.

Tessman, Lisa. 2001. "Critical Virtue Ethics." In *Feminists Doing Ethics*, ed. Peggy DesAutels and Joanne Waugh, 79–99. Lanham, MD: Rowman & Littlefield Publishers, Inc.

Tessman, Lisa. 2005. *Burdened Virtues: Virtue Ethics for Liberatory Struggles*. Oxford: Oxford University Press. https://doi.org/10.1093/0195179145.001.0001.

Thornton, Bruce. 2015. "Three Cheers for Political Incivility." *Hoover Institution*, September 22, 2015. https://www.hoover.org/research/three-cheers-political-incivility.

Tischler, Barbara L. 2016. *Muhammad Ali: A Man of Many Voices*. New York: Routledge.

Treanor, Brian. 2014. *Emplotting Virtue: A Narrative Approach to Environmental Ethics*. Albany: SUNY Press.

Tronto, Joan. 1993. *Moral Boundaries: A Political Argument for an Ethic of Care*. New York: Routledge.

Tuan, Yi-Fu. 2008. *Human Goodness*. Madison: University of Wisconsin Press.

Uelmen, Gerald. n.d. "The Price of Free Speech: Campus Hate Speech Codes." Character Education, Markkula Center for Applied Ethics. Accessed October 17, 2017. https:// www.scu.edu/ethics/publications/iie/v5n2/codes.html.

United Nations. 2006. "Convention on the Rights of Persons with Disabilities." Article 24 Education. https://www.un.org/development/desa/disabilities/convention-on-the -rights-of-persons-with-disabilities/article-24-education.html.

University of San Diego. 2004. *Mission, Vision, and Values*. February 22, 2004. https://www .sandiego.edu/about/mission-vision-values.php.

University of Virginia. 2014. *Mission Statement*. January 14, 2014. http://www.virginia.edu /statementofpurpose.

Van Hooft, Stan. 2006. *Understanding Virtue Ethics*. Chesham, UK: Acumen.

Van Zyl, Liezl. 2015. "Eudaimonistic Virtue Ethics." In *The Routledge Companion to Virtue Ethics*, ed. Lorraine Besser-Jones and Michael Slote, 183–195. New York: Routledge.

Virginia Historical Society. 2017. "Thomas Jefferson and the Virginia Statute for Religious Freedom." Accessed November 7, 2017. https://www.virginiahistory.org/collections -and-resources/virginia-history-explorer/thomas-jefferson.

Wagner-Peck, Kari. 2013a. "Chuck Klosterman's Response to My Letter." *A typical son* (blog), November 12, 2013. https://atypicalson.com/2013/11/12/chuck-klostermans -response-to-my-letter/.

Wagner-Peck, Kari. 2013b. "An Open Letter to Chuck Klosterman, New York Times, Ethicist." *a typical son* (blog), November 7, 2013. https://atypicalson.com/2013/11 /07/an-open-letter-to-chuck-klosterman-the-new-york-times-ethicist/.

Wagner-Peck, Kari. 2014. "I Am the Author of the Open Letter to Chuck Klosterman Regarding the R-word." *Huff Post, The Blog*, November 21, 2103, updated January 25,

2014. https://www.huffingtonpost.com/kari-wagnerpeck/i-am-the-author-of-the-op_b_4319577.html.

Wald, Eli, and Russell G. Pearce. 2011. "The Obligation of Lawyers to Heal Civic Culture: Confronting the Ordeal of Incivility in the Practice of Law." *University of Arkansas at Little Rock Law Review* 34 (1): 1–52. https://lawrepository.ualr.edu/lawreview/vol34/iss1/1.

Walker, Margaret Urban. 2014. "Historical Accountability and the Virtue of Civic Integrity." In *Virtue and the Moral Life*, ed. William Werpehowski and Kathryn Getek Soltis, 39–55. Lanham, MD: Rowman & Littlefield.

Walker, Rebecca L. 2007. "The Good Life for Non-Human Animals: What Virtue Requires of Humans." In *Working Virtue: Virtue Ethics and Contemporary Moral Problems*, ed. Rebecca L. Walker and Philip J. Ivanhoe, 173–189. Oxford: Oxford University Press.

Walker, Rebecca L., and Philip J. Ivanhoe. 2007a. "Introduction." In *Working Virtue: Virtue Ethics and Contemporary Moral Problems*, ed. Rebecca L. Walker and Philip J. Ivanhoe, 1–39. Oxford: Oxford University Press.

Walker, Rebecca L., and Philip J. Ivanhoe. 2007b. *Working Virtue: Virtue Ethics and Contemporary Moral Problems*. Oxford: Oxford University Press.

Walker, Samuel. 1994. *Hate Speech: The History of an American Controversy*. Lincoln: University of Nebraska Press.

Walton, Douglas. 2006. *Fundamentals of Critical Argumentation*. Cambridge: Cambridge University Press.

Wang, Amy B. 2017. "Lawmaker Apologizes after Saying Leaders 'Should Be LYNCHED' for Removing Confederate Statues." *Washington Post*, May 22, 2017. https://www.washingtonpost.com/news/post-nation/wp/2017/05/22/lawmaker-says-louisiana-leaders-should-be-lynched-for-taking-down-confederate-statues/?utm_term=.45d5a343137c.

Weber Shandwick. 2016. "Civility in America 2016: U.S. Facing a Civility Crisis Affecting Public Discourse & Political Action." https://www.webershandwick.com/news/article/civility-in-america-2016-us-facing-a-civility-crisis.

Welch, Kathleen Ethel. 1999. "Ethics, Rhetorical Action, and a Neoliberal Arts." In *Ethical Issues in College Writing*, ed. Fredric G. Gale, Phillip Sipiora, and James L. Kinneavy, 75–89. New York: Peter Lang.

Welch, Nancy. 2012. "Informed, Passionate, and Disorderly: Uncivil Rhetoric in a New Gilded Age." *Community Literacy Journal* 7 (1): 33–51. https://doi.org/10.1353/clj.2012.0028.

White, Richard. 2008. *Radical Virtues: Moral Wisdom and the Ethics of Contemporary Life*. Lanham, MD: Rowan and Littlefield.

Wilhoit, Stephen. 2009. *A Brief Guide to Writing Academic Arguments*. New York: Longman.

Williams, Bernard. 2002. *Truth and Truthfulness*. Princeton: Princeton University Press.

Williams, Patricia. 1987. "Spirit-Murdering the Messenger: The Discourse of Fingerpointing as the Law's Response to Racism." *Miami Law Review* 42:127.

Wollstonecraft, Mary. [1793] 1989. "A Vindication of the Rights of Women." In *The Works of Mary Wollstonecraft*, 2nd ed., vol. 5, ed. Janet Todd and Marilyn Butler, 61–266. New York: New York University Press.

Wood, Allen W. 2011. "Kant and the Right to Lie." *Eidos* 15:96–117.

Wood, Thomas, and Ethan Porter. 2016. "The Elusive Backfire Effect: Mass Attitudes' Steadfast Factual Adherence." August 5, 2016. https://papers.ssrn.com/sol3/papers.cfm?abstract_id=2819073. https://doi.org/10.2139/ssrn.2819073.

Wu, Albert W., Thomas A. Cavanaugh, Stephen J. McPhee, Bernard Lo, and Guy P. Micco. 1997. "To Tell the Truth: Ethical and Practical Issues in Disclosing Medical Mistakes to Patients." *Journal of General Internal Medicine* 12 (12): 770–775. https://doi.org/10.1046/j.1525-1497.1997.07163.x.

Yagelski, Robert P. 2009. "A Thousand Writers Writing: Seeking Change through the Radical Practice of Writing as a Way of Being." *English Education* 42 (1): 6–28.

Yale University. 2017. *Mission Statement of Yale University.* http://catalog.yale.edu/ycps/mission-statement/.

Zagzebski, Linda Trinkaus. 1996. *Virtues of the Mind: An Inquiry Into the Nature of Virtue and the Ethical Foundations of Knowledge.* Cambridge: Cambridge University Press. https://doi.org/10.1017/CBO9781139174763.

Zagzebski, Linda Trinkaus. 2010. "Exemplarist Virtue Theory." *Metaphilosophy* 41 (1–2): 41–57. https://doi.org/10.1111/j.1467-9973.2009.01627.x.

Zarefsky, David. 2005. *Argumentation: The Study of Effective Reasoning.* 2nd ed. Chantilly, VA: The Teaching Company.

ABOUT THE AUTHOR

JOHN DUFFY is an associate professor of English at the University of Notre Dame, where he serves as the O'Malley Director of the University Writing Program. He has published on the ethics of writing, the rhetoric of disability, and the historical development of literacy and rhetoric in cross-cultural contexts. He recently co-edited the essay collection *Literacy, Economy, and Power*, and his book, *Writing from These Roots*, was awarded the 2009 Outstanding Book Award by the Conference on College Composition and Communication. He teaches courses in rhetoric, writing, and literature.

INDEX

ing of, 20; of rhetorical interpretation, 14; of rhetorical practice, 14; rhetorical virtues, 96–117 (*see also* Rhetorical virtues); skills and, 66–67; in Writing Studies, 14

Virtue ethics, 12–13, 22, 63–95; applied virtue ethics, 89–93 (*see also* Applied virtue ethics); Aristotelian virtue ethics, 70–74 (*see also* Aristotelean virtue ethics); consequentialist ethics versus, 69–70, 89; defined, 67–70; deontological ethics versus, 69–70, 89; "emotivism" versus, 69; feminist virtue ethics, 78–84 (*see also* Feminist virtue ethics); non-Western virtue ethics, 84–89 (*see also* Non-Western virtue ethics); rhetorical virtues, 96–117 (*see also* Rhetorical virtues); science compared, 68–69; sentimentalist virtue ethics, 74–77 (*see also* Sentimentalist virtue ethics)

Virtue Ethics: A Pluralistic View (Swanton), 69

Virtue Ethics and Confucianism (Angle and Slote), 85

Virtues in Action: New Essays in Applied Virtue Ethics (Austin), 95*n*9

Virtues Project, 74

Virtus (Roman god), 65

W

Wagner-Peck, Kari, 130–132

Wald, Eli, 26

Walker, Margaret Urban, 105

Walker, Rebecca L., 15, 90

Walton, Douglas, 16

Washington Post, 4, 29

Waters, Maxine, 30

Weber Shandwick (public relations firm), 6

Weinberg, Francine, 99

Welch, Kathleen Ethel, 43, 57

Welch, Nancy, 16

Wendell, Barrett, 50

What Are the Virtues? (Foot), 63

"What Do Women Want in a Moral Theory?" (Baier), 94–95*n*4

"A Whisper of AIDS" (Fisher), 14

White, E.B., 49

White, Richard, 13, 14, 110

White supremacists, 27, 29–30

"Why Confucius' Ethics is a Virtue Ethics" (Sim), 85

Will, George, 29

Williams, Patricia, 26

Wilson, Joe, 28

Winch, Peter, 127

Wisconsin Walleye War, 111–112

Wollstonecraft, Mary, 78–79

Wood, Thomas, 19

Working Virtue: Virtue Ethics and Contemporary Moral Problems (Walker and Ivanhoe), 90

World Trade Towers, 30

WPA Outcomes Statement for First-Year Composition (3.0), 10, 97

Writing: Aristotelian virtue ethics and, 73–74; consequentialist ethics and, 53–56, 61; deontological ethics and, 49–51, 61; ethics and, 61–62; feminist virtue ethics and, 83–84; non-Western virtue ethics and, 88–89; postmodern ethics and, 56–61, 61–62. *See also specific topics by name*

Writing Arguments: A Rhetoric with Readings (Ramage, Bean, and Johnson), 106–107

"Writing as Moral and Civic Thinking" (Stotsky), 56

The Writing Lab (newsletter), 56

"Writing Pedagogies of Empathy: As Rhetoric and Disposition" (Leake), 136*n*2

Writing Studies: civility and, 15; current state of, 20–21; postmodern ethics and, 56, 58–59; public argument and, 8–12; use of term, 23*n*2; virtue in, 14

X

Xin, 86

Xueji (Confucius), 128

Y

Yagelski, Robert, 144

Yale University, 139

Yiannopoulos, Milo, 27

Yoga ethics, 84

Yogasutra, 84

Z

Zagzebski, Linda, 128–129

Zarefsky, David, 115